Education studies:
An issues-based approach

Editors

John Sharp

Stephen Ward

Les Hankin

LearningMatters

First published in 2006 by Learning Matters Ltd.

British Library Cataloguing in Publication Data

A CIP record for this book is available from the British Library

ISBN–10: 1 84445 047 3
ISBN–13: 978 1 84445 047 3

The right of the authors and editors to be identified as the Authors of this Work has been asserted by them in accordance with the Copyright, Designs and Patents Act 1988.

Cover design by Topics – The Creative Creative Partnership
Project management by Deer Park Productions, Tavistock
Typeset by Pantek Arts Ltd, Maidstone
Printed and bound in Great Britain by Bell & Bain Ltd, Glasgow

Learning Matters Ltd
33 Southernhay East
Exeter EX1 1NX
Tel: 01392 215560
Email: info@learningmatters.co.uk
www.learningmatters.co.uk

Contents

Editors and contributors   vii

Acknowledgements   ix

Introduction   1

Part 1: The nature of education   3

Chapter 1 What is education?   5
Keira Sewell and Stephen Newman

Chapter 2 What is worth knowing in Education Studies?   12
Andy Pickard

Chapter 3 Community education: innovation and active intervention   20
Viv Kerridge and Ruth Sayers

Chapter 4 Education and the free market   29
Nigel Tubbs

Chapter 5 The mystery of learning   37
John Sharp and Barbara Murphy

Chapter 6 Education and integrating Children's Services   47
Pat Hughes

Part 2: Learning and teaching   57

Chapter 7 Schools and classrooms   59
Denis Hayes

Chapter 8 The child, family and society: Early Years in context   67
Wendy Bignold

Chapter 9 Polarisations in English   75
Ruth Hewitt and Elizabeth Hopkins

Chapter 10 Mathematics for the future   83
Mark Patmore

Chapter 11 Science and society   91
Richard Walton

Chapter 12 Technology and education: debates, contexts   98
and computers
John Potter

Chapter 13 The nature of higher education   106
Stephen Ward

Part 3: Themes in education   115

Chapter 14 Lifelong learning   117
Steve Bartlett and Diana Burton

Chapter 15 Leadership in education   125
John Sharp and Graham Meeson

Chapter 16 Race and education   134
Nasima Hassan

Chapter 17 From special needs to inclusive education   142
Carol Smith

Chapter 18 Faith in education: what place for faith   150
communities in schools?
Kate Adams and Mark Chater

Chapter 19 Education for citizenship and democracy   159
Howard Gibson

Chapter 20 Comparative education   167
Les Hankin

Chapter 21 Globalisation and global education   176
Les Hankin and Wendy Bignold

Index   184

Editors

John Sharp is a Professor of Education and Programme Leader for Education and Subject Studies at Bishop Grosseteste College in Lincoln.

Stephen Ward is Head of Education and Childhood Studies at Bath Spa University.

Les Hankin led the development of the Education Studies degree pathway at Liverpool Hope University. He has worked extensively on Hope's teaching projects in India and Africa.

Contributors

Kate Adams is a Senior Lecturer in Education Studies at Bishop Grosseteste College. Her research interest lies in children's dreams and spirituality.

Steve Bartlett is Professor of Education Studies at the University of Wolverhampton. He has written a range of books and articles in the field.

Wendy Bignold is Vice Dean of Education at Liverpool Hope University. Her main research interest focuses on diversity and inclusion.

Diana Burton is Professor of Education and Dean of the Faculty of Education, Community and Leisure at Liverpool John Moores University. She has written a number of papers and books covering a range of issues within Education Studies.

Mark Chater was until very recently a Reader in Education at Bishop Grosseteste College. He now directs Religious Studies and Theology on behalf of the QCA.

Howard Gibson lectures at Bath Spa University and enjoys thinking about the areas where political philosophy, language and educational issues meet.

Nasima Hassan is a Senior Lecturer in Education at Liverpool Hope University. She has worked in India and South Africa with disadvantaged communities in developing inclusive education and she researches Muslim faith schools.

Denis Hayes is a Reader in Education at the University of Plymouth. He has a special research interest in student teachers' experiences on school placement and their motivation for teaching.

Ruth Hewitt is a Senior Lecturer in Education and Subject Studies at Bishop Grosseteste College where she specialises in the teaching and learning of English.

Elizabeth Hopkins is a Senior Lecturer at Bishop Grosseteste College. She is interested in dynamic English teaching and work-related learning as a means of engaging disaffected pupils.

Pat Hughes is a Senior Lecturer at Liverpool Hope University and a non-executive Director of a Primary Care Trust (NHS) heavily involved in the integration of Children's Services.

Viv Kerridge is a Senior Lecturer in Drama at Bishop Grosseteste College. She specialises in applied drama.

Graham Meeson is a Senior Lecturer in Education Studies at Bishop Grosseteste College. He is particularly interested in leadership and management in educational settings.

Barbara Murphy is a Senior Lecturer in Education Studies at Bishop Grosseteste College. Her interests include unpicking the multifaceted dimensions of learning, understanding and memory.

Stephen Newman is a Senior Lecturer in Education at Bradford College. His research interests include philosophy, philosophy of education and educational policies and politics.

Mark Patmore is a Senior Lecturer in Mathematics Education at Nottingham Trent University. He is currently working with intending and practising secondary maths teachers.

Andy Pickard is Academic Division Leader for Education and Community Studies at the Institute of Education, Manchester Metropolitan University.

John Potter is a lecturer in ICT in Education with a research interest in learner agency, digital media and new technology.

Ruth Sayers is a Principal Lecturer at Bishop Grosseteste College where she specialises in drama in the community.

Keira Sewell is a lecturer in Primary Education at the University of Southampton. She is particularly interested in education beyond the classroom and how this enhances provision.

Carol Smith is a Senior Lecturer in Education Studies at Bishop Grosseteste College. Her main interest is SEN and children with Specific Learning Difficulties.

Nigel Tubbs teaches Education Studies at the University of Winchester where he is Professor of Philosophical and Educational Thought.

Richard Walton is a Reader in Education in the Centre for Science Education at Sheffield Hallam University. He is particularly interested in the relationships between learning in formal and informal settings.

Acknowledgements

John Sharp and Barbara Murphy wish to thank to Donald Clark for his kind permission to reproduce the Learning Styles questionnaire which appears in Chapter 5.

John Potter would like to thank Peter Twining for his kind permission to reproduce the table that appears in adapted form in Chapter 12.

Introduction

What is education and why is it so important? Where does education take place and when? How is education studied? These are fairly obvious questions to ask you'd think, but questions which are actually quite difficult to answer. Just go right ahead and try for yourself or, better, try with a group of friends. It's not so easy, is it! Among the many stumbling blocks we'd hope you'd encounter are the great scope, diversity and complexity not only of the content of education as a subject discipline itself, but of the processes by which education takes place and the social, cultural, political and historical contexts in which it occurs. But it's this very scope, diversity and complexity that makes Education Studies so exciting and attractive, and which will be addressed here.

About this book

This book is intended to inform and support your own learning and personal and professional development as you go about studying education, whether you are in the first or final year of a formal course of Education Studies, teacher training at university or college, or even undertaking research at a higher level and studying for a masters degree or doctorate. We hope that you will be introduced to this book as a 'core text' by your own tutors, who might use it in an intellectually rigorous and systematic manner in lectures, seminars and tutorials, or you might find it essential as a background reader for self-study.

Features of the book include:

- **21 chapters written and presented in an authoritative and informative, yet readable and accessible way by contributors from a great many institutions around the country, each bringing their own interest and expertise to bear on the issues raised and considered;**

- **research boxes and pause-for-thought boxes to help promote critical reflection and analysis and a deep exploration of ideas;**

- **fully referenced text to provide further reading for those who wish to pursue issues under consideration further.**

The chapters presented here are arranged into three logically consistent groupings, though in reality the nature of the subject matter in each overlaps considerably:

- **the nature of education;**

- **learning and teaching;**

- **themes in education.**

The nature of education

Education is something that we tend to take for granted as what happened to us in schools. But when we come to study education we find that there are many different ideas about what education and schooling should be. The chapters in the first section are intended to challenge your ideas about the nature of education. They begin by getting to grips with what education is about and what it means to study education as a university subject. They then go on to look at the nature of learning, education in the community and the implications for schools of the government's *Every Child Matters* agenda.

Learning and teaching

Education Studies and teacher training are very definitely not one and the same but they are joined at the hip to a greater or lesser degree. It all depends on who you ask! Whether as a reader of this book you go on to teach or to make a career in one of the newer branches of the education profession, you will certainly find the curriculum chapters interesting and informative, and free of the shackles and narrow confines of the compliance-driven culture typical of most courses leading to qualified teacher status. This is important in an increasingly vocationalised world driven by measurable outcomes and generic transferable skills. This section begins and ends with an introduction to schools and classrooms and concludes with a look at colleges and universities. Questioning the very basis upon which any curriculum is established, that is, understanding a curriculum's theoretical, philosophical and idealogical underpinning, is as important as getting trained to deliver one. Some might say more so.

Themes in education

The final section of the book looks carefully at those all-encompassing themes that shape the educational landscape and influence our increasingly uncertain lives. Globalisation, with its opportunites and threats, is explored in terms of market forces, cultural and ethnic dominance and the responses society must make as it changes and adapts to meet new challenges. The motifs of lifelong learning, citizenship, faith and inclusive regard for all members of society are interwoven here. All entail the mantle of responsibility, as citizens and, for some of us, as leaders. Coursing through all the universal themes set out in these chapters is a concern for identity and the fulfilment of the individual.

Part *1*

The nature of education

Chapter 1

What is education?

Chapter 2

What is worth knowing in Education Studies?

Chapter 3

Community education: innovation and
active intervention

Chapter 4

Education and the free market

Chapter 5

The mystery of learning

Chapter 6

Education and integrating Children's Services

Chapter *1*

What is education?

Keira Sewell and Stephen Newman

Introduction

Ask anyone what 'education' means and the answers are likely to be varied. Many primary-aged children might suggest that it 'helps them to learn', whereas secondary-aged children often think that 'education helps to get a job'. Adults have varied views, often based on their own experiences of the education system. Thus the term 'education' is not an easy one to define, often being wrapped up with the ideas of 'schooling', 'learning' and 'training'. This chapter examines the debates about the nature of education and the possible definitions or meanings of 'education'. It looks at the different ways philosophers have analysed education and it asks you to do some philosophical analysis of your own in thinking about the different 'language games' played by educational thinkers and policy-makers.

Defining education

The notion of education has taxed the minds of philosophers since the times of Plato and Socrates and, despite the multitude of definitions put forward, Matheson and Wells (1999) have argued that we are still no nearer reaching one that is wholly satisfactory. Gregory (2002) has suggested education is concerned with equipping minds to make sense of the physical, social and cultural world, while Peters has proposed that when we use the term 'education' it brings with it the implication that there is an intention to transmit, in a 'morally acceptable' way, something considered worthwhile (Peters, 1966). Yet, can we really equip young minds with the ability to make sense of a world which will look very different in ten or twenty years? Who determines what is, and what is not, worthwhile and on what do they base such decisions? What is meant by Peters's phrases 'intentionally transmitted' and 'morally acceptable'? It is no easier to answer these questions if we take Hirst's (1965) view that liberal education has value for an individual because it fulfils the mind rather than fulfilling vocational or utilitarian needs.

One of the difficulties in defining education lies in the interchangeability of those terms associated with it. Where some may see the term 'schooling' as synonymous with the term 'education', or suggest that the relationship between learning and teaching is causal (Carr, 2003), Gregory (2002) has indicated that the terms are distinct and that the relationship between the two cannot be assumed. Indeed it is this distinctiveness that enables individuals to determine their own education on leaving a schooling system that they may believe has failed them.

> *Pause for thought* | what has education done for you?
>
> Draw a timeline from birth to current age and consider the effects of education on your own development. To what extent have formal and informal systems and processes enabled you to progress? Consider your future and identify your personal needs for education. What contexts will enable you to meet these needs?

Schooling, education, learning, training

The argument that the notions of 'schooling' and 'education' are distinct raises the question of whether education can simply be assigned to *product*, or whether it is the process of education that is of paramount importance. However, if education is regarded as a process, a further question arises: what should this process entail? There may initially appear to be a strong argument in support of learning playing a fundamental role, particularly if learning is taken to mean the acquisition of knowledge, understanding or skills that were not previously held. Perhaps the starting point for this debate should therefore be learning rather than education; that is, that the type of learning taking place may determine whether we refer to education or training or even schooling.

This regress of questions continues in the notion of training. Becker (1964) described training as focusing on the development of technical abilities that are linked to specific vocations or are generic across the field of employment. More recently, Cohen (1982) described it as applying to a specific and limited learning goal. Thus attention turns to the nature of technical abilities, what defines limited learning goals, and whether training promotes a different kind of learning than education.

Papadopoulous (1998) acknowledged the many possible interpretations of the term education, arguing that it can be regarded as an all-embracing term, serving a number of different purposes in ways that recognise both product and process. He has suggested that education is variously seen as promoting:

- **economic prosperity;**
- **employment;**
- **scientific and technological progress;**
- **cultural vitality in a society increasingly dominated by leisure activities;**
- **social progress and equality;**
- **democratic principles;**
- **individual success.**

Pause for thought | the meaning of the term 'education'

What do you think of Papadopoulous's summary of education? Are there any aspects of education you think he has ignored? Is there anything he has included you would wish to exclude? Try ranking this list in order of priority. What has influenced your decisions? Who is education for? Is it primarily for the good of society or for the good of the individual? Think of some of the ways in which the term 'education' is used. Do they share any common feature(s)?

A philosophical approach

The remarks thus far have illustrated that there is little, if any, consensus about any one precise meaning of the term 'education'. Not only does the term seem to have many meanings but the search for criteria for the term that are relevant for all the meanings also seems fraught with difficulty. It seems far from easy to identify any 'core' meaning that each and every use of the term 'education' must share.

An alternative approach that may be helpful in considering the question of 'what education is' takes as its starting point the reminders provided by Wittgenstein, particularly those provided in his *Philosophical Investigations* (hereafter referred to as *PI*, Wittgenstein, 1953). Wittgenstein suggested that most terms get their meanings from the contexts – the 'language-games' – in which they are used. He proposed that most words do not have fixed meanings, and hence uses; rather, they are like tools in a toolbox and can be used for varied purposes. If someone makes a mistake in their use of a term, then the relevant criteria from the appropriate language-game can be made explicit in an attempt to provide clarification. Thus the judgement of whether a use is appropriate comes from the context in which the word is used.

Instead of considering the term 'education', let us consider the term 'chair' as an apparently more straightforward example. Is there a core or central meaning of that term? Perhaps your instinctive first thoughts lead you to think that there is. But a chair may differ in size, shape, colour; it may have legs, it may have none. A chair may seat one person, or maybe more than one (think of young children, perhaps). A chair might be used to mean a professorial post in a university, or a person convening a meeting. Interestingly, however, in spite of this diversity of meanings, there is no apparent confusion when this term is used in our everyday language. This is, in everyday life, far from being a puzzling or surprising fact. This example suggests that the criteria for deciding whether the use of the term 'chair' is appropriate come from the context, rather than from the term 'chair' itself.

The notion that words do not have fixed meanings is closely allied to that which suggests that words can have more than one meaning. Take as a further example the term 'games'. Wittgenstein suggested that the uses of this term form a network where there may be overlaps of meaning between some of the uses, but that there is nothing in common to all uses of the term 'games'. Wittgenstein also suggested that this network of similarities can be characterised by the phrase 'family resemblances'. The same notion can be taken to represent a series of related 'language-games', each 'consisting of language and the actions into which it is woven'; as before, some of these language-games are closely related, others are not.

Pause for thought | meanings and contexts

A further example: 'red' (like other ordinary words) takes its meaning from the way it is actually used. The use of the word depends not just on a shade of colour, or on an object being described, but also on the context. Think, for example, of the differences between the uses of 'red' in the phrases 'red paint', a 'red pillar box', someone with 'red hair' and 'being in the red'. Consider the uses of the term 'white' in 'white coffee', 'white wine', 'white skin' and 'white paint'. Try to make up some phrases of your own using the word 'deep', but where 'deep' has different meanings.

The meanings of 'education'

Having considered some of the examples with which Wittgenstein highlighted the issues, let us return to consider the implications for attempting to define 'education'. With these ideas in mind, we can see that if the social context provides the structure for understanding the use of language and meanings then, in asking the question 'what is education?' we may expect a range of diverse answers, depending on the contexts in which the question is asked and answered. We should not expect 'education' to have one fixed meaning; rather we may expect the term to have many meanings, meanings that may change.

Does this mean that we can never answer the question 'why do you call this "education"'? Not at all. But according to Wittgenstein such a definition would be context-specific, and probably given for a 'special purpose'. Thus, one interpretation of the term 'education' in *this* context may be to conceptualise education as involving developing expertise in various language-games. At a general level this may be all that can be said; such an interpretation is meant to be descriptive rather than prescriptive and is explicitly context-specific. In this sense, to engage in education is indeed to be involved in a social process of meaning making.

Consider, for example, trainee teachers. The purpose of their training is to prepare them to meet the professional competences expected from someone entering teaching. However, Lang (1995) has argued that we cannot assume a commonality in the individual belief systems of trainees and that teacher education must be reflective, providing opportunities for trainees to examine and explore the values, beliefs and attitudes that underpin their approach to education and identify those factors that may determine how they resolve conflict. Such an approach, it is argued, enables them to move beyond mute acceptance of policy and procedure to a deeper understanding of the philosophies and principles that underpin these and an appreciation of the extent to which their own values and beliefs support or inhibit putting them into practice. Newman (1999) supported this distinction, characterising teacher *training* as a means of developing a beginning teacher's ability merely to follow the rules of a language-game, and teacher *education* as a way of developing

> *a critical practitioner: someone who is capable of thinking about what they do, justifying and explaining it where appropriate, and adapting their playing and their understandings [of language-games] to varying circumstances.* (p159)

As a further example, consider the teacher who needs to manage a bully/victim problem. Training might equip them with the skills of carrying out school policy and procedure but would not address some of the deep-rooted feelings, values and beliefs that affect the way they resolve conflict. Education, it is suggested, can explore these feelings and, while not always promoting change, at the very least can raise awareness of the presence of these feelings, of the ways in which they may determine responses, and help to develop the ability to articulate and justify particular actions in a way appropriate to the context (that is, the language-game being played).

Education for differences

If education has many meanings, which vary according to context, then it would be appropriate to consider the notion that education should not be limited to one context. Such a decision thus frees us to consider the range of educational opportunities available to us throughout our lives.

On one level it is likely that all of us will have experienced the traditional contexts of *formal* education. These contexts are normally long-term, extending from primary through to higher education, and include institutions such as schools, colleges and universities. They frequently involve a government-set or institutionally-devised curriculum, and assessments that lead to nationally or internationally accepted awards or qualifications. Such outcomes appear to be valued by all generations, even though younger generations no longer see qualifications as the passport to high level or even stable employment (Aro et al, 2005).

Despite the high esteem in which the outcomes of formal contexts are held, however, for some, these traditional contexts of formal education, far from being neutral in their approach, seek to impose a particular view of knowledge, of language, of relationships and of reasoning on those who attend them (Giroux, 1985). Schools are thus regarded as instruments of 'social control' (Freire, 1972), serving to reinforce the interests of a particular dominant group and to work against the interests of those who are less dominant. This perception of traditional contexts of education as authoritarian (Meighan, 2005) perhaps helps to explain the increasing interest in alternative forms of education, such as home tuition, spearheaded by such groups as Education Otherwise. Just how alternative these approaches are is often determined by the curriculum offered and the methods and contexts of delivery. As Webb (1990) has noted, provision at home may vary considerably in terms of motive, method and aims, ranging from delivery of the statutory curriculum in the home environment through to a much more individually determined learning programme delivered in a variety of contexts including museums, galleries, science centres, field study centres, or even on extended trips around the world. Whilst the first type of provision might appropriately be described as 'home schooling', the latter types are more likely to be identified as non-formal or informal education.

Even within the traditional contexts of so-called formal education there are examples of different forms of education. Thus, for example, some schools (such as Summerhill) may not subscribe to all that others may consider to be the characteristics of formal education. Similarly, activities such as yoga classes, cookery classes, music lessons and evening classes may take place within the physical context of a school but may sometimes be characterised as non-formal in their purpose. Other contexts could include driving lessons, youth clubs, guide and scout groups, play schemes and holiday camps.

Informal education might be characterised as describing contexts that are neither formal nor non-formal. Examples might include museums, galleries and science centres, which see their function as public education rather than education limited to a specific clientele. Both non-formal and informal education can perhaps often be characterised by an emphasis on choice in that they provide opportunities into which learners can opt, and which may sometimes include opportunities for learners to set their own learning outcomes.

Perhaps some contexts that deliver or support the delivery of statutory curricula are best described as 'alternative' forms of formal education. These include such contexts as 'Playing for Success', 'Learning by Achievement', field study centres and themed museum visits. Such contexts often support learning in a way that could not be achieved within the classroom and often rely heavily on the theory that learners learn best when immersed *in situ,* where they have access to specific artefacts, experiences and approaches.

However, the description of a year-long trip by a family across Europe designed to provide access to such experiences as learning a new language, experiencing a different culture, learning about a country, trying new foods, and so on as an 'alternative form of formal education' would not seem appropriate. While possibly contributing to the statutory curriculum, such experiences go far beyond it, often resulting in outcomes that are difficult to quantify. Yet it could be argued that the development of additional skills, knowledge and understandings of the whole family could not be achieved in any other way. However, to describe such learning as *informal* seems unsatisfactory as the objectives of such a trip may be clearly defined and the route planned to specifically achieve these.

Other approaches, such as e-learning, provide opportunities to access information in a place other than the classroom, thus providing access to the curriculum for a range of learners at different times. Technologies, such as the internet, may also enable learners to access learning contexts that may otherwise be impossible; for example, viewing the Antarctic via a webcam at Davis Station. Access to the world wide web also opens up a wealth of opportunities for individualised informal learning that allows learners to determine their own interests and outcomes. Some uses of such resources, we may wish to argue, are 'educational'; others not. Such arguments may depend on our view of education and the purpose it serves. For example, playing on a computer game may develop children's ICT skills but not all may wish to describe such an activity as 'educational'.

The past two decades have seen the rapid growth of a new generation of enterprises such as the Eden Project (in Cornwall), the Jorvik Viking Centre (in York), Dynamic Earth (in Edinburgh), Eureka! (in Halifax) and Odyssey (in Belfast). These can be characterised by their clear objectives (often related to collective citizenship and the promotion of change), the utilisation of a resource base (physically impressive, exciting and incapable of being replicated in schools), the adoption of an interactive approach, and an ability to respond to a wide range of clients. In exploring the distinct nature of these enterprises, Peacock (2005) suggests the term 'peri-formal' as a means of identifying their unique contribution to education which neither formal nor informal contexts can achieve.

Research box

how do different users use interactive resources?

Much has been made of the interactive, hands-on nature of activities in constructivist, child-centred learning within schools and this debate has informed the ongoing development of museum education. However, the extent to which such an approach can develop conceptual knowledge and understanding is a matter for debate; museums and other peri-formal providers recognise that different users engage with resources in different ways. One example of this was demonstrated by research carried out by Fernández and Benlloch (2000) in Spain, who looked at participant use of the travelling interactive display *'Ver para no creer'* ('seeing, not believing'). The focus of their research was the collection of quantitative behavioural data relating to the duration of visit, duration of group conversations and reading behaviour. Their results indicated that different users interact with the exhibit in markedly different ways. Lone users approach the exhibit calmly, reading the information at appropriate points to enable them to make sense of their interactions. Groups of adults have a much more light-hearted approach, with one of the group members usually dominating the interaction while others in the group read the display panel and observe their actions. Children in groups normally commence interaction without reading the display panels whilst the adults in their group attempt to guide their actions in order to help them manipulate the exhibit rather than explaining the concepts underpinning it. Conversations are brief and limited to 'doing' rather than 'understanding'. Once the exhibit has been demonstrated they move on. Learners therefore appear to take what they want at that moment from the activity offered, suggesting that less formal contexts for education not only have to address the needs of a broader range of learners, but that they also may have difficulties in ensuring learning is both 'hands-on' and 'brains-on'.

Meighan and Siraj-Blatchford (2003) discussed the notion of flexitime education that allows learners to spend part of their time in a formal education context, such as a school, and part elsewhere. Such an approach enables learners to take advantage of the range of learning contexts available, including e-learning. In the United States there is increasing interest in the development of Independent Study Programmes, designed to meet the needs of individual learners, and in the development of learning systems that have as a central premise the notion that learning can take place anywhere and can be directed by the learners themselves (see Meighan and Siraj-Blatchford, 2003). Meighan and Siraj-Blatchford have recognised the benefits of these approaches, they also point out that the notion of flexitime is not readily accepted; whilst current legislation allows a child to be educated at home or at school, permission for each flexitime arrangement requires separate negotiation. It could be argued that legislation in the UK inhibits the development of flexible approaches such as these. Perhaps some of the responsibility lies with the legislation laid down in the Education Reform Act 1988, which devolves funding to schools based on numbers of pupils in school, the 'bums on seats' approach. As a consequence, schools may be unwilling to formalise a flexitime arrangement or maintain places for pupils on extended trips, no matter how educational such arrangements may be. The extent to which schools may use visits to other educational contexts to support curriculum delivery is also influenced by the need to fund such visits, either through the limited budget available or by relying on voluntary contributions from parents or carers. While many museums (for example, the Natural History Museum in London) have removed or reduced entry prices for educational parties, the cost of transport to and from such venues may preclude schools from making full use of the opportunities they offer.

It seems probable that developments in the use of information and communication technology will facilitate online and 'virtual access' to many such resources, thus helping to widen participation and extend access to these facilities. Good use is already being made of this in education programmes for children in the Australian outback, and Meighan (2000) reported on the success of 'cyber schools' in Canada. If Gregory's (2002) view of education is accepted, an education that hopes to enable learners to make sense of the physical, social and cultural world must at least keep pace with the changes in that world, and many would see change as both necessary and inevitable. However, while it would seem obvious that educational institutions will need to make full use of funding strategies, educational policies and technological initiatives in order to initiate change, it is important to remember that education is deeply embedded in national culture (Wood, 2004). Attempts at educational change will need to reflect this and, as a consequence, approaches used in one country may not necessarily be transferable to another. For example, despite the increase in home education in countries such as the United States, the UK, Australia and Canada, this approach is still rare in the Netherlands (Bluk, 2004), perhaps because parental expectations demand that education takes place in schools.

Summary and conclusions

It is evident that strategic thinking that goes well beyond current educational policy will be required to make best use of the opportunities available to us in the UK. At present, government funding is used mainly to support formal educational contexts, such as schools, leaving other providers, such as the peri-formal, to rely on grants, funding by industry, or the National Lottery.

Given that the term 'education' has a variety of meanings and can take place in many contexts, those who seek to open up the opportunities afforded by adopting more flexible and context-specific descriptions of education will need to be able to argue their case, to be able to play the various language-games of policy-makers, funding agencies, opinion-shapers, educators and others. Traditional views of education may then be replaced by a recognition that a diversity of approaches is possible, where the criteria of 'education' will vary depending on the context, and where explanation, persuasion and justification have an accepted and expected place.

References

Aro, M, Rinne, R, Lahti, K and Olkinuora, E (2005) Education or learning on the job? Generational differences of opinions in Finland. *International Journal of Lifelong Education*, 24(6): 459–474.

Becker, GS (1964) *Human capital: a theoretical and empirical analysis, with special reference to education*. New York: National Bureau of Economic Research.

Bluk, H (2004) Performance in home schooling: an argument against compulsory schooling in the Netherlands. *International Review of Education*, 50(1): 39–52.

Carr, D (2003) *Making sense of education*. London: RoutledgeFalmer.

Cohen, B (1982) *Means and ends in education*. London: George Allen and Unwin.

Fernández, G and Benlloch, M (2000) Interactive exhibits: how visitors respond. *Museum International*, 52(4): 53–59.

Freire, P (1972) Education: domestication or liberation? *Prospects*, 2(2), reprinted in Lister, I (1974) *Deschooling*. Cambridge: Cambridge University Press.

Giroux, HA (1985) Introduction, in Freire, P *The politics of education: culture, power and liberation*. London: Bergin and Garvey.

Gregory, I (2002) The aims of education, in Davies, I, Gregory, I and McGuinn, N (eds) *Key debates in education*. London: Continuum.

Hirst, PH (1965) Liberal education and the nature of knowledge, in Archambault, RD (ed) *Philosophical analysis and education*. London: Routledge and Kegan Paul.

Lang, P (1995) Preparing teachers for pastoral care and personal and social education: to train or educate? *Pastoral Care*, 13(4): 18–23.

Matheson, D and Wells, P (1999) What is education?, in Matheson, D and Grosvenor, I (eds) *An introduction to the study of education*. London: David Fulton.

Meighan, R (2000) *Natural learning and the natural curriculum*. Nottingham: Educational Heretics Press.

Meighan, R (2005) *Comparing learning systems: the good, the bad, the ugly, and the counter-productive*. Nottingham: Educational Heretics Press.

Meighan, R and Siraj-Blatchford, I (2003) *A sociology of educating*. London: Continuum.

Newman, S (1999) *Philosophy and teacher education: a reinterpretation of Donald A. Schön's epistemology of reflective practice*. Aldershot: Ashgate.

Peacock, A (2005) The emergence and characteristics of peri-formal education, Paper presented at the seminar on non-formal education, King's College, London, June 2005.

Peters, RS (1966) *Ethics and education*. London: George Allen and Unwin.

Papadopoulous, G (1998) Learning for the twenty-first century: issues, in Delors, J (Chair) *Education for the twenty-first century: issues and prospects. Contributions to the work of the International Commission on Education for the Twenty-first Century*. Paris: United Nations Educational, Scientific and Cultural Organisation.

Webb, J (1990) *Children learning at home*. Lewes: Falmer Press.

Wittgenstein, L (1953) *Philosophical investigations*. Oxford: Blackwell.

Wood, K (2004) International perspectives: the USA and the Pacific Rim, in Ward, S (ed) *Education studies: a student's guide*. London: RoutledgeFalmer.

Chapter 2

What is worth knowing in Education Studies?

Andy Pickard

Introduction

Knowledge studied at secondary schools, colleges and universities is often held to take two forms: academic and vocational. Historically, Education Studies has occupied a particularly important space in the academic/vocational divide. The subject has been strongly associated with the vocational business of training teachers while wanting to be sufficiently academic and theoretical to justify placing such training inside the universities. Epistemology is the philosophical study of knowledge, and the need for Education Studies to be both a practical and theoretical study of education has been epistemologically challenging for the subject. This chapter is concerned with the epistemological implications of the development of a 'new' Education Studies, independent of teacher training. While Education Studies graduates will doubtless go on to occupy a number of diverse roles within education, the subject itself is freed from the requirement to vocationally train its students. Nevertheless, as will be argued, the subject inherits much of its content from teacher training. The nature of the knowledge bequeathed to Education Studies is examined in this chapter and conclusions drawn about the educational experiences of Education Studies students.

Teacher education and Education Studies

Education Studies as a distinctive subject emerged first in the 1960s as a key element in the newly created Bachelor of Education degree. Students following such degrees would study typically a main subject (or possibly two), together with Education Studies. Teaching practice in schools and associated university and college courses in 'professional studies' were regarded as important, especially by the students, but hardly requiring the intellectual rigour commensurate with the award of a degree. Education Studies itself was subdivided into three contributory disciplines, all with good academic pedigrees – philosophy, sociology and psychology – with the history of education as an occasional syllabus element. Each of these disciplines offered a distinctive way of understanding education; together they added up to what was worth knowing about the theory of education. In other words, they were the subject's epistemology.

This somewhat crude resumé will be familiar to teacher educators and most teachers trained in the period before the mid-1980s. What has been less discussed, and rather taken for granted, is the extent to which the 'new' Education Studies programmes outside of teacher training remain dependent upon the epistemological framework developed in the 1960s.

The feel of heritage-style restoration and refurbishment of the subject is perhaps best illustrated by the textbooks designed to support Education Studies programmes. Two notable contributions to the genre illustrate this point. Bartlett, Burton and Peim (2001), for example, suggested that the following key questions are central to Education Studies as a discipline:

What is education and what are its purposes? How does learning take place and how far is achievement dependent upon natural ability or social factors such as income, gender and race? The attention of the student is also drawn to educational policy and political issues surrounding education. (p.viii)

As the authors acknowledge, these are essentially philosophical, psychological and sociological questions, albeit ones that the authors intend should be taught in a multidisciplinary way.

Similarly, Ward in *Education studies: a student's guide* (2004) has informed those who will be studying the subject that they will be 'learning psychology, sociology, history, philosophy, ethics, politics, economics and international and global relations'. This may appear as a daunting list, but he defends Education Studies against the accusation of 'dabbling' in other disciplines by arguing for a 'synthesis' of different knowledge in order to understand education. How such a synthesis occurs remains something of a mystery. Ward cites understanding maths teaching as an example of an area of education which can be explained by reference to diverse educational knowledge. The problem is, of course, that any specific moment of maths teaching (or any other kind of teaching) may be 'explained' by almost anything. The pragmatic and the contingent – the weather outside, whether the teacher has had time to prepare, the child who is feeling queasy – will loom at least as large in trying to understand a moment in time as the wider generalities of educational theory. In any educationally practical moment, therefore, if synthesis happens, it will be between the practitioner's understanding of what is educationally right and desirable and the immediate practical possibilities of the moment.

Epistemologically, the new textbooks being written to support Education Studies are best seen as being located in a long-standing tradition of liberal education. This is hardly surprising. Stuart Hall (1986) has described liberalism as deeply embedded in 'English common sense and political culture'. He also points to the ways in which liberalism was a progressive social ideology, as opposed to the old order of society, in that it has consistently favoured an 'open meritocratic society'. Liberalism, according to Hall, has been instrumental in encouraging us to see ourselves as self-sufficient beings and he cites as central John Stuart Mill's creation of a developmental model of humanity whereby people are capable of infinitely developing their individual powers in a society whose purpose must be to facilitate this life-long educative process. Small wonder, therefore, that liberalism has had a dominant position in educational thinking, where it has been grafted on to a philosophical tradition that the pursuit of knowledge is both a good in itself and characteristic of the mind. Thus the arch-exponent of liberal education in the 1960s and 1970s, Paul Hirst (1965), argued that 'whatever else liberal education is, it is not a vocational education'.

Hirst's views were hugely influential in the emergence of Education Studies as a university subject, helping to provide an academically rigorous element to the training of teachers. Nevertheless, Hirst and his fellow philosophers of education were not without their critics who, Carr (2005) argues, saw liberal educators as too neglectful of the historical, cultural, social and political contexts of education. Some believed that liberal education was little more than an elaborate defence of the status quo and the privileged careers of its exponents.

The dust has long since settled on these ancient epistemological battles but they remain relevant to Education Studies in two important respects. First, Education Studies in the past 20 years of the twentieth century, both inside teacher training and increasingly outside, began to address educational contexts in a serious fashion. The political processes of educational policy-making, for example, began to be studied critically. Secondly, educational philosophy itself began to engage with educational practices in a philosophical way. To work outwards from what teachers and others did in classrooms and other educational locations in order to discover philosophical dimensions became much more commonplace. The effect of this was to blur the distinction between the strictly vocational – the practical world of the classroom – and the academic – the theoretical world of books, libraries and the lecture theatre. While the new Education Studies has fully embraced the first of these developments – a liberal education enhanced by a strong engagement with education contexts – it continues to neglect the second. What kind of Education Studies would be created if practice itself is seen as intellectually rich, central to the new Education Studies, and the academic/vocational division consequently blurred, provides the substance of what follows.

Pause for thought | what knowledge do you think is worth knowing?

Liberal educators see education as a transaction. In other words, teachers, including university tutors, possess tried and tested knowledge which they pass on to their students. Reflect on your own experience in this respect. Write down briefly the areas of knowledge which you have acquired from teachers in this way. How do you know that the knowledge you have acquired is true? Why do these areas of knowledge matter to you? How would you cope if you did not have this knowledge?

Theory and practice in Education Studies

The previous section began with an assertion that teacher education in the 1960s and 1970s afforded status to 'theory', with practice via school placements being necessary but of relatively low intellectual stature. To a remarkable degree the 1980s and 1990s reversed this. Schools become partners with universities in the training of teachers and the Teacher Training Agency was created to oversee teacher training. This it did and still does, primarily through the publication of 'standards' that defined what counts as classroom aptitudes and skills for beginning teachers. These are rigorously policed by OFSTED, and inevitably the curriculum of teacher training has been largely transformed in a 'standards' direction, with Education Studies and main subjects being squeezed to find the space.

Crook (2002) linked these changes to the decline of a disciplines-based Education Studies, although in the same journal McCulloch (2002) told a more optimistic story of robust survival of psychology, philosophy and sociology. Neither is much interested in the epistemological aspects and the function of introducing them here is to draw attention to the significance of the relationship between theory and practice which has been the dominating issue of teacher training in the past 20 years. It is a question that has major epistemological implications for programmes in Education Studies, but one that has been largely neglected so far in the literature about the subject. Wilkin (1996) saw teacher education as being shaped by a dialogue between the ideologies of politicians and those of teacher trainers in which the meaning of both theory and practice was central. The concern with practice was not forced upon teacher trainers but rather the reverse.

It is the intention of this chapter to focus on the discussions that sought to make practice academically respectable, viable and rigorous. Three major and influential epistemologies of practice emerged from the reconfiguration of conceptualisation of teacher education in this period. They were:

- **reflective practice;**
- **critical social science;**
- **action research.**

Epistemology is the theory of what counts as knowledge, and each of these ways of thinking about practice generated new educational knowledge. Of course, they were also paralleled by a far more pragmatic endeavour by teacher trainers to accommodate their programmes to an intrusive and auditing government. It is hardly surprising that these epistemologies emerged more strongly in the context of teacher research and programmes for serving teachers. Initial teacher training was largely corralled by the 'Standards' and OFSTED.

Reflective practice

Reflective practice encouraged teachers to think deeply about their everyday experiences. The term implicitly combines the practical world of the classroom with that of the university (a place to think, but in many respects, reflective teaching was as much a state of mind as it was a fully fledged epistemology. The exception is the work of Donald Schön. His *The reflective practitioner: how professionals think in action* (1983) has been most frequently cited as the intellectual begetter of reflective practice. Schön's book is emphatically epistemological. The whole *raison d'être* for reflective practice, as Schön saw it, was as a response to a crisis in professional knowledge. He argued that existing professional knowledge was rooted in technical rationality and scientific positivism. By this he meant that professionals were supposed to acquire proven knowledge which could then be applied to a range of diverse situations, irrespective of unique contextual features. For Schön, this way of thinking about professional knowledge was simply unable to cope with the complexity of modern problems. He points to the ways in which successful professional practice is often intuitive, pragmatic and imbued with the 'knowledge in action' kind. The book is an extended analysis of the ways in which a range of professionals work through problems whereby the 'unique and uncertain situation comes to be understood through the attempt to change it, and changed through the attempt to understand it'.

Schön's work helped those working in teacher training to frame practice in analytical ways. It was a world where the practitioner's biography mattered, where meanings were made in the process of practising rather than simply given, and one in which each problem had its unique aspects. Yet, in spite of its strengths, Schön's work has limited application to Education Studies. This is partly because, while his general argument – the crisis of professional knowledge – was clearly epistemological, the detail of this was never followed through conceptually. His model is very much an 'in-practice' one. He has little to say about anticipated situations or envisaged practice of the kind that is crucial to Education Studies students. Such students will be thinking about their own educational experiences; they will be beginning to anticipate future educational employment; they may even be carrying out small-scale educational research activities. What seems unlikely is that they will be vocationally involved in the day-to-day business of educational practice which is necessary to give Schön any kind of purchase on the epistemology of the new Education Studies.

Critical social science

By the mid-1980s the idea that teachers could research their own practice as a legitimate form of educational research was flourishing in several universities. Some of this research owed something to Schön's work as outlined above; rather more of it was rooted in action research, a brief review of which will follow. However, small-scale classroom-orientated teacher research also provoked a critical reaction as being not 'real research' and for ignoring broader academic dimensions. Some key elements in this reaction were encapsulated in Carr and Kemmis's *Becoming critical: education, knowledge and action research* (1986).

In contrast with other epistemologically orientated texts, Carr and Kemmis certainly did not wear their philosophy lightly. The book was conceived as an attempt to provide teachers as a research 'movement' with a 'theoretical rationale' which would 'clarify its meaning, arm it against criticism and promote its future progress'. This theoretical rationale drew upon critical social science and the work of the German philosopher Jürgen Habermas in particular. He distinguished between the following:

- **knowledge that is about technically controlling objects;**
- **knowledge that is of a practical interest kind enabling practitioners to understand and interpret;**
- **emancipatory knowledge, which produces an objective understanding of the cultural, social and political frameworks in which communication and social action occur.**

Carr and Kemmis sent out a clear message that emancipatory knowledge should be the goal of teachers' research and the criteria by which its relevance was judged. In the past 20 years, *Becoming critical* has been much quoted, especially by teacher researchers, much praised, sometimes misused and occasionally abused. In a recent reflective piece on the book, Carr and Kemmis (2005) have asserted that while the intellectual, political and educational world has moved on, the value of emancipatory knowledge as the basis for teacher research remains.

Is it conceivable that the epistemology of *Becoming critical* would also serve as an epistemology for Educational Studies? Is it possible to envisage a curriculum organised around the notion of moving from technical educational problems, through an investigative approach to educational issues, towards a much broader view of education to include social and political processes. Such an epistemology certainly has the appearance of the development and rigour required of a university subject. Unfortunately these academic strengths are at the cost of engagement with the lived-in realities of practice itself. *Becoming critical* always feels like a template laid across the complexity of an educational experience, suppressing individuality and setting authority outside of practice in favour of 'academia'. If Education Studies is to deliver knowledge worth knowing then it has to be rooted in the ways in which the students of the subject understand and develop educational practices in a rigorously intelligent way.

Action research

The object of Carr and Kemmis's critique was action research, which they believed lacked a 'theoretical rationale' and, it has to be said, there is a strong whiff of 'hang theory, let's get on with the job' about some exponents of action research. It seems sufficient for teachers to point to some improvement in their practice, linked to clearly articulated and defensible research methods, to legitimise action research. The result is that epistemological issues remain buried somewhere in a plethora of case studies.

However, this is too simple. John Elliott (1987), for example, has identified the work of the German philosopher Hans-Georg Gadamer as a major influence on the action research tradition. Gadamer was concerned with hermeneutics, i.e. the ways in which interpretation of experience generates knowledge. Self-consciousness and language distinguish human beings from other species and make the interplay of interpretation of experience through the use of language the proper object of philosophical enquiry. Thus, the practices of teachers involve choices within concrete situations. These choices in turn involve values and beliefs which are intimately linked to teachers' sense of themselves as teachers. Understanding becomes an 'in-the-moment' thing. In other words, meanings of educational situations do not just exist – they are made by those involved in these situations.

This may sound a little impenetrable. It helps to think in terms of everyday examples, such as going on holiday. You plan a holiday with some idea of yourself as a holiday-maker – sunglasses, white sand, glass of tequila in hand, that kind of thing. You then experience the holiday itself, which usually involves some adjustments in your concept of being on holiday. You then return home with your sense of yourself as a holiday-maker reaffirmed ('I know I like sea and sun') or modified in some way ('I never thought I would enjoy that kind of holiday'). Holidays now mean something different for you.

Educational action research involves a similar process. Teachers examine their typical practices as teachers with a view to improvement. The outcome is that their sense of themselves as a teacher is affirmed, modified or even occasionally, transformed. An epistemologically developed version of action research, relocated away from classroom preoccupations and synthesised with critical social science, might serve as the theoretical basis of Education Studies. The remainder of this chapter builds on that notion.

> *Pause for thought* | a (very) small-scale research enquiry
>
> Educational research can be done on a very small scale indeed. It is essential that the researcher is curious and wants to find the answer to some questions. Also, research is characterised by being systematic and publicly available. One area of curiosity could be how texts such as this one are read. Begin with reflecting on how you are reading this chapter. Are you reading it word by word or skim reading? What ideas are you picking out as being significant and why? If it is your own copy rather than a library copy, do you highlight extracts of text? How do you intend to use the knowledge you have gained? Now, try to turn this reflective piece into research by discussing your reading with three other readers. On the basis of this comparison can you draw any conclusions about the similarities and differences among students reading academic texts? Who are you going to share your conclusions with?

A phenomenological epistemology for Education Studies

The previous section drew attention to the importance of Gadamer to the development of action research. Gadamer was a phenomenological philosopher. Phenomenologists are concerned with the ways in which human beings deal with everyday life in creative and pragmatic ways. The ways we understand and interpret ourselves and the world around us, phenomenologists argue, is a matter of experience. This is a very different philosophy from the idealist tradition that dominates western thinking whereby the rational mind arrives at objective truths and applies these to practice. It was this latter view which dominated liberal education and seems to dominate current ways of thinking about Education Studies whereby students will learn the 'right' educational knowledge to be applied subsequently in some yet-to-be-determined vocational setting. What happens then when a phenomenological pebble is dropped into this idealist pond?

Phenomenology means starting with the knower, rather than assumptions about the known. In other words, it means paying serious attention to Education Studies students. Their sense of themselves in practical educational situations as learners, as potential educational workers in many different ways, and as citizens whose informed perspectives on educational issues should influence policy-making, should be the heartbeat of Education Studies as a subject. Nor should this be an adjunct or kind of afterthought to the main business of teaching students about education. The major educational issue should be Education Studies students themselves.

A justification for this can be found in the philosophy of the German Martin Heidegger, whose writing from the first half of the twentieth century has influenced more recent philosophers, notably Richard Rorty, Jacques Derrida, Michel Foucault and Pierre Bourdieu. This influence is in spite of the romantic and nationalistic tendencies in Heidegger's writing which enabled him to prosper under Nazism. His emphasis on everyday experience as a source of meaning and intelligibility and his rejection of the notion that action is based on beliefs and desires rather than 'skilful coping' is a familiar phenomenological refrain. What is distinctive about Heidegger is his focus on the relationship between being and time. Heidegger argued that our sense of ourselves develops out of a range of possibilities we see as open to us. We make choices which make us what we are and we do so in the full knowledge of our own mortality – eventually we are all dead. It is the intelligibility of this process which interested Heidegger and which is relevant to the attempt to describe a phenomenological epistemology for Education Studies.

Heideggerian phenomenology seems to offer three significant contributions to such an epistemology. The first has been stated by Dreyfus and Hall (1992), who suggested that Heidegger 'by focusing on the ways of revealing in our everyday lives, can account for the meaningful interconnectedness or resonance in our practices'. Heidegger points to the dynamic quality of existence and the restless nature of internal life. This sense of struggle derives from the ways in which we try to maintain a consistent sense of ourselves as we are buffeted by our passage through the world. This brings us to Heidegger's second contribution. The extent to which we are able to achieve this sense of coherence and consistency is described by Heidegger as 'authenticity'. In contrast, 'inauthentic beings' become lost in the world, in the sense that they become creatures of circumstance, driven by whatever social conformities happen to surround them. Authenticity is one of the most troubling of concepts for some present-day philosophers, who see it as an elevation of rationality, a re-statement of the old notion of the enlightened individual, superior to the rest of humanity. This is troubling for them because it ignores the complex ways in which people can be intelligent. Emotional intelligence, or visual intelligence, for example, are the kinds of intelligences which seem to be marginalised by authenticity. It also seems to imply some final settled state of affairs which are 'authentic'. This too jars with our experience of life as ever-changing and moving.

However, Heidegger can be read differently – more softly. In this reading, authenticity is about a sense of 'fittingness', a sense of appropriateness in practical conduct which is subscribed to by an individual and recognised as such by others.

The notion of a public dimension to our professional conduct means paying serious attention to the contexts in which practices take place. Meaning-making is a public as well as a private act. This is where the kind of critical social science subscribed to by Carr and Kemmis and others re-enters the picture. In order to understand the context in which actions take place it is necessary to examine seriously the ways in which educational ideas and practices are socially defined. However, the door through which one enters this critical world is not that of liberal education (students must know these things) or a hierarchical notion of emancipatory knowledge. The door has to be created by the student who sees the relevance of engaging critically with social definition of education because it matters to their being as an educationalist.

The third and possibly most crucial Heideggerian contribution to Education Studies epistemology relates to time. Education Studies students are not teacher training students and, therefore, do not have an immediate school context in which to locate themselves. Education contexts for them are anticipated. Anticipating a state of affairs or a set of experiences which are not here and now, has inevitably to be envisaged in abstract and generalisable terms. At the point of writing this piece, the readers are not present. However, you can be imagined in general terms as students of Education Studies. You are envisaged as being interested in education and what underpins the subject. You are likely to harbour some ambition to work in an educational setting in some capacity in future. You are intelligent enough to undertake a degree and you are reading this text in the belief that it will help you succeed in that ambition. As a collective you will be gender and ethnically mixed and drawn from a variety of backgrounds. When this text was being written none of you was present but you still influenced the writing. This was what Heiddegger meant by being and time.

What all of this means epistemologically for Education Studies is that the subject needs to be constructed around the relationship between what is educationally here-and-now and what is educationally around the corner. This needs to be done on both a general subject curriculum level and on an individual student level. The extrapolation from the here-and-now to points in the future requires students to have opportunities to exercise imagination but not in an excessively fanciful way. Phenomenological analysis requires detailed appraisal of current practices and convincingly argued projections into the future.

Pause for thought | an anticipatory exercise

Think about yourself in five years' time. You have graduated with your degree in Education Studies and you are working in an educational setting – it could be a school as a teacher or it could be in an administrative role in an office, or it could be in a children's centre. How do you envisage yourself to be in that role? What will have changed about you in those five years in order to undertake the role? What will have stayed the same? Explain to yourself why it will be necessary to change in some respects.

Summary and conclusions

The major points made in this chapter are as follows:

- **Education Studies as a free-standing subject outside teacher training is a relatively new subject for most universities to offer students;**
- **the major issue facing Education Studies is epistemological, i.e. what counts as knowledge in the subject;**
- **Education Studies has inherited much of its content from teacher training and is, therefore, dominated by a liberal education tradition, built on a theory-to-practice model;**
- **this dependence on educational theory as the mainstay of Education Studies ignores the transformation in ways of critically thinking and analysing educational practices developed in the past 20 years;**

- **reflective practice, critical social science and action research constitute three major epistemologies in that they create new ways of knowing about education;**
- **an Education Studies rooted in a phenomenological epistemology will transcend the vocational/academic divide to create a subject really worth knowing and studying.**

The implications of this chapter are all contained in the final bullet point above and they relate to what is learned in Education Studies, how it is assessed and what counts as achievement in the subject:

- **a phenomenological approach means focusing on the everyday educational experiences of Education Studies students;**
- **practically, this means requiring students to offer thoroughly detailed and analytical accounts of their past, current and anticipated educational experiences, including those located in family, work and cultural settings;**
- **these understandings of students' own educational lives as learners will be contextualised, i.e. they will relate to the general ways of thinking about and experiencing education, many of which are contained in the other chapters in this volume;**
- **they will examine the implications of this phenomenological analysis for their own projected futures working in a potential variety of roles in multi-professional educational contexts;**
- **the intellectual attributes of the subject will also be phenomenological, i.e. the quality of the students' analysis will reside in their abilities to describe their current educational experiences, relate these to the contextual educational world around them and project into future educational roles in a coherent, critical and systematic way.**

Such a transformed epistemology would ensure that Education Studies was relevant to students and built upon knowledge worth knowing.

References

Bartlett, S, Burton, D and Peim, N (2001) *Introduction to education studies*. London: Paul Chapman.

Carr, W (ed) (2005) *The Routledge Falmer reader in philosophy of education*. Abingdon: RoutledgeFalmer.

Carr, W and Kemmis, S (1986) *Becoming critical: education knowledge and action research*. Lewes: Falmer Press.

Carr, W and Kemmis, S, (2005)

Crook, D (2002) Educational studies and teacher education. *British Journal of Educational Studies*, 50(1): 57–75.

Dreyfus, HL and Hall, H (1992) *Heidegger: a critical reader*. Oxford: Blackwell.

Elliott, J (1987) Educational theory, practical philosophy and action research. *British Journal of Educational Studies*, 35(2): 149–69.

Hall, S (1986) Variants of liberalism, in Donald, J and Hall, S (eds) *Politics and ideology*. Milton Keynes: Open University Press.

Hirst, P (1965) Liberal education and the nature of knowledge, in Archamult, RD (ed) *Philosophical Analysis and Education*. London: Routledge and Kegan Paul.

McCulloch, G (2002) Disciplines contributing to education? Educational studies and the disciplines. *British Journal of Educational Studies*, 50(1):100–19.

Schön, DA (1983) *The reflective practitioner: how professionals think in action*. New York: Basic Books.

Ward, S (ed) (2004) *Education studies: a student's guide*. London: RoutledgeFalmer.

Wilkin, M (1996) *Initial teacher training: the dialogue of ideology and culture*. Lewes: The Falmer Press.

Chapter 3

Community education: innovation and active intervention

Viv Kerridge and Ruth Sayers

Introduction

This chapter is concerned with education that occurs in the broader community rather than in a formal educational institution. It highlights the theoretical aspects of community education and consider its roots, function and importance. Set alongside the philosophical exposition will be a number of illustrations to place community education within a drama and theatre context, as we perceive a constructive and vibrant connection between the two. There is a strong tradition of using drama and theatre in active community projects and a coherent theoretical basis which explains its usefulness and illustrates its effectiveness. The chapter introduces interventionist techniques designed to enable communities to recognise and negotiate external restrictions. Distinctions are drawn between theatre-in-education, community theatre and educational drama. The political perspective offered includes a consideration of the financial, social and political pressure placed upon the development of community education and the level of attention and funding given to mainstream theatre as opposed to 'people's theatre', including street arts. The professional perspective offers a practical guide to establishing community projects with regard to ethical, philosophical and logistical frameworks.

Background

Formal education is a relatively new construct whereas some sense of community is fundamental to human development. Many of our life skills are absorbed *in situ* by informal means; that is by the family or community. Humans learn many things effectively, if sometimes painfully, from observation and trial and error. Traditionally, crafts and trades worked on an apprenticeship basis through active learning, and formal theoretical assessment was not part of the process. There was of course nothing idyllic about this arrangement; it too was subject to economic restrictions and dictated to by the basic need to survive. Community cooperation and education are difficult to untangle. Even formal education generally takes place in the local community, and educational institutions form communities of their own in which personal relationships and individual identity play a significant part in the learning process. To this extent it is misleading to suggest that education, in its broadest sense, can be anything but a community issue. So what is it that differentiates 'education in the community' from formal education?

Formal education is taken here to mean that which takes place in schools and other educational institutions. It undergoes constant development, or at least change, according to such criteria as pressures of finance, local and global pressures, government priorities and pedagogical fashion. Formal education can be flexible and fluid or very closely prescribed. Education in the community is also an umbrella term for a wide variety of activities which vary in terms of formality from drop-in play sessions for mothers and toddlers to fully accredited lifelong learning courses. It is also closely connected with community development and the connection between social welfare, community and education.

A trawl of the internet uncovers a wealth of Community Education Centres throughout the UK which offer a vast array of services such as:

- **education–business partnerships (which put schools in touch with potential business sponsors);**
- **links with local services (police, social services, health services);**
- **learning resource services (facilities such as desktop publishing, video editing, internet access);**
- **community cafes (or other relaxation areas where people can socialise and pick up information leaflets on local facilities);**
- **activities for the elderly;**
- **parents' groups (often with speakers and facilitators of parenting skills);**
- **basic skills sessions;**
- **youth organisations;**
- **professional advice (grant aid and advice on funding and training for community initiatives);**
- **citizens' advice sessions;**
- **free legal advice sessions;**
- **a range of classes at a variety of levels.**

Some of these centres are based in community schools, libraries or other public buildings, whilst some have their own separate premises, such as welfare halls and local institutes. These are open to all local residents; some of the facilities are free and others are subsidised. Many of these facilities may seem more 'community' orientated than 'educational'.

Pause for thought | community education

Look through the list of services. How many of them seem to you to be educational? Which do you consider to be community services? Are any of them difficult to differentiate? Do you think that any of the functions on the list help to 'create' a sense of community or do they 'service' a local area?

The history of community education

This level of provision is not a new phenomenon. During the second part of the nineteenth and the whole of the twentieth centuries, there was a strong tradition of working people's clubs and institutes throughout the country. In his fascinating history of British working class intellectual life, Rose (2002) referred to the miners' institutes of South Wales as: '*One of the greatest networks of cultural institutions created by working people, anywhere in the world*'.

He mentions that, by the time of the Second World War, the Tredegar Institute Library circulated 100,000 books per year, and many of these institutes had cinemas and film societies, and had staged numerous concerts and cultural performances. There is evidence that these libraries stocked a vast range of books on a variety of subjects and that people's reading habits included the classics and social and political texts. Whilst some of the people who benefited had aspirations beyond their cultural background, the majority used it as a form of personal enrichment and empowerment.

In addition to the wide range of cultural pursuits there was a strong tradition of political debate which often manifested itself through drama. Throughout the 1930s, radical theatre groups such as the 'Red Megaphones' in Salford (MacColl, 1973) were producing agit-prop theatre performances for the working classes in order to raise awareness of political, social and ideological issues. They used street theatre as a way of delivering their message. Their work was inspired by similar experiments in America led by the 'Living Newspaper' units that had been established as part of the Federal Theatre Project during the 1930s (Witham, 2003).

Susan Mansfield (cited in Allen and Martin, 1992) traces both the lesser-known contribution that women made to the development of community education and the patriarchal values which manifested themselves as powerfully in community education as they did in the school system. The Suffrage Movement and the socialist Sunday Schools raised the political awareness and confidence of women; the Women's Cooperative Guild, moved from an association concerned with women's traditional role, to a campaigning body which championed women's education. Later, movements such as the Townswomen's Guilds and the Women's Institute included education programmes, and campaigned for women's issues. The Suffragette Movement used drama in the form of propaganda sketches and full-length plays to further their political aims.

These movements and institutions and others like them across the country were largely self-generating and run by those they served. Rose notes that while the miners' libraries and other facilities were fed by the Miners' Welfare Fund set up by parliament to tax coal production and direct the revenue to the institutions, the miners themselves controlled the budget. They enjoyed a high level of cultural and intellectual freedom and were instrumental in the development of a culturally and politically aware populace beyond the jurisdiction of formal educational institutions. This is in contrast to many current community education centres, which offer similar facilities but are often run *for* the community rather than *by* them, and rely on local authorities for subsidy. The system of applying to a variety of bodies for funding ensures certain standards, but places a variety of obligations on the centres which may be counter-productive or restrictive. Such restrictions have been placed on theatre programmes that have been specifically designed to address community needs.

Theatre-in-education, often referred to as TIE, began in the UK in the 1960s. The history of TIE has been influenced by the political and economic context of each decade. Prior to the Education Reform Act of 1988, local education authorities were major funders. During the late 1970s and early 1980s there was little accountability and considerable freedom in designing programmes of work. A company was able to work for several days, or even weeks, with one class of students. With the implementation of Local Management of Schools as part of the 1988 Education Reform Act with the resulting restrictions, companies began to search for alternative sources of funding, often resorting to short-term projects designed to address a single issue quickly.

Emerging pressures

Michele Erma Doyle (cited in Richardson and Wolfe, 2001, p4), referring to youth and community workers, remarked on the pressure of external expectations on the field of informal education. She notes that both adult education and youth work are under increasing pressure to focus on formal accreditation of learning. She recognised that community workers need to be aware of the underlying educational theory to their work and laments the 'how-to' nature of the current literature which detracts from their professionalism. This, she suggested, is a direct result of the impact of the National Curriculum and its concentration on what is learned and how it is learned:

> This 'product' approach to learning [is] in contrast to the traditional focus of informal education which ... has focused on relationships and thus on the process by which learning happens, rather than on what is learnt. (p6)

These observations are reminiscent of the philosophy of Paulo Freire and his reference to formal education as 'the banking concept of education': a storing process where students build up deposits of knowledge supplied by the teacher (Freire, 1970). The 'banking concept' can be perceived as a restriction on the educator, who is required to teach a highly prescribed curriculum. Freire called for educators to abandon the deposit system of education and to replace it with 'the posing of the problems of human beings in their relations with the world'. This approach is seen, at least in part, in a number of community initiatives. The national strategy plan for neighbourhood renewal launched in 2001 as a government initiative recognises that:

> neighbourhood renewal starts from a proper understanding of the needs of communities, and that the most effective interventions are often those where communities are actively involved in their design and development. This includes community of interest, such as people who are black or from minority groups, as well as geographically defined communities. (White, 2002, p1)

Theoretically at least, the sense of grass roots participation in community planning and development is seen as a positive and necessary step. Lawton (1995) referred to 'The Third Way', a political philosophy adopted by New Labour at the turn of this century which recognised the impossibility of sustaining the Welfare State as chief provider, and sought to combine the complexities of capitalist globalisation and free markets with a social obligation on behalf of the state to support individuals and communities to help themselves:

> *The basic ideas entailed in the Third Way focus is on empowering individuals, families and communities to lift themselves out of poverty, unemployment and social exclusion by a combination of individual responsibility, education, social support and welfare to work initiatives.* (p95)

This recognises that, if people are to play an active part in local democracy, new skills and attitudes need to be developed. Government initiatives such as the citizenship curriculum in schools brings a new focus on community and active citizenship into the twenty-first century. A report of a Liverpool City Council initiative on a neighbourhood renewal skills and knowledge programme offers the following insight:

> *Most people associate learning with formal education, in schools, universities or a training course. But neighbourhood renewal is a new challenge, and everyone involved will need to develop new skills. For some this may involve individual training. But it also means learning from experience, learning jointly with other partners, and talking to people facing similar challenges.* (White, 2002, p23)

This advocates discussion, involvement and personal and group commitment. While obviously challenging, the approach to learning is empowering and life-enhancing on both an individual and community level. Freire (1970) referred to 'problem-posing education' and contends that people, when challenged with problems that relate in a direct way to their own or their community's well-being, will feel obliged to respond to the challenge. By presenting challenges as personal and yet universal, the individual is encouraged to develop a sense of connection and personal involvement with the community. If this connection becomes proactive, it can in turn lead to the decentralisation of power and closer, interactive communities of responsible citizens who are involved and confident enough to make a difference. This approach has been developed in the work of Brazilian theatre practitioner Augusto Boal. Boal's Marxist interventionist theories, influenced by Freire, were used frequently by TIE practitioners during the latter part of the twentieth century. One example is the work of Kaos Theatre Company, whose 1993 TIE programme was designed to address issues central to a growing understanding of AIDS and was constructed to encourage young people to recognise the epidemic and to change their views before they entered adulthood. Phil Morle (1993), artistic director of the project, worked alongside the company to create a series of workshops that began with an exploration of Boal's 'Image Theatre'.

Pause for thought | proactivity

It is interesting to note that, for very different reasons, many western governments in pursuit of 'the Third Way' should mirror a number of the pedagogical recommendations of a revolutionary such as Freire. Consider for a moment what the advantages of proactive communities might be and the disadvantages for both

- a community?
- a government?

What is a community?

The concept of community is multifaceted and fluid. The term is often used to describe:

- **physical proximity, as in neighbourhood;**
- **civic identity, as in a populace;**
- **collective identity, as in unity, cooperation and shared interest.**

A sense of locality may well be fundamental to an individual's sense of identity, but this can be negative as easily as it can be positive. A sense of belonging, being recognised and accepted is psychologically healthy, but many people at some point in their lives feel marginalised or stifled by a community that is based purely on proximity. However, locality can provide a network of support. In addition to locality, there is a broader sense of community which operates on a less personal level. This includes such things as a wider regional or national identity, or a shared language and loose classifications such as the 'black', 'gay', or 'asylum seeker' community. In normal, unstressed situations these broad classifications tend to remain on a level of recognition rather than meaningful engagement. Nicholson (2005) pointed out that these broader identities can obscure enormous differences and frequently ignore multiple identities. Each individual belongs to a number of communities some of which satisfy a transitory need, others which are more lasting. Sometimes people from different locations and from different backgrounds find a common cause which initiates a sense of community, if only for a short time.

An increasing form of community identification, described by Nicholson as 'the paradigm shift from communities of locality to communities of identity', involves a sense of community dictated less by geography and more by interest and common experience, beliefs or values. This concept is made easier by effective communication services. To some extent this is an 'imagined' community of shared identity with no material existence.

> *Pause for thought* | overlapping community
>
> The concept of community is not singular. Consider for a moment how many 'communities' you belong to and write them down. How far do they overlap? If you have left a community, how much of it have you absorbed and taken with you? Have you ever felt on the margins of a community? Have you ever felt restricted by a community you belonged to? Does community imply exclusiveness? Compare your ideas of community with someone else's.

Community intervention

Asking communities to become more active and to take more responsibility socially, educationally and politically, is a form of intervention. Its success depends on how far individuals are able to identify with community issues, which will depend to some extent on how clearly they understand them and on how much influence they believe they can have. People's apparent indifference to global, national and local issues often stems from a sense of powerlessness and a lack of confidence that they can have any influence whatsoever. Offering practical information or education about how society functions and how individuals and communities can access legal, financial and social services is helpful, but there are more empowering ways of educating people which enhance confidence, offer insight and actually build a sense of community identity.

Neelands (2004) has developed the notion of social justice within the 'people's theatre', which he sees as participatory and active, belonging to all people within a community. Instead of defining form or genre, he refers to a living partnership between and within theatres, linking cultures together. He believes that stories are the building blocks of theatre and asserts that all communities share the common belief in the power of stories to help their youth make sense of the world. Neelands's vision included artistic transformations at the heart of theatre, with actors transformed through roles and the spaces they inhabit, transformed into imaginary worlds. Even time is transformed and made symbolic through theatrical events, an aspect expanded by Schechner (2003). As well as being a stimulus for artistic action, Neelands has a vision of the 'people's theatre' within the social dimension, going

> *beyond the recognition of cultural differences in our artistic work to include the opportunity for our social and economic differences to be publicly and socially negotiated in the interests of social justice.* (p33)

Any kind of interventionist strategy can potentially damage as well as liberate. Practitioners are accountable for the effect that their work has on the communities they service, as these examples demonstrate.

Research box

monitoring the challenge

To what extent should participants be 'projected into' or protected from controversial material and methodologies? The balance between challenge and support is the key to this issue. The first example is an exposition of the HIV/AIDS workshops, mentioned earlier, through the perspective of the director Phil Morle (1993). In an 'anti-intellectual' approach to learning, the Kaos Theatre Company used theatre games, contact improvisation and sculpting and physical manipulation of participants. The director encouraged participants to use their hands and eyes instinctively, without taking time to plan and think ahead. Although Boal's theories were evident in this process, the deliberate avoidance of intellectual engagement with the form does not appear to have adhered to his practice in all respects.

> *If individuals think in their heads first and then attempt to translate this into physical imagery, the result is compromised by limitations of translation, causing a constraint of the potential image and ultimately the debate.* (Morle, 1993, p3)

Trusting in the language of imagery was central to the process in order to allow unconscious feelings to surface. The validity of such devices could be questioned since they do not offer protection to participants and encourage potentially embarrassing unguarded responses. Tensions could arise between the company delivering the workshop and the group leader entrusted with care of the group.

There are many examples of interventionist theatre programmes using Boal's Forum Theatre to address issues allied to the citizenship agenda (Dwyer, 2004). One such programme was the Brisbane Dracon project (O'Toole and Burton, 2005), which focused on the role of acting in helping young people towards a cognitive understanding of the nature, causes and dynamics of conflict and bullying. Students were given the skills to take control of their own conflicts and conflict agenda, with an assumption that educational drama techniques have 'considerable potential to motivate and assist students to understand the causes of conflict.'

Community drama programmes claim to have had a positive impact in the area of social inclusion and social regeneration. Increasingly, such programmes have been expected to produce evidence of social outcomes as well as artistic realisation, taking theatre into new socio-cultural territory. Typically a company might be expected to produce statistical evidence about the participants and audiences serviced. London Bubble Theatre Company has placed these issues at the centre of its community programmes with the belief that the arts have the capacity to break down barriers of class, culture, age and gender. *The Making of George* (Owen, 2004) was a collaborative project which sought to meet the objectives of the Southwark Community Cohesion Pathfinder Programme, a regeneration initiative. There was a meeting of social aims between funders and artists, but a tension emerged between a non-arts funding source and an arts programme. This community play could not rely simply on the benefits of bringing together people aged 15–75 from the area in a vibrant and innovative arts event. It also needed to produce evidence of social outcomes.

The community play is a medium for communities to take ownership of their own regeneration and is also an interventionist theatre form. The term defines a collection of voluntary non-professional actors working together to create a performance, usually based on a local issue or story. It clearly falls under the mantle of educational theatre within the community and allows groups who inhabit the same cultural context to share their stories and learn to understand each other's problems, breaking down the barriers between groups and opening a dialogue with excluded groups in society. Van Erven (2001) wrote of a series of community plays throughout the world and suggests that the artistic processes involved in community theatre evolve under particular socio-cultural conditions. Whilst scripts are often used in community theatre, there is an emphasis on oral stories and personal recollection. Spare Tyre Theatre Company, a community group formed to develop performance with people aged 65 to over 80 years old, offers an example of the function of the community play in social inclusion, empowering and valuing the experiences of a social group who might otherwise feel socially excluded (Irving, 2003).

The status of the community play and street arts when set against mainstream theatre belies its significance in the lives of individuals. Gardner (2003) commented that street arts events are virtually ignored. Yet the 'Streets of Brighton' Festival draws in an audience of more than 100,000 people. In France, the 'Cinescenie' at Puy de Fou is performed on the largest outdoor stage in the world, with 1,000 actors, aged from five years old upwards, a team of 300 staff and 100 animals in each show. Almost 7 million spectators have seen the event since its inception in 1978. The pastoral setting is combined with cutting-edge technology to exciting effect, with surround sound, laser, pyrotechnics, water screen and projections. Despite its scale, reporting of such an event is minimal beyond the region in which it is performed. Kershaw (1999, 2003) advocated greater radicalism in street performance and wants to move away from spectacle and towards dialogue, which might result in greater critical attention.

Setting up a community project

'Education in the community' offers an exciting opportunity to make a difference to the lives of others, especially when using vibrant interactive methodologies such as drama and theatre. It also places a number of practical and professional demands on those charged with establishing such projects. Effective protocols are required to ensure that etiquette, ethical concerns and equal opportunities are in place that will provide respect for participants. When higher education students work in the community, additional issues affect the project such as health and safety, assessment and support. The complexities involved in setting up an educational community project are outlined below.

If a facilitator undertakes a project with an established group, he or she suspends the relationship between the group and their usual leader. Initiating a positive relationship between the 'normal' group leader and the facilitator of the project is vitally important.

If a facilitator hopes to establish a freestanding community group, he or she must decide whether or not to approach an umbrella organisation in order to recruit volunteers. Gaining access to a target group within a church or prison, for example, could be achieved through access to regular meetings, enhanced through an advertising campaign. Both the emerging group and the facilitator in this situation have the security of working within clearly established rules and codes of practice. The facilitator will be required to observe the policies and procedures of the host organisation and will have the responsibility of ensuring that participants in the project do the same. A positive aspect of this situation is that individual rights and responsibilities are assured, with behaviour contracts in place and minority interests preserved. Individual needs are addressed through existing legislation and the whole group, including the facilitator, is protected by the organisation's public liability insurance, health and safety legislation and risk assessments.

It is possible, however, that the umbrella organisation may inhibit the behaviour of the participants and promote an atmosphere that the facilitator finds inappropriate. For example, there may be codes relating to appearance and use of language that meet the needs of the organisation in its day-to-day operation but prevent the facilitator from achieving the atmosphere required for learning outcomes to be realised. If interventionist drama theories are to be employed in the liberation of individuals from aspects of their lives that cause oppression, it is inappropriate to work within oppressive regimes. Yet if the organisation is sponsoring the work, its aims and values cannot be ignored even when they contradict those of the facilitator.

Given these negative possibilities, the facilitator may elect to establish a 'freestanding' community group, perhaps to celebrate a single event, such as a community festival or national celebration. Arts events in this category could include a community play, torch-lit procession, street party, exhibition or entertainment for a village fete. Such events would be more likely to emerge from within a locational or geographical community group than an interest group. If the facilitator is an insider, then local loyalties, friendships and shared understanding will provide the pressure and motivation for the formation of the group. A disadvantage of the local leadership arrangement is that the group may fall victim to historical rivalries and disputes and may find it hard to attract funding.

Further observations, following logically from comments above about the establishment of a freestanding community group, relate to the increased risk accepted by the facilitator. Without the cushion of respectability and legislative support offered by an institutional framework, the lone facilitator may lack even basic facilities, such as meeting or rehearsal space.

Having identified a community group, the facilitator must produce a detailed project outline. This might include:

- **targets;**
- **earning outcomes;**
- **identified target-group needs;**
- **timelines;**
- **budget;**
- **outcomes;**
- **legislative issues;**
- **research;**
- **risk management;**
- **workshop plans and content;**
- **resource needs;**
- **partners' interests;**
- **review processes.**

A professional contract is needed in order to clarify roles, responsibilities and liability. It is essential that all partners are aware of the function, scope and expected outcome of the community project and that an appropriate balance is struck with participants between ownership and accountability.

Summary and conclusions

There is a rich history of education within communities in non-formal settings. This goes beyond the accumulation of facts and information and deals with ideas, aspiration and personal and community identity. While it is vulnerable to outside manipulation, it is also responsive to positive intervention.

Intervention can be political, social or educational. Communities may be empowered to accept or reject intervention and can develop their own strategies for change from within. Theatre and drama structures are ideal for active intervention as they offer physical examples which can be viewed, deconstructed and re-negotiated. They also allow effective and cognitive responses to occur simultaneously, encouraging rounded engagement. Intervention is always value-laden and so any attempt to work within communities using active learning methods demands a level of self-awareness on the part of the facilitator in order to avoid imposing attitudes and assumptions.

It has been suggested that communities work most effectively when they form self-supporting units and also that theatre can be a powerful medium for initiating responses. Since theatre programmes can sometimes seem transitory and imposed, and also risk unearthing sensitive issues for vulnerable members of society, there is perhaps greater benefit in using sustained, active drama methodology to empower communities to solve problems. A well-prepared drama project in which a single facilitator moves into the community and works within it, as described above, is therefore an effective vehicle for building a confident, proactive community.

References and further reading

Allen, G and Martin, I (1992) Histories of community education: a feminist critique, in *Education and community*. New York: Cassell.

Boal, A (1998) *Theatre of the oppressed*. London: Routledge.

Boal, A (1999) *The rainbow of desire*. London: Routledge.

Dwyer, P (2004) Making bodies talk in Forum Theatre. *Research in Drama in Education*, 9: 9–23.

Freire, P (1970) *Pedagogy of the oppressed*. London: Penguin.

Gardner, L (2003) Out of the ashes. *Street Arts: A Users Guide*, I: 8–10.

Irving, E (2003) Old age ain't no place for sissies. *Mail Out: National Magazine for Developing Participation in the Arts*, 3: 9.

Kershaw, B (1999) *The politics of performance*. London: Routledge.

Kershaw, B (2003) Seeing through the spectacle. *Street Arts: A Users Guide*, 1: 10–13.

Lawton, D (1995)

Lawton, D (2001) *Education for citizenship*. London: Continuum.

MacColl (1973) Grass roots of theatre workshop. *Theatre Quarterly*, 9: 58–68.

Morle, P (1993) Art can save lives: drama and AIDS. *Journal of National Drama*,12(1): 2–4.

Neelands, J (2004) The opening address to the 5th World Congress of IDEA. *Drama Journal*, 12(1): 31–8.

Nicholson, H (2005) *Applied drama*. Hampshire: Palgrave Macmillan.

O'Toole, J and Burton, B (2005) Education acting against conflict and bullying: the Brisbane Dracon Project 1996–2004. *Research in Drama Education*, 10(3): 269–84.

Owen, L (2004) The Making of George. *Drama Journal: One Forum, Many Voices*, Winter 12(1): 5–7.

Richardson, LD and Wolfe, M (2001) *Principles and practice of informal education*. London: RoutledgeFalmer.

Rose, J (2002) *The intellectual life of the British working classes*. New Haven, CT: Yale University Press.

Schechner, R (2003) *Performance Theory*. London: Routledge.

Van Erven, E (2001) *Community theatre: global perspectives*. London: Routledge.

White, L (2002) *Neighbourhood renewal, case studies and conversations*. London: NIACE.

Witham, B (2003) *The Federal Theatre Project: a case study*. Cambridge: Cambridge University Press.

Chapter *4*

Education and the free market

Nigel Tubbs

Introduction

The idea of a free market in educational provision lies at the heart of some of the most fiercely contested issues within education. Whether debating equality of opportunity, the liberty of parents to choose their child's school, or the quality of teaching in both schools and universities, the free market is ubiquitous; its effects are felt everywhere. In this chapter we will explore some of the ways in which the free market has shaped and continues to shape such discussions.

Kant's principles

It is important for students of education to explore the *principles* that lie behind ideologies of the free market and those that oppose them. We will use here Immanuel Kant's definition of a principle. He argued that there are two types of principles. The first is a *subjective principle*. This is characterised by personal taste and desire, and is often characterised by justifying itself as 'I want …' By definition this kind of interest is *particular* to each person. It cannot therefore be made a law, applicable *universally* for everyone, because it is wrong to impose *my* particular desires/ends/purposes/motives on those of someone else.

Secondly, Kant noted that there are *objective principles*. These are 'laws' regarding what *everyone ought* to do. For example, it is an objective principle, universally applicable to all persons, that everyone must pay taxes. This can be called objective because:

- **it applies to all people regardless of their subjective desires;**
- **the purpose is not individual or particular, but universal.**

It is in this struggle between the universal interest and the particular interest that debates about the role of the free market in education are fought out.

What is the free market principle?

A free market is one in which the law of supply and demand is allowed to operate without restriction and intervention by government. In other words, something will be made and supplied for people to buy and use if there is a demand for it and if they are prepared to pay for it. A successful business satisfies this demand and makes money. A failing business supplies something for which there is no demand and goes bust.

The principle of the free market, also known as *laissez-faire* economics, is held by its supporters to be the best way to run a society because the real needs of everyone (the universal) are met – people are fed, jobs are created, homes are built – and money and time are not wasted on producing things no one wants. In addition, if there is competition among those who produce and supply the goods, then this should ensure quality and value for money. Profit is the incentive to make things; therefore the profit motive can be trusted to supply what society needs because it will only respond to real needs. In this sense, the free market operates in the universal interest; that is, it is in the best interests of everyone.

Adam Smith

The most famous representative of the principle of the free market is Adam Smith (1723–90). He outlined the way he believed the free market should organise society in his book the *Wealth of nations*, published in 1776. For our interests, Part 5 of the book gives some details on how the free market should be applied to education.

Smith (1977) argued that 'in every profession, the exertion of the greater part of those who exercise it is always in proportion to the necessity they are under of making that exertion'. Or, in other words, people only work hard because their wages depend upon the result of their work: *no result — no payment*. Extra incentives to work hard are, he says, 'rivalship and emulation', or in other words, competition between people. We can add here that, for Smith, if people are paid according to their individual ('particular') worth, then the universal interest is best served.

His view, then, was that the only way to ensure quality in teaching and lecturing is for the tutor to be 'voluntarily chosen by the student', who should also be able to 'change him for another without leave first asked'. The opposite, he says, leads to lectures in which the tutor and the students know that he is 'speaking or reading nonsense or what is very little better than nonsense', and to lectures which students therefore desert or attend only with 'contempt or derision'. He noted wryly that

> the discipline of the college ... may enable him to force all his pupils to the most regular attendance upon the sham lecture, and to maintain the most decent and respectful behaviour during the whole time of the performance. The discipline of colleges and universities is in general contrived, not for the benefit of the students, but for the interest, or more properly speaking, for the ease of the masters. Its object is, in all cases, to maintain the authority of the master, and whether he neglects or performs his duty, to oblige the students in all cases to behave to him as if he performed it with the greatest diligence and ability. (p249)

His conclusion was that quality in education can only be assured where the reward of the tutor 'depends principally [or entirely] upon the fees or honoraries of his students'. We might add here that Smith sees universal state provision of education with guaranteed salaries as unlikely to be an incentive to quality teaching. A greater spur to hard work would be to reward each teacher on their merits rather than regardless of them. Reward the particular, and the universal will look after itself.

Pause for thought | is lecturing an easy life?

Do Smith's worries apply as much to today's lecturers in universities as they did in Smith's day? Do lecturers have an easy time of it because they will get paid no matter what the standard of their lectures? Would their performance be improved if the students could pay them according to their merit, and refuse them payment if their lectures were not up to scratch?

Lowe's Revised Code of 1862

It is not hard to follow this theme of 'payment by results' over the following 230 years. Perhaps the most famous example in the nineteenth century is Robert Lowe's Revised Code. Robert Lowe believed in free market economics. His Revised Code, and in particular, payment by results, put this philosophy of the free market into practice. Government spending on education had increased from £20,000 in 1833 to £668,000 in 1859 and this alarmed many in the government. A way of cutting back was to let the market take over and only give government money to those teachers who produced pupils able to pass in six standards of the three Rs. To this end, Lowe introduced testing and league tables in the proficiency of the three Rs of all children of six years and over in state-assisted elementary schools. Each child could earn the school the sum of 12 shillings while successful examination performance earned a further 8 shillings. Of his Revised Code, Lowe said, 'hitherto we have been living under a system of bounties and protection; now we propose to have a little free trade [another way of saying free market]' (Curtis, 1948). The system lasted until 1896.

> *Pause for thought* | no change?
>
> It is probable that some readers have already made for themselves a comparison between the Revised Code and the situation that exists today. Do we not now also have league tables, testing and, in certain ways, payment by results?

The free market and parental choice

One idea that represents the free market in education is that of 'vouchers'. The principle is very simple: every parent gets a voucher from the government to 'spend' with the school of their choice. In 1975 the *Black Papers* made the following case:

> *It could be argued that the introduction of state controlled and provided education from 1870 onwards was all a mistake ... If the 1870 Act had simply provided the poor with a 'ticket' or a voucher to buy education then the rapidly expanding private schools would have quickly met all the remaining demand.*

> *The time [1975] would seem ripe for the establishment of at least two full voucher experiments in Britain ... A non-transferable voucher could be issued for each pupil and the parent would be able to pay it into the school of his choice, either state or private. The school would in turn exchange the vouchers for cash from the state or the local education authority at a value equal to the average cost of state education in that area for the relevant age. Popular schools would continue to expand and unpopular schools would decline and close.* (Cox and Boyson, 1975, p27)

When Keith Joseph became Secretary of State for Education in 1981 it seemed as if vouchers would indeed be introduced. Joseph, in 1982, spoke warmly of the idea:

> *The voucher, in effect, is a cash facility for all parents, only usable in schools instead of money. It would come from the tax payer, and it would give parents, however poor, a choice of schools regardless of how much the schools cost, be they in the private sector or the maintained, that is, the public sector. The idea of the voucher is a noble idea. It is the idea of freeing parents from all money considerations in choosing a school for their children.* (Chitty, 1989, p184)

However, vouchers have never yet been introduced into compulsory education.

A more recent intervention into the debate about parental choice and the free market has been made by Harry Brighouse. He has made the case for enhancing parental choice 'by prohibiting state schools from selecting students, and forcing Local Education Authorities to pay for transportation' (Brighouse, 2002). His argument is that there are already market forces at work in deciding which children can get into which schools. Even though most children might still attend their local school, Brighouse argues that the market determines who can and who cannot afford to live in the neighbourhood. Thus, 'middle-class and wealthy parents who are unsatisfied with their children's schools have a choice. They can move to the neighbourhood within their district where most of the middle-class and wealthy children go'.

By definition, since this option is available only to some parents, the principle of the free market here can only attend to the *particular* interests of some parents. In addition, it could be said that schools operate the selection of pupils because the neighbourhood has already selected their intake through the housing market. House prices here act as the voucher. Against those who would argue that choice itself is the problem, and would allocate students to their local school, Brighouse argued that the only way to offer real choice to poorer parents in poorer neighbourhoods is to open up choice completely. Working-class parents, he said, are just as capable as middle class parents of selecting good schools if only they were to be given the chance to choose. Anything that 'effaces the barriers between districts can be expected to contribute to equality'.

Brighouse's argument is interesting in that he thinks that only a completely free choice of school by parents, with transportation subsidised by local education authorities (LEAs), can overcome the inequalities that exist in the free (housing) market. James Tooley, on the other hand, argued that the free market is not sufficiently involved in parental choice of schools. He argued that it is the profit motive that can best regulate against failing schools. If schools could be chosen by customers along the same lines as they choose which supermarket to shop in, then, very quickly, those schools that nobody wanted would go out of business. Whilst the brand name, say, of Waitrose, is a guarantee to customers of high quality, there is no such way of identifying quality across the country in terms of schools. So, Tooley would support the creation in the free market of privatised schools – perhaps owned by different companies – so that schools, like supermarkets, could be identified and available in all areas. Parents would know exactly what they were getting because the branding would guarantee particular qualities, approaches, etc. Tooley says, 'if we abhor "sink" schools and want a guarantee of quality for all children, no matter what their parental circumstances, then the solution is competing education companies with strong brand names providing for them '.

The free market and the 1988 Education Reform Act

There is a second way, after parental choice of schools, in which the free market has been introduced into education. This time it was, and continues to be, around ways to guarantee the quality of teaching. The 1988 Education Reform Act introduced (among other things) the following features:

- **a national curriculum;**
- **tests for all children at 7, 11, 14 and 16;**
- **publication of test results school by school;**
- **open enrolment (schools would have to accept pupils according to parental choice).**

There are ways in which the Act can be seen as putting the free market into education. For example, since all pupils were to be taught the same curriculum, they could all be tested across common standards. The publication of the results of those tests, school by school, would enable parents to compare schools' performance and then use this information to decide for themselves the best school for their children.

Lawton (1992) has argued that the 1988 Act made vouchers unnecessary because league tables of schools' results would ensure that the parent, the consumer, would have all the power: 'market forces could be encouraged by the simple mechanism of attaching a price to every pupil and encouraging schools to compete for the pupils'.

It is important that we note here how notions of 'freedom' and 'choice' are seen by supporters of the free market as best protected by a lack of government planning and intervention. Consumers have most freedom and choice in the market place when they can make their own mind up about what to buy. It is their money, and this spending power ought to ensure that only quality commodities (in this case, good schools) are available. Consumer power is thought by free marketeers to be the only way of genuinely ensuring that teachers are accountable in education and are motivated to produce excellent schools. The fear of a school closing because it is not getting enough students, and then being labelled a 'failing school' should be enough incentive to ensure that the teachers in such schools improve their performance. Here, the market will ensure that standards are raised because, as we saw with Adam Smith above, teachers' jobs will depend upon it. This fear of unemployment will be much more powerful in raising standards than any notion of 'professionalism' or central planning could be. When parents choose the best schools for their children, then, through the law of supply and demand, good schools would grow and bad, unpopular, failing schools would close. The free market will ensure high quality schools and high quality teachers because it will introduce competition between schools for students.

Criticisms of the free market in education

Criticisms fall into three types: political, educational and moral.

Political critiques

The main thrust of political critiques of the free market is centred around notions of equality of opportunity. We have seen already that Brighouse discerns a huge advantage in educational opportunity to those families that can afford to move into houses within the catchment area of 'good schools'. Gipps (1993) has made a similar point:

> *As is becoming increasingly clear, the concept of market choice allows the articulate middle and educated classes to exert their privilege (whilst not appearing to). Both the market and the chooser are operating in terms of self-interest, and the result is exclusion and differentiation, rather than freedom and choice. Choice is not to be confused with selection. How the system copes with unchosen schools and unselected children is likely to be a major dilemma.* (p35)

Lawton was equally sceptical:

> *A free market in education is likely to be inferior to a system planned by professionals, because a free market is only efficient if there is perfect information − or at least very good information − as well as the ability to pay. Many parents are not in a position to know what is on offer, nor to know how to judge its quality, nor to pay for what they would like. Given the situation, to talk of the free market is either naive or hypocritical; it can be argued that what parents want may not always be in the best interests either of the children or of the community as a whole.* (p86)

His conclusion was that 'a completely free market in education would be unfair to some individuals and economically inefficient for society as a whole'. Chitty's (1992) conclusion was that:

> *There is no indication that the infusion of market values will do anything to raise the standard of education in the country. The free-market philosophy underpinning the Education Reform Act has everything to do with competition and privatisation and very little to do with a genuine extension of educational opportunities.* (p42)

These critics are united in their fear that, left to the free market, education will continue to privilege affluent middle class parents who can afford to play the system, and continue to disadvantage poorer parents who must accept the school they find in their neighbourhood. This is compounded when schools are able to select pupils because they are oversubscribed. In this situation, all the power of choice that was supposed to be with the parents moves quickly back to the schools. This creates a self-fulfilling prophecy, where the good schools select the 'best' students, and these schools flourish, while less popular schools slip into a spiral of decline, left only with those students that the good schools have already rejected. Behind this critique, we can say that the combination of the housing market and the over-subscription of popular schools operates by definition in the particular interests of some, but cannot be said to operate in the universal interest, that is, in the interests of everyone. As long as there are winners and losers, this aspect of the free market in schooling falls foul of Kant's requirement that an objective principle represent the universal interest or the interest of all.

At the time of writing this chapter the government produced its White Paper called *Higher Standards, Better Schools for All* (DfES, 2005). Its proposals incorporate Brighouse's demand for LEAs to pay the transportation costs of pupils from poorer families which, in turn, should provide these families with greater choice of local schools. The principle claimed for this by Prime Minister Tony Blair in his Foreword to the White Paper is 'to put parents in the driving seat for change in all-ability schools that retain the comprehensive principle of non-selection'. Specifically, the proposal to pay for 'transportation costs addresses the problem that while the affluent can buy choice ... [the new proposals] will ensure that choice is more widely available to all within an increasingly specialist system, not just to those who can pay for it', (DfES, 2005). It remains to be seen whether the freedom for schools to set their own admission policies will really extend choice to the poorest families.

Educational critiques

Critiques of the free market on educational grounds tend to stress the overpowering sense of the rigidity and conformity that the National Curriculum and testing bring with them. Davies and Edwards (2001), for example, have argued that schooling has itself become defined in market terms, that is, as the main way to ensure that future citizens learn the skills necessary for success in the global market place. Education is now not only run on free market principles, its very function serves the demands of that market. The student is seen less in educational terms and more in terms of training to meet the needs of industry and commerce. They remark that for New Labour 'it is clear that the overwhelming imperative is to recast education primarily, if not exclusively, as an instrumental means of ensuring economic success in an increasingly competitive global market'. Overall, they conclude that the influence of the free market within schools is 'a seriously flawed logic that renders it [New Labour's educational policy] ill equipped to meet the challenges of the twenty-first century'.

Moral critiques

Equally powerful critiques of the effects of the free market in education are made in moral terms. One such critique is from the current Archbishop of Canterbury, Dr Rowan Williams. In his book *Lost icons* (2000), Williams noted an ambivalence within the very notion of 'choice'. 'Real choice,' he says, 'both expresses and curtails freedom.' In beginning to separate market choice from real life choices, he notes that the latter are not like choosing what to buy on a supermarket shelf. Applied to parental choice of schools, Williams draws attention to how the 'choice' made by one parent may impact on the lack of choice left to another. In addition, those schools that are chosen by parents, and are therefore able to 'attract customers away from competitors' mean that the schools left behind can enter 'a spiral of failure … and the consequen[t] diminution of real choice for some parents'.

Williams's concern here was that we do not understand the effects that the choices made by one person or family have upon the decline of choice for others. We are not encouraged to worry about others, only that we get what we want. The free market's heralding of consumer choice, in education at least, 'encourages us to ignore the contexts and effects of such choice'. In other words, we are being encouraged to think only of ourselves and our own needs, regardless of the effect they may have on others. This, said Williams, is part of a wider social problem where in reality choice becomes 'the successful assertion of will'.

Thus, for Williams, rather than being the solution to many of society's problems, the rhetoric of choice within a free market needs to 'be stripped of its false innocence', that is, stripped of the idea that one family's choices don't affect other families' choices. He worries that adults seem content to remain uninformed about how their choices make a difference to others, and that 'choice for one group is preserved or defended at the cost of the freedom of others to choose what they want or need'. In the ideology of the free market, then, Williams concludes that choice is debased, reduced from its moral imperative to always consider others to a world where, we might say (though Williams does not put it quite like this), 'I get what I want and damn everyone else'.

Pause for thought | the price of choice

Do you agree with Williams? Do all our choices have effects in the world that we are mostly unaware of? Are all our so-called free choices in fact already compromised by the conditions that make them possible? If so, what are we to do: carrying on choosing and forgetting about others, or perhaps restrict our own freedom of choice trying to improve the situations of others?

Summary and conclusions

What kind of conclusion can we arrive at, then, when thinking about education and the free market? Is it, on the one hand, the only efficient and effective way of getting the best schools for all pupils? Or, on the other hand, is it merely an ideology that favours the haves over the have-nots, and enshrines and perpetuates privilege and discrimination in the education system? As future Education Studies graduates, this can be expected of you. This thinking can be aided by returning to Kant's definition of an objective principle and thinking how it might apply here and what can be learned from it.

Suppose we think it unfair that the free market be used in education only to benefit those with enough money to make choices and that, therefore, we support the universal interest by letting communities, through LEAs, decide which child attends which school. At the same time, this opinion should make us nervous because it will remove the right of parents to choose and replace it with the decisions of local politicians. To ensure everyone is treated the same we have removed the right for anyone to choose at all.

On the other hand, we might take the view that freedom to choose is more important than any LEA policy. We support the free market, therefore, because it restores that choice. However, we are also slightly nervous because we recognise that while some will have choice, others won't.

Put bluntly, if we support the universal interest, we suppress particular needs and if we support individual choice we prioritise the choices of the few over the (universal) needs of the many. It seems that whichever choice we make we cannot satisfactorily meet the universal interest *and* individual needs. What are we to do?

Perhaps returning to Rowan Williams might help here. Rather than see the problem as requiring one answer, perhaps one should recognise the need for a better understanding of the nature of making choices. It is true, on the one hand, that every choice has implications beyond the locality of the choice. If we choose a pair of trainers, we must also recognise that they may be produced by children working in sweat shops around the world being paid very little. We cannot help that. But we can gain a clearer understanding of the implications of choosing those trainers. Similarly, and on the other hand, if we support equality of opportunity through universal education policies which apply to everyone, we must also recognise the dangers this holds for individual freedom of choice. We can gain a clearer understanding of the ways in which equality of opportunity may well reduce the choices that others have. Or, if we support freedom of choice over the universal needs of everyone, we must recognise how getting what we want may well mean others losing out.

Politicians and policy-makers, it seems, seldom commit themselves to expressing the difficulty of choosing between the universal and the particular. For political reasons they are expected to have unambiguous statements on everything. Thankfully, Education Studies students need not be so restricted. We can remain open to learning about the contradictions that appear in the relation between the universal and the particular when seeking to apply principles. Indeed, this provides us the opportunities, in our studies, to look ever more deeply into what more can be learned from such contradictions.

References

Brighouse, H (2002) A modest defence of school choice. *Journal of Philosophy of Education*, 36(4): 653–9.

Chitty, C (1989) *Towards a new education system*. Lewes: Falmer.

Chitty, C (1992) From Great Debate to Great Reform Act: the post-war consensus overturned, in Rattansi, A and Simon, B (eds) *Rethinking radical education: essays in honour of Brian Simon*. London: Lawrence and Wishart.

Cox, CB and Boyson, R (eds) (1975) *Black Papers 1975: the fight for education*. London: Dent.

Curtis, SJ (1948) *History of education in Great Britain*. London: University Tutorial Press.

Davies, M and Edwards, G (2001) Will the curriculum caterpillar ever learn to fly?, in Fielding, M (ed) *Taking education really seriously: four years hard labour*. London: RoutledgeFalmer.

DfES (2005) *Higher Standards, Better Schools for All*. White Paper, 25 October.

Gipps, CV (1993) Policy-making and the use and misuse of evidence, in Chitty, C and Simon, B (eds) *Education answers back: critical responses to government policy*. London: Lawrence and Wishart.

Kant, I (1956) *Critique of practical reason*. New York: Macmillan.

Kant, I (1990) *Foundations of the metaphysics of morals*. New York: Macmillan.

Lawton, D (1992) *Education and politics in the 1990s: conflict or consensus?* London: Falmer Press.

Smith, A (1977) *Wealth of nations*. London: Everyman.

Tooley, J (2003) Why Harry Brighouse is nearly right about the privatisation of education. *Journal of Philosophy of Education*, (37)3: 427–47.

Williams, R (2000) *Lost icons*. London: Morehouse Publishing.

Chapter 5

The mystery of learning

John Sharp and Barbara Murphy

Introduction

Learning is widely regarded as a lifelong activity which may occur intentionally or otherwise in a range of different learning environments, including schools, colleges, universities and the workplace. At times, of course, learning takes place with remarkable ease. Committing a simple fact to memory and being able to recall it on demand, or completing a relatively simple practical task successfully having been shown how to do it only once or twice, rarely presents much of a challenge. More often than not, however, what we are expected to learn, or indeed have to learn, is considerably difficult and requires effort. But can we be said to have learnt something if, for example, we take copious notes during a lecture and then repeat them back in an examination? Have we learnt something better if we get good grades in assessed coursework? Have we learnt anything at all if we cannot transfer our knowledge from one context to another? This chapter examines how we come to know what we know by reviewing evidence from within the fields of neuroscience, cognitive psychology and education itself. It also looks critically at learning styles and the growing use of learning style questionnaires as a practitioner-based activity in schools.

What do we mean by learning?

According to Driscoll (2000), most authors share a common view of learning which can be defined as a 'persistent change in human performance or performance potential' that cannot be ascribed to growth or maturation. Fortunately, the results of learning are often observable in the outcomes of human behaviour and taxonomies of learning outcomes are well known. Bloom's taxonomy of learning outcomes, for example, consists of six levels of activity which start with a demonstration of knowledge before working their way through comprehension, application, analysis and synthesis to evaluation (Bloom et al, 1956). The higher the taxonomic level, the more advanced the learning and intellectual challenge involved. By way of contrast, Gagné's taxonomy of learning outcomes is broader and considers learning in terms of a variety of cognitive, social, affective and psychomotor factors (Gagné, 1985). While Driscoll's definition of learning is valuable in helping to identify learning in terms of human performance and potential, it does not help to understand how knowledge is acquired in the first instance.

Learning and the brain

The origin and acquisition of knowledge in humans has been a matter of intense philosophical debate which can be traced back at least to Plato. Historically, views have tended to fall within one of three main camps: nativists considered all individuals to be born with the knowledge they needed and that anything else was acquired by some innate or inherited characteristic; empiricists considered all individuals to acquire knowledge out of experience; and rationalists considered all individuals to acquire knowledge by engaging in reasoning. Today, individuals are considered to be born at least partly 'hard-wired' with an architecture of the mind which facilitates cognition, rather than with a mind full of knowledge *per se*. Understanding that architecture is fundamental to understanding how we learn.

Summarising from the work of Greenfield (1997), the human brain is a creamy-brown coloured organ which reaches full development in late adolescence or early adulthood. Visual inspection of the brain reveals three immediately obvious components, each of which can be identified just prior to birth:

- **the cerebrum;**
- **the cerebellum;**
- **the brain stem (which runs into the vertebrae or bones of the neck and spine as the spinal cord).**

The cerebrum, the outermost layer of which is referred to as the cerebral cortex, is particularly striking and consists of two almost symmetrical and highly convoluted cerebral hemispheres (Fig. 5.1). These hemispheres, together with their frontal, temporal, parietal and occipital lobes, are connected by a number of inter-cortical nerve fibres including the corpus callosum. Different regions of the brain, including the sub-cortical structures hidden from view by the cerebral cortex itself, are responsible for the bewildering array of different brain functions, from the receipt and processing of information from receptors located all over the body (the sensory areas) to the coordination of almost every action that the body performs, voluntarily or involuntarily (the motor areas). Some regions carry out combined functions that link sensory and motor information and are active when interpreting experiences, concentrating, problem-solving, decision-making and reasoning (the association areas). Brain function also determines just 'who we are'.

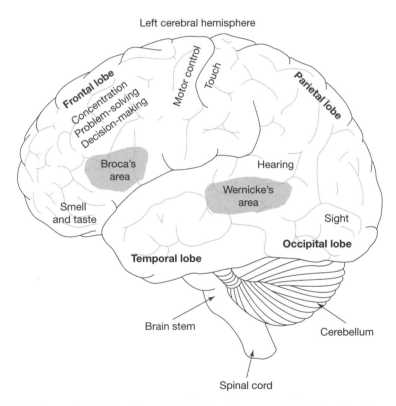

Figure 5.1 The human brain showing main structural components and functional areas

While the techniques available to study learning and the human brain are wide and varied, non-invasive neuro-imaging has proved particularly productive. Positron emission tomography or PET scans, for example, have revealed that different regions of the brain are active when carrying out related but subtly different language tasks, including hearing words (Wernicke's area and the auditory cortex), speaking words (the motor cortex), seeing words (the visual cortex) and generating words (Broca's area). PET scans have also revealed that language development and comprehension are lateralised and gender-specific. That is, they involve both hemispheres of the brain in different ways and to different degrees in men and women, statistically at least. But knowing about which areas of the brain are active as we perform very specific tasks is one thing. Determining the exact nature of that activity and how it results in learning is something else.

According to O'Shea (2005), the adult brain as a whole, but particularly the cerebral cortex, is densely packed with cells of different types, including an estimated 100 billion neurons. Neurons come in different shapes and sizes and do different jobs. A 'typical' brain cell, however, measures less than about one tenth of a millimetre across and consists of the following elements:

- **a squat cell body or soma which contains the nucleus;**
- **a number of dendrites which branch out from the cell body and taper;**
- **a single axon which extends outwards from the cell body and ends in an array of synaptic terminals or synapses.**

What appears to distinguish neurons from other cells in the human body is their ability to network with each other and communicate. This is made possible by a whole series of signals that begin with action potentials or electrical currents generated in the bodies of neurons themselves and transmitted along their axons. These action potentials arrive at synaptic terminals where they stimulate the release of chemicals called neurotransmitters. As neurotransmitters cross the gap or synaptic cleft between the axon of one neuron and the dendrite of another, synapses are said to 'fire'. This electrochemical means of communication between neurons is the neuroscientific basis of learning. Even learning a simple fact, however, is a process thought to involve not two but entire populations of neurons distributed around the brain and networked in ways that we cannot even begin to imagine. But there is little point in learning something if you simply forget it. The constant firing of synapses and the connections they make allow certain synapses to become temporarily strengthened, forming short-term memories which may last only a few seconds. Further firing, however, results in a remodelling of synapses themselves which become strengthened on a more permanent basis. The adaptability of neurons and the brain to learn and remodel itself in this way is referred to as 'plasticity'. The effects of plasticity are particularly evident in neuro-imaging studies of the brains of musicians which reveal enhanced development in areas that correspond to how particular instruments are played (Weinberger, 2005).

Compelling as it may seem, and despite all of the advances made within the field of neuroscience in recent years, the working of the human brain is simply far too complex to formulate any sensible, practical, everyday educational application in its broadest sense. Indeed, the range of 'neuro-myths' surrounding the brain and education remain an endless source of entertainment to neuroscientists themselves (Blakemore and Frith, 2002; Geake and Cooper, 2003; Goswami, 2004).

Pause for thought | fact or fiction?

In his book *The brain's behind it*, Smith (2002) points out that it is incumbent upon educators to show responsibility to ask more precise questions of neuroscientists and their findings and vice versa if only to question and eradicate the great variety of neuroscientific and educational fallacies that have arisen over the years. Together with a friend or a group of colleagues, consider what you believe to be the truth or otherwise in some of Smith's examples:

- the brain cells you get at birth are those you have for life;
- there are critical periods within which specific brain development occurs;
- you only use 10 per cent or less of your brain;
- your brain is like a sponge;
- stress stops you learning;
- your memory is perfect;
- your left brain is logical, your right brain creative;
- listening to Mozart makes you intelligent;
- children can only concentrate for two minutes more than their chronological age;
- male and female brains are so different we ought to teach boys and girls in different ways.

Now consider the personal and educational implications of your beliefs. Of course, not all of these statements are true ... but which ones? Would you be surprised to find out that most are actually half-truths, distortions or just plain wrong? Take a look at Smith's commentary on the matter and reflect upon the significance of his findings. For particularly accessible and valuable insights into the complexities of the brain and how it works see Ratey (2001) and Rose (2003).

Modelling memory

While the complexities of learning and memory formation at the level of the neuron are considerable, learning and memory are widely regarded as emergent properties of the human brain which can be investigated in other more readily observable ways. From a series of highly controlled laboratory-based experiments and recourse to how computers work as a suitable metaphor, the limitations of which are well understood if often overlooked, psychologists have modelled the human cognitive system in terms of at least three inter-connected storage areas. These include:

- **sensory memory;**
- **short-term or working memory;**
- **long-term memory.**

Summarising from the work of Eysenck and Keane (2005), learning and memory formation not only involve the processing and storage of information but other processes, including attention, perception, encoding and retrieval (Fig. 5.2).

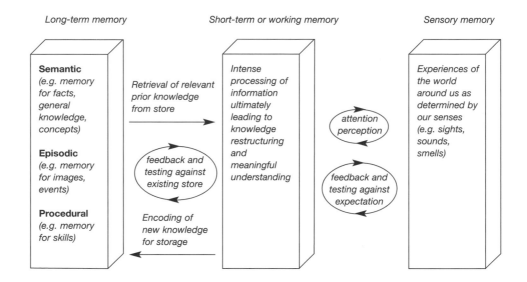

Figure 5.2 Cognitive model of learning and memory

In their studies of learning and memory, cognitive psychologists often represent the organisation and representation of declarative or 'knowing that' knowledge, the main focus of our attention here, using the schema construct (the cognitive psychologist's equivalent of a neuronal network). A schema of an object such as a book, for example, is an idealised knowledge package that contains all of the information elements associated by an individual with that object. Because a schema is regarded as an organising structure for knowledge, it is convenient to consider a schema's information elements to be organised and represented in memory in terms of concepts. In classical theories of concept formation, concepts have attributes. Attributes define what it is to be a member of a concept and concept learning takes place by association (similarity, contiguity and contrast). Explanation-based views of concepts and concept formation, however, are more useful when dealing with the complexities of attributes and the relations that exist between them which together give rise to higher levels of cognitive functioning. Theories of knowledge acquisition based upon the schema construct and the semantic networks they form assume that schema are not static and that their content, the arrangement of that content and the relations between information elements change as knowledge acquisition and concept learning take place (the cognitive psychologist's equivalent of plasticity). Of course, human learning involves more than information processing. People also deal with meaning and making sense of the world and the events going on around them. Interestingly, the most influential factor affecting the rate, accuracy and effectiveness of knowledge acquisition and concept learning, including what we forget, is what a learner already knows.

Cognitive psychologists have long used information processing as a means to explore potential instructional sequences and events for teaching. According to Gagné and Driscoll (1988), as one of many possible examples, these include:

- **gaining attention (alertness);**
- **activating motivation by introducing objectives (expectancy);**
- **stimulating the recall of prior knowledge (retrieval to short-term or working memory);**
- **presenting stimulus materials (selective perception);**
- **providing learning guidance (encoding and entry to long-term memory storage);**
- **eliciting performance (responding);**
- **assessing performance and providing feedback (reinforcement);**
- **enhancing retention and transfer (cueing retrieval).**

> *Pause for thought* | the condition of learning
>
> Think of a lecture or tutorial you have attended recently, a seminar you have led, or a class you have taught. On reflection, can you identify any of the instructional events outlined by Gagné and Driscoll (1988)? Did they occur in any particular order? Consider the learning environment you found yourself in or created for others, the tasks you were asked to complete or gave others to do, and the social organisation and interactions of the people present. Can you define any of the effective teacher characteristics involved? What about the learners? What does all of this tell you about cognition and the condition of learning?

Learning in an educational context

If the picture of learning painted in earlier sections seems somewhat clinical, we only have to look towards schools, classrooms and a curriculum area like science to add a little 'mess'. Science is a particularly valuable curriculum area to consider, as learning theory in science education has advanced far beyond the global theorists such as Piaget and Vygotsky into constructivism in a domain-specific way (Driver et al, 1994). Research into children's ideas in science education, for example, seeks to consider how children conceptualise the objects, events and phenomena of science by eliciting their knowledge and understanding of them. Much work in this area, and across the primary and secondary age phases in particular, has demonstrated repeatedly that scientific knowledge cannot be transmitted easily from one individual to another (e.g. didactically from teacher to child) but must be constructed through acts of personal and social cognition by learners themselves (Duit and Treagust, 2003). The emergent properties of knowledge acquisition and concept learning in science education are now well established:

- **children form their own ideas about the world in which they live long before any formal teaching takes place in school;**
- **children's ideas frequently differ from the science taught at school and the ideas of scientists themselves;**
- **children's ideas can be strongly held and resistant to change even in the most supportive, caring and stimulating of teaching and learning environments;**
- **children's ideas can and do change as a result of learning science at school but often in unanticipated ways;**
- **children often share similar ideas as a result of shared experiences, the use of language, and interpersonal relationships.**

More importantly, perhaps, the emergent properties of knowledge acquisition and concept learning in science resonate well with the features of learning and memory presented earlier from within the fields of neurosciences and cognitive psychology and established links have already been made, if only in the broadest and most qualitative way (Anderson, 1997; Mayer, 2002).

Research box

the chaos in learning science

Basing their work on constructivist premises, and extrapolating from the non-linear principles of dynamical systems theory and chaos, Luffiego et al. (1994) have presented an advanced schema-based model of learning science involving the evolution of a conceptual schema in order to describe the state of a learner's cognitive system before, during and after teaching or instruction. While the application of dynamical systems theory and chaos to matters of an educational nature might at first seem unusual, their extension from the realms of mathematics and computing into many other disciplines has met with some success, particularly in terms of explaining the sometimes odd behaviour and predisposition of evolving systems that tend towards disorder and unpredictability, however brief that tendency might be (i.e. learning is limited, selective and incomplete). According to Luffiego et al., the human cognitive system is an open, dynamic and non-linear system capable of selecting, storing and processing information, and this system exhibits extreme variability between individuals as a result of the sensitivity of initial cognitive states (the 'butterfly effect'). Luffiego et al. have suggested that the conceptual schema within most cognitive systems are in fact powerful information 'attractors' for they exhibit general stability and resistance to change and give rise ultimately to 'final-states' of knowledge (which emerge as children's ideas). As a result, learning science may take place along similar or widely divergent and unpredictable pathways resulting in errors and misconceptions as well as scientific conceptualisation. Some empirical evidence which lends some support to the notion of chaos in cognition has already been provided by Bloom (2001) and Sharp and Kuerbis (2006). At the very least, Luffiego et al. have provided a new language of learning, at best a whole new paradigm within which to explore science education in new and exciting ways.

However, learning science as a process of conceptual change (or learning in any other cognate discipline for that matter) may be overly simplistic. Science at school is an intellectual, practical, creative and social endeavour which seeks to help children and young adults better understand and make sense of the world in which they live. Science education involves them in thinking and working in particular ways in the pursuit of reliable scientific knowledge. If, as Driver et al (1994) have suggested, children are to be enculturated into science, then intervention and negotiation of meaning with a teacher are essential if the tools and conventions of the scientific community are to be made fully available. As Driver et al. have also noted, 'the challenge is one of how to achieve such a process of enculturation successfully in the round of normal classroom life', particularly when 'the science view that the teacher is presenting is in conflict with the learners' prior knowledge schemes'. This, of course, places considerable demands on the curricular expertise of teachers. Linder (1993) has also argued from both cognitive and phenomenographic perspectives that individuals could construct a repertoire of conceptions of objects, events and phenomena ('domains of knowledge'), the one eventually chosen and used depending on the context, social, scientific or otherwise, for which it is required ('mode of perception'). Linder has proposed that learning by 'conceptual appreciation' might be more appropriate than learning by conceptual change. But teaching, like curriculum development, is also strongly influenced by culture and ideology, not just how children learn (Millar and Osborne, 1998; Sharp and Grace, 2004). Hodson (1998), for example, has suggested that with child-centred, process-driven or discovery-led pedagogies it is often commonplace to find, say, children at school in Key Stage 1 constructing a knowledge of the world around them which is far from scientific, but that anything is allowed to count as science provided the children are working cooperatively and in a warm and friendly learning environment. As Hodson correctly noted, however, not all investigations and enquiries are scientific and not all forms of knowledge and understanding arising from them are equally valid from a scientific point of view. In secondary schools too, while it is accepted that practical work undoubtedly contributes towards securing interest, curiosity and progress in science, scientific knowledge and understanding cannot always be developed through practical work alone.

VAK or VAK-uous?

In much the same way as meta-cognition, or learning how to learn, has grown in prominence as an effective learning strategy in educational circles over the years, the whole concept of learning styles has made an equally impressive recent appearance. Despite a long history and solid research pedigree from within the field of cognitive psychology, the apparent trivialisation of learning styles and their determination in schools throughout the UK is perhaps something of a concern. Much of this trivialisation revolves around the notion that an individual's learning style can somehow be reduced to only three independently assessed modalities – visual, auditory and kinaesthetic or VAK – and that this can be identified using a simple research instrument in the form of a self-assessment questionnaire. More worryingly is the notion that the outcome from such a simple questionnaire could then be used to inform teaching or curriculum development to better match an individual's needs. Often implicit within this position is a view that working within a learner's preferred learning style will ultimately lead to improvements in various cognitive and intellectual abilities. Some sources go further, suggesting that there is a clear link between learning styles and 'multiple intelligences theory', when actually neither rests on firm foundations, or that justification for learning styles can be found in how the brain works (Perks, 2004). In a special issue of the journal of *Educational Psychology* devoted to learning style issues, Cassidy (2004) has already pointed out that 'whilst educators in all fields are becoming increasingly aware of the critical importance of understanding how individuals learn, it is equally important that any attempts to integrate learning style into educational programmes are made from an informed position'. With background provided by Cassidy and the extensive review provided by Coffield et al (2004), we aim the following criticisms at VAK as it appears in schools to stimulate discussion and debate.

Origin and terminology

Despite the history of learning style research, which can be traced back through the psychology literature for some 40 years or more, the exact origin or source of derivation of VAK and VAK instrumentation used in schools remains uncertain. Indeed the range of instruments to be found and the variation between them can be quite startling. Few have found their way into schools with any indication of provenance and few come with any literature explaining how they should be used and interpreted. Even those that do, including the commercially available VAK questionnaires found on the internet, need to be interrogated critically. While the closest learning style questionnaire with a school-centred focus is thought to be the Learning Style Inventory, or LSI, provided by Dunn et al (1989), this bears no resemblance to the VAK-type found in schools. Indeed, the LSI actually attempts to match an individual's learning style to the emotional, sociological, physical and psychological elements of the learning environment. Not only might those setting out to investigate using learning styles be daunted at the range of models, instruments and theoretical perspectives actually available, they might be equally daunted at the confusing terminology and definitions that also exist. Of course, there are mixed views about the nature of learning styles and there is no general agreement on a definition. Dunn and co-workers, for example, define learning style as the way students begin to concentrate on how they process, internalise and remember new and difficult academic information. Riding and Raynor (1998) add that a learning style might equally be defined as the process used by an individual to respond to the demands of a learning activity. The VAK instruments found in schools measure neither of these things rigorously.

Validity, reliability and dimensionality

The development, design and range of applicability of all sophisticated learning style instruments from within psychology like LSI have been rigorously used and tested. Even then, the validity and reliability of some instruments remain the subject of controversy, the seriousness of which is closely related to the importance of the claims they make. From the most cursory glance at VAK instrumentation used in schools, some questions asked of individuals would appear to probe attitudes towards learning, learning habits, learning preferences, personality and sociability. These are very different things. Some questions also appear to be so generally expressed as to be of little relevance to education or learning style at all. In addition to undermining validity, these features also raise doubts over dimensionality and whether or not VAK instrumentation measures one or a number of different learning attributes. The difficulty of establishing whether an individual's preferred learning style affects performance or an individual's performance affects learning style should not be overlooked.

Universality

VAK instrumentation in schools adopts a 'one size fits all' stance. Schools and the classrooms are, however, diverse learning environments filled with individuals with diverse learning needs taught by teachers with their own ideologies and philosophies of education. The demands imposed by each curriculum area are also diverse and children in schools rarely work in isolation but in groups, and develop rapidly throughout the primary and secondary years. Most teachers and other educators agree that the choice an individual makes regarding how they approach a task is largely automatic and derived from prior experience and may vary according to each and every learning situation or context. What is less clear is whether or not such traits remain constant over time. It would seem unreasonable, therefore, to claim that any preferred learning style made available by a single VAK questionnaire would provide any meaningful insight into any individual's needs on a day-to-day or even longer-term basis.

Pause for thought | determining your own preferred learning style

The following questionnaire in three parts has been adapted from the work of Clark (1998). Its inclusion here is for illustration and discussion and it should not be taken or used out of context.

Read each statement carefully and use the following Likert-type scale to score your response. Add all of the scores in each part together and record them as indicated (each part has a minimum score of 6 and a maximum score of 30). Are you a visual, auditory or kinaesthetic learner?

Score 1 – almost never applies
Score 2 – applies once in a while
Score 3 – sometimes applies
Score 4 – often applies
Score 5 – almost always applies

Part 1: visual
(a) I take lots of notes and like to doodle.
(b) When talking to someone else I have the hardest time handling those who do not make good eye contact with me.
(c) I make lists and notes because I remember things better if I write them down.
(d) I need to write down directions so that I may remember them.
(e) When recalling information I can see it in my mind and remember where I saw it.
(f) If I had to explain a new procedure or technique I would prefer to write it out.

Total score:

Part 2: auditory
(a) When I read I read out loud or move my lips to hear the words in my head.
(b) When talking to someone else I have the hardest time handling those who do not talk back with me.
(c) I do not take lots of notes but I still remember what was said – taking notes distracts me from the speaker.
(d) I like to talk to myself when solving a problem or writing.
(e) I remember things more easily by repeating them again and again.
(f) If I had to explain a new procedure or technique I would prefer telling about it.

Total score:

Pause for thought | continued

Part 3: kinaesthetic

(a) I prefer to start working on tasks without listening to instructions first.
(b) I take notes and doodle but rarely go back and look at them.
(c) My working space appears disorganised to others.
(d) I like to move around – I feel uncomfortable sitting for too long.
(e) If I had to explain a new procedure or technique I would prefer to demonstrate it.
(f) With free time I am most likely to exercise.

Total score:

Look at the statements again carefully. Do you think they measure learning style or something else? Do you really think your learning style can be determined so easily? Even if it could, what does your profile mean? What if it's mixed? At what point does an apparent preference actually become significant?

In learning style research, most authors, recognising the significance of their work, do advocate a balanced and sensible approach that involves using a carefully chosen variety of teaching strategies which consider a variety of styles with the aim of providing all individuals with the opportunity to learn in different ways. But is this not just good practice? Even the most 'traditional' primary classroom provides an active learning environment with children's senses stimulated in all kinds of different ways and even the most 'traditional' lecture is more likely to be a multimedia event than a recital. At best, and within academic journals, some published studies involving rigorously tested psychological learning style instruments do report improved understanding and self-reflection of individuals as learners themselves. But the majority of such studies involve adults not children. Cassidy (2004) reminds us, 'for those working within an educational setting wishing to utilise learning style to promote more effective learning, whether through individual or group profiling, design of instructional methods, or identifying learner preferences, operationalising learning style is a necessary but highly problematic endeavour'. VAK in schools, if it is ever to be taken seriously and beyond generalisation at an intuitive level, has a long way to go.

Summary and conclusions

Learning is hard work and far from straightforward. Developments from within the fields of neuroscience, cognitive psychology and education have shed a great deal of light on how we learn and how we come to know what we know, yet at the same time confirming that learning is a profoundly complex process. While tempting, making close links between all three fields is a hazardous activity. Even when neuroscientists, cognitive psychologists and educators appear to explore similar things, they usually do so in very different ways and at very different levels of abstraction. The harsh truth is that even relevant findings from within each field are all too often ambiguous and hotly debated. Occasionally, and in our search to unlock the mysteries of learning and how best to maximise our own learning potential and that of others, we all have to be reminded at times not to simply believe, rely upon or readily accept without question what we are told. This in itself is a part of learning. Of course, what we learn and learn to do throughout a lifetime is vast, extending well beyond the simple acquisition of knowledge. Some of the many factors that contribute to this can be identified but a great many others elude us still. Even in formal learning environments such as schools, colleges, universities and the workplace, the extent to which we reach our full potential as learners is often about opportunity rather than ability, and knowing when and how to seize it. To achieve our full potential we also have to learn how to learn, to acquire good learning habits and to take or share responsibility for our own learning as well as the learning of others. There are no short cuts, no quick fixes and no magic bullets.

References

Anderson, OR (1997) A neurocognitive perspective on current learning theory and science instructional strategies. *Science Education*, 81: 67–89.

Blakemore, SJ and Frith, U (2002) The implications of recent developments in neuroscience for research on teaching and learning. Available at **www.icn.ucl.ac.uk/sblakemore/SJ_papers/ESRCmainreport.pdf** (accessed 12 May 2006).

Bloom, BS, Englehart, MD, Furst, EJ, Hill, WH and Krathwohl, DR (1956) *Taxonomy of educational objectives. Handbook I: Cognitive domain*. New York: McKay.

Bloom, JW (2001) Discourse, cognition and chaotic systems: an examination of students' argument about density. *Journal of Learning Sciences*, 10(4): 447–92.

Cassidy, S (2004) Learning styles: an overview of theories, models and measures. *Educational Psychology*, 24(4): 419–44.

Clark, D (1998) Visual, auditory and kinaesthetic survey. Available at **www.nwlink.com/~donclark/hrd/vak.html** (accessed 1 December, 2005).

Coffield, F, Moseley, D, Hall, E and Ecclestone, K (2004) *Should we be using learning styles? What research has to say to practice*. Learning and Skills Research Centre. Trowbridge: Cromwell Press.

Driscoll, MP (2000) *Psychology of learning for instruction*. Boston, MA: Allyn and Bacon.

Driver, R, Asoko, H, Leach, J, Mortimer, E and Scott, P (1994) Constructing scientific knowledge in the classroom. *Educational Researcher*, 23(7): 5–12.

Duit, R and Treagust, DF (2003). Conceptual change: a powerful framework for improving science teaching and learning. *International Journal of Science Education*, 25(6): 671–88.

Dunn, R, Dunn, K and Price, GE (1989) *Learning styles inventory*. Lawrence, KS: Price Systems.

Eysenck, MW and Keane, MT (2005) *Cognitive psychology*. Hove: Psychology Press.

Gagné, RM (1985) *The conditions of learning*. New York: Holt, Rinehart and Winston.

Gagné, RM and Driscoll, MP (1988) *Essentials of learning for instruction*. Englewood Cliffs, NJ: Prentice Hall.

Geake, J and Cooper, P (2003) Cognitive neuroscience: implications for education. *Westminster Studies in Education*, 26(1): 7–20.

Goswami, U (2004) Neuroscience and education. *British Journal of Educational Psychology*, 74: 1–14.

Greenfield, S (1997) *The human brain*. London: Phoenix.

Hines, M (2004) *Brain gender*. Oxford: Oxford University Press.

Hodson, D (1998) *Teaching and learning science: towards a personalized approach*. Milton Keynes: Open University Press.

Linder, CJ (1993) A challenge to conceptual change. *Science Education*, 77(3): 293–300.

Luffiego, M, Bastida, MF, Ramos, F and Soto, J (1994) Systemic model of conceptual evolution. *International Journal of Science Education*, 16(3): 305–313.

Mayer, RE (2002) Understanding conceptual change: a commentary, in Limón, M and Mason, L (eds) *Reconsidering conceptual change: issues in theory and practice*. Dordrecht: Kluwer.

Millar, R and Osborne, J (1998) *Beyond 2000: science education for the future – a report with ten recommendations*. London: King's College.

O'Shea, M (2005) *The brain: a very short introduction*. Oxford: Oxford University Press.

Perks, D (2004) The shattered mirror: a critique of multiple intelligences theory, in Hayes, D (ed) *The RoutledgeFalmer guide to key debates in education*. London: RoutledgeFalmer.

Ratey, J (2001) *A user's guide to the brain*. London: Abacus.

Riding, RJ and Rayner, S (eds) (1998) *Cognitive styles and learning strategies*. London: Fulton.

Rose, S (2003) *The making of memory: from molecules to mind*. London: Vintage.

Sharp, JG and Grace, M (2004) Anecdote, opinion and whim: lessons in curriculum development from primary science education in England and Wales. *Research Papers in Education*, 19(3): 293–321.

Sharp, JG and Kuerbis, P (2006) Children's ideas about the Solar System and the chaos in learning science. *Science Education*, 90(1): 124–47.

Smith, A (2002) *The brain's behind it: new knowledge about the brain and learning*. Stafford: Network Educational Press.

Weinberger, NM (2005) Music and the brain. *Scientific American*, 291(5): 66–73.

Chapter 6

Education and integrating Children's Services

Pat Hughes

Introduction

In 1973, a primary school pupil named Maria Colwell was murdered by her stepfather. In the subsequent inquiry it was shown that a significant number of public services, including education, were involved with the family and that many of them were unaware of each other's work. As a direct result, area child protection committees (ACPCs) were set up to ensure that the same thing never happened again. Operational structures were put in place and designed to promote communication between different aspects of service provision. Twenty seven years later, in 2000, Victoria Climbié, another primary school pupil known to at least 12 agencies, was also murdered by her carers. The resulting inquiry again demonstrated that the services worked in an uncoordinated way. During the 27-year interim between the deaths of Maria and Victoria, many other children identified formally as being 'at risk' were failed by the very services set up to prevent the occurrence of such neglect and abuse.

This chapter explores the implications of the most recent attempt to 'join together' different areas of Children's Services to provide a more effective service for children and young people. It has direct implications for anyone taking Education Studies, as the subject broadens to include other educational professionals with a particular interest in children's well-being.

Teachers

Compulsory education has always played an important role in providing formal educational and pastoral services for children and young people. Teachers have often been the only individuals who maintained substantial contact with individual children, apart from their parents and carers. Teachers have always felt this duty of care, as school log books from the nineteenth- and twentieth centuries document (Purkis, 1993). This care might have been demonstrated in different ways from those of today, but it was nevertheless an integral part of the teacher's role.

The role of the teacher has changed considerably since those first years of compulsory schooling. Schools are now charged with becoming learning communities (Pariser, 2000) and teachers encouraged to see themselves as lead learners (Greenhalgh, 2002). The increase in the number of allied educational professionals working in classrooms has meant that many class teachers, particularly in primary schools, are now leaders of small teaching teams within their own classroom. The great majority have had no training in such a role and, if the integration of Children's Services is to be truly effective, these key classroom practitioners will need to have support in working as a teaching team and being able to liaise with other agencies involved with children. Once teachers become confident about their changing role in children's learning it should provide greater opportunities for interaction with individual and small groups of children; wider opportunities for developing trusting relationships, creating a sense of belonging and creating an understanding of responsibility and 'the real world'.

Pause for thought | society change and implications for the teacher's role

Contemporary society has changed and with it the need for schools to respond. It is important not to have a false nostalgia about the past, but to note that society has changed, will continue to do so, and that those in it must adapt and change as well. Schools prepare children for a changing and unpredictable future, as well as for living in sometimes difficult conditions in the present.

Dryden and Vos (2002) in *The learning revolution* identified the major trends that will shape the future:

- continued change in family units – both nuclear and extended;
- a greater awareness of how learning develops;
- the growth of the internet and its potential;
- the changing shape of work and leisure;
- a growing underclass often associated with ethnicity and underachievement.

How might each of these trends influence the teacher's role in relation to those they teach?

Allied educational professionals

Today there are far more people working in schools who are not teachers than those who are. Some are employed directly by the school, others are employed by other agencies but work in school. And of course there are those who work in schools in a voluntary capacity. A useful definition for allied educational professionals employed by schools is 'professionally trained staff who work in schools, usually with teachers, to support learning'. The majority of these are on the school payroll and have a job description and/or responsibilities for supporting pupils' learning. These include learning mentors, bilingual support workers, higher level teaching assistants (HLTAs), classroom assistants (CAs), teaching assistants (TAs), parent support workers and parent mentors, special needs assistants (SNAs), behaviour management workers, nursery nurses, library staff, technicians and counsellors. Campbell and Fairbairn (2005) looked at several of these, including some of those who may not actually work in a classroom, but who take children out of the classroom. Of course, not all schools employ all these people, and some may employ others as well. The nomenclature varies from school to school and from one local authority to another. This certainly makes it more confusing when Education Studies students are on placement in school and may wonder about the varying titles, roles and responsibilities of those working with pupils. What joins all these allied educational professionals together is their general remit to break down children's and young people's barriers to learning. They must be seen, recognised and paid as an essential element in improving children's lives. At the time of writing they form some of the most poorly paid workers in the education sector.

The expanding role of the allied educational professional in school

The image of the Victorian teacher is of someone often standing alone in a school hall, surrounded by large numbers of children sitting on chairs, supported only by pupil teachers and monitors. Today's schools are very different in the support provided for learning. It is this difference which will be a key element in the real success of integrating Children's Services. The growth of the allied worker, sometimes known as 'the paraprofessional', was heralded by the 1994 Code of Practice for children with special educational needs (SEN). Among other things this Act:

- **standardised funding of support for children with SEN;**
- **standardised diagnosis and management of children with special needs in mainstream schools;**

- **resulted in pupils having statements of need with money attached;**
- **introduced special needs support workers.**

This, and later legislation, increased the number of professionals working directly with children and young people in both primary and secondary schools. The inclusion agenda rapidly increased the number of statemented children and during 1997–2001 doubled the number of support assistants (Goddard, 2005). This was largely a result of pupils coming into mainstream schools from special schools. These statemented pupils may have individual support for all or part of the day (Hall, 2005).

The late 1990s saw the next major increase in the numbers of allied professionals in primary schools with the introduction of the National Teaching Strategies in 1998 (literacy) and 1999 (numeracy). One of the features of the recommended pedagogy in the both the National Literacy Strategy (NLS) (DfEE, 1988) and the National Numeracy Strategy (NNS) (DfEE, 1999) was more focused small group teaching. Most schools responded to this challenge by employing support assistants to work with small groups. Again, initially these workers were mainly untrained and teachers took on the role of training them to work with the strategies. This changed when the National Strategies themselves adapted to responses by schools by providing training directly for teaching assistants. It was often linked to assistants working with booster groups and specific intervention strategies, such as the Additional Literacy Strategy (ALS), Further Literacy Strategy (FLS) and Springboard for Mathematics (Goddard, 2005). These latter initiatives were written to be 'delivered' by support workers. This quickly increased the professionalism of classroom assistants as teachers recognised their increased involvement in pupil learning, rather than simply concentrating on the management of pupil behaviour when working with small groups. It was recognised formally by many schools who changed their job description from 'classroom assistant' to 'teaching assistant'. There is no doubt that these classroom-based allied professionals working with groups of children have a unique and integral role to play in identifying potential issues related to pupils' basic needs. They are also probably the very people in whom vulnerable children and young people are most likely to confide.

The increased numbers of allied professionals involved directly in teaching pupils, often in smaller groups, has resulted in the development of training for allied professionals. In 1995 the specialist teaching assistants (STA) programme was set up. This provided paid day release for STAs and focused on English, mathematics and behaviour management. Those taking the course had to have English and mathematics at GCSE and this was a strict admission requirement. The training resulted in an 'A' level equivalence qualification. Many of those who did the course successfully were encouraged to move on to degree courses, some of which were specially designed for them.

Another professional development route from 2004 was the higher level teaching assistant (HLTA), and those applying again had to have English and mathematics. This route largely replaced the STA and the cynic might say that this was because it was much cheaper for central government to run. Initially a 50-day training programme was planned, but this was replaced with a three-day assessment programme to ensure that specific standards had been met.

In secondary schools there was a recognised shortage of teachers in particular subject areas and specialist training was given in addition to the HLTA assessment. The HLTAs were initially seen by central government as the most highly qualified of the teaching assistants and able to cover classes by themselves. Central government's workforce remodelling agenda was intended to push this forward, although many schools proved reluctant to pay the true cost of employing an HLTA because, for slightly more outlay, they could employ a newly qualified teacher (NQT) (Goddard, 2005). The unions representing teachers and the allied professionals have been engaged in a long debate about the rapidly decreasing distinction between teachers and allied professionals. For most allied professionals pay and conditions are not nearly as attractive as those for qualified teachers (QTS), and in many schools they are paid on a part-time pro-rata basis rather than for 365 days a year like teachers.

Other allied professionals, such as learning mentors and counsellors, have a wider whole-school brief. Learning mentors, for example. emerged in the Excellence in Cities (EiC) programme. The first learning mentors were trained and employed to tackle 'specific problems' facing children in cities. The DfES saw them as key personnel in helping individual pupils to overcome barriers to learning and acting as an advocate for pupils (Hughes, 2005). The guidance and the National Training Programme for learning mentors recognised that many of these barriers to learning involved basic needs such as those identified by Maslow (1962).

identifying basic needs

Maslow (1962) suggested that needs vary in order of importance. Lower order needs, such as hunger and thirst, take precedence over higher order needs, such as realisation of personal potential. It is the failure of lower order needs that often forms the major barrier to learning for children and young people.

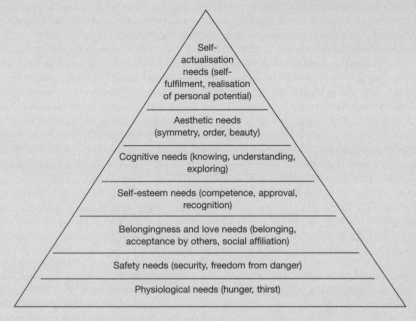

Self-
actualisation
needs (self-
fulfilment, realisation
of personal potential)

Aesthetic needs
(symmetry, order, beauty)

Cognitive needs (knowing, understanding,
exploring)

Self-esteem needs (competence, approval,
recognition)

Belongingness and love needs (belonging,
acceptance by others, social affiliation)

Safety needs (security, freedom from danger)

Physiological needs (hunger, thirst)

Figure 6.1 Maslow's hierarchy of human needs areas

Each of these basic needs strands can be linked to different elements of the role of anyone working with children. Learning mentors, for example, are nearly always involved in monitoring attendance. After all, schools cannot make a difference to lives if pupils do not attend. They frequently run breakfast clubs to fulfil physiological needs, and work on anti-racist, anti-bullying and other safety strategies. They also work with individual and small groups of children and young people who have barriers to learning linked to needing to belong and having self-esteem. Increasingly, they are used by schools to make the formal and informal liaison between schools and other children's services (Hughes, 2005).

Educational support workers and external providers

Schools are often involved in working with agencies that are able to give them extra support and advice. These can be separated between educational support workers and external providers. Educational support workers are those whose services are based within the sphere of education such as the Education Welfare Office (EWO), the educational psychologist and the Connexions Service for careers support. Educational support agencies tend to focus their work around general welfare issues, attendance, behaviour, educational progress, social and emotional development, career moves and ethnic minority issues. Then there are the external providers. These are a range of agencies who may be involved in assessing the needs of children or young people and their families, or offering them practical support. The key agencies vary from area to area and are frequently subject to both name and funding changes. They include health and social services, charities involved with children and/or their families, faith agencies and communities, and housing agencies. More legalist services such as the police and courts are increasingly employing trained personnel to work with school pupils. This may be with whole-school groups, but is often as a preventative measure with small 'at risk' groups. In addition to these, there are the agencies that arise as a result of government initiatives: for example SureStart for early years and Extended Schools. These agencies are particularly vulnerable to changes in funding, personnel and remit.

It does not take too much imagination to see how any one child in a school may be in contact with 'educational' professionals from a variety of agencies. This support may be at an individual level – particularly for those in secondary schools – or it may be linked to the child or young person as a part of their family unit. Those working in school with the very same children may in practice have no idea about this.

Pause for thought | multi-agency involvement

Since the Maria Colwell case, there has been a rapid growth of agencies working with families, carers, children and young people. Contact with one agency, such as social services or the Citizens Advice Bureau for example, will often result in families being put in touch with other forms of help. It is useful to unpick the challenges presented by this multi-agency approach and look at one particular example to gain an understanding of how many agencies could be involved with one particular child and his family.

John's attendance is inconsistent and he often appears tired. His class/form teacher has become concerned that he is mixing with a group of older boys (including his brother) who are known to truant and be involved with petty crime.

- What support may John get in school, either formally, i.e. via a learning mentor, or informally, e.g. a welfare assistant who knows his family?
- What other educational support services may be involved?
- What other agencies could be involved with John's family?

Every Child Matters

After the death of Victoria Climbié, the government commissioned an inquiry report (Laming, 2003). This was rapidly followed by a government response on how children should be kept safe and later by a Green Paper entitled *Every Child Matters* (DfES, 2003). It made a series of recommendations to improve multi-agency working, acknowledging that child protection could not be separated from policies to improve children's lives as a whole. This report recognised, really for the first time, the problem of children 'falling through the cracks' between different services. It went much further than the last-minute patching and bureaucracy that were identified as existing child protection procedures. It recorded that too often children experienced difficulties at home or at school but received 'too little help too late, once problems have reached crisis point'. Whether many of those working hard with individual children and their families would agree with this widespread condemnation of their efforts was not examined.

Every Child Matters covers children and young people from birth to age 19. In education terms, this encompasses several distinct sectors:

- **under-5s provision within schools and nurseries (both within the public and private sector) and under-5s within their own homes or in the homes of others paid to look after them;**
- **those in compulsory education between the ages of 5 and 16 (this also includes those who have been excluded from schools, those being educated at home and those for whom formal education is being provided in settings other than school such as behavioural units and 'Oasis' units for excluded children);**
- **those in post-compulsory education such as further education, higher education and other training settings.**

It also covers all those outside these educational settings, in particular those whose basic skills were seen as an ongoing matter for concern.

The privilege and challenge for all of those working within the education sector is that they are in the forefront of working with children and young people. Indeed, teachers and other educational professionals working in these sectors may see more of children and young people than their parents do. From an estimated child population of 11 million, this will cover the 50–100 children and young people who die from abuse or neglect every year, the 25,700 who are on the child protection register, the 59,700 looked after children, the 300,000 to 400,000 children in need and the 300,000 to 400,000 vulnerable children (DfES, 2003).

Translated into local terms, one local authority with a population of about 150,000 audited their own child population from the data they had already collected. It was estimated that in any one year they had approximately:

- **254 children in the care of the local authority;**
- **145 children on the Child Protection Register;**
- **156 children who are known as young carers (youngest aged 3);**
- **430 children with enduring mental health problems;**
- **2,699 reported incidents of domestic violence, where children were either involved or watching;**
- **30–50 children under the age of 18 going into the local accident and emergency unit of the hospital every month;**
- **63% of under 5s with dental decay;**
- **18.3% of girls and 8.8% of boys aged 11 upwards who smoke;**
- **90 babies born to teenage mothers, of whom 25% smoke.**

> *Pause for thought* | collecting data
>
> All local authorities (LA) gather data about the children within their jurisdiction and, with the development of more integrated Children's Services, it is much easier to access. It may, for example, be produced as part of their Public Health Annual Report. Issues within local areas vary and indeed within different parts of local areas. Education Studies has long been concerned with the politics of education (Bartlett and Burton, 2003; Matheson, 2004; Ward, 2004), and identifying local figures provides an opportunity to look for statistics on national sites, such as the Deputy Prime Minister's Office, as well as local sites, such as your own local authority's website. Identify those areas which might collect such data and see if they have their public documents online. If not, it is possible to request it by telephone. The absence of easy access to these statistics is also important. After all, access to school league tables is extremely easy and it should be as easy to access numbers of vulnerable children. Indeed, it is often possible to show direct relationships between the two when examining your own authority or one in which you have had a placement.

The Every Child Matters agenda

The influential government report which followed the 2003 Green Paper extended its remit into an agenda for change. The report had the title *Every Child Matters: Change for Children* (DfES, 2004). This covers all children from birth to age 19 and is given legal force in the Children Act 2004. It establishes five outcomes for children and young people:

- **be healthy;**
- **stay safe;**
- **enjoy and achieve;**
- **make a positive contribution;**
- **achieve economic well-being.**

Within this Outcomes Framework, as it is known, each outcome was extended by five specific aims; for example, for achieving economic well-being the aims were identified as:

- **engaging in further education, employment or training on leaving school;**
- **being ready for employment;**
- **living in decent homes and sustainable communities;**
- **having access to transport and material goods;**
- **living in households free from low income.**

Support for each of these aims is targeted at parents, carers and families. In the case of the achieving economic well-being outcome, this is to support them in becoming economically active. There are national targets and other indicators to be judged through inspection.

For schools, the OFSTED inspection framework is changed to include all five of these outcomes (OFSTED, 2005). The final OFSTED reports are required to 'evaluate the extent to which each area is meeting the … five outcomes for children and young people'. The Every Child Matters agenda also permeates the Self Evaluation Form (SEF) which head teachers are required to complete every year.

The Every Child Matters agenda recognises the need to have some practical (operational) guidelines. The 2004 Children Act gave a particular leadership role to local authorities in setting up the arrangements to secure cooperation among local partners. It appointed a Children's Commission for England; required every local authority to have a Director of Children's Services and a senior local councillor to be a lead member for Children's Services. It was believed that this would lead to a high profile administrative structure which would improve services for children and young people. The Act also provided guidelines for inter-agency arrangements. These had to involve, among others, schools, GPs, health centres, local culture, sports and play organisations and the voluntary and community sector.

Some challenges for integrating Children's Services

There is little about all this with which anyone can disagree. The framework for it gives a vision of what children's lives should be. It is possible to question it from a philosophical point of view and to be suspicious of the neatness of five outcomes each with five aims, all fitting neatly onto an A4 sheet. It has become strategic policy, but like many such political ideals, the operational structures may take time to come into practice. Birth to nineteen is a long period of time and few governments, let alone policies, last so long.

There have been challenges in the past to multi-agency working, including (EiC/DfES, 2003):

- **a shortage of operational workers in many of the public services involving children – administrative workers as well as those 'in the field';**
- **time and resource pressures which affect communication – busy people are often unavailable and attempting to contact them can result in frustration;**
- **gender and status issues – for example female day care workers and support assistants not feeling that their views are being taken seriously;**
- **misunderstanding of professional roles resulting in agencies having stereotypical and unrealistic views of others;**
- **fear of criticism by another agency worker which can result in defensiveness and withdrawal;**
- **problems left to fester with no one taking responsibility for their resolution.**

Children's Workforce Strategy

The challenges of the Every Child Matters agenda were recognised to some extent in the many supplementary documents that followed the original Green Paper; one was the key provisions in the Children's Workforce Strategy (2005). This looked at the whole issue of workforce remodelling and training. It aimed to build on good practice already taking place, recruiting high quality staff into the children's workforce, retaining people by offering better development and career progression; strengthening inter-agency and multidisciplinary working and promoting stronger leadership and management.

A key reform of this workforce remodelling is a Common Assessment Framework (CAF) for children with additional needs: a pre-assessment checklist with a standard form for recording. Training for this workforce was intended to cross agencies and services and to involve a common core of skills and knowledge (DfES, 2005). Training should cover:

- effective communication;
- knowledge of children's and young persons' development;
- safeguarding and promoting the welfare of the child;
- supporting transitions;
- multi-agency working;
- sharing information.

Multi-agency and multidisciplinary professional development at this national level represented an important change. It was an attempt to move professionals working with children out of their 'own professional silos' (Coyne, 2005). In schools this has meant that all staff had to be included in professional development. The Training and Development Agency (TDA) increased its centralised power and training potential across the whole schools-based workforce.

There has always been concern that such centralised training can be over-prescriptive and involve briefing personnel with government directives, rather than engaging them in fundamental issues of operational practice. In order for such training to be truly successful for those undertaking it, it needs to be dynamic and responsive to the changing needs of those providing it. Providers for continuing professional development need to listen and respond as well as to brief.

For those working either directly or indirectly in the education sector, this workforce remodelling did represent a real opportunity to engage, first, with other professionals in the same sector and secondly with other professionals working in related sectors. Whether this will achieve the very ambitious outcomes outlined in *Every Child Matters* remains to be seen.

Pause for thought | looking at implications for educational professionals

Workforce remodelling initiatives have been triggered by the Every Child Matters agenda but a number of challenges have hindered them in the past. Professional development in this area has been deeply involved with the theory of change initiatives and how they can be managed (NHS Institute, 2005). This has been linked with the belief in lifelong learning that is seen as essential and which has to be developed early in a child's life (Bartlett and Burton, 2003). Choose any educational setting with which you are familiar and identify some implications for professional development and lifelong learning that are involved with:

- an understanding of multi-agency working in relation to Children's Services;
- a common core of skills and knowledge;
- information sharing;
- creation of a multi-agency lead professional;
- workforce reform and professional development.

You then might like to look at what is happening in your own educational setting.

Summary and conclusions

The child protection legislation in the past has seemed to be aimed at those working in social services and health with a nod towards education: attendance at a case conference or a request for a school report. The education service has often been seen as an 'add-on' in terms of integrated services. Yet looking at the increasing number of allied professionals working in schools, it is clear that many of them are involved directly in helping to reduce the need for legislation to aid the children in their care. Any vision for education involves 'making a difference' to children's and young people's lives. The rationale behind the Every Child Matters agenda was presented as a vision for the start of the twenty-first century. All those working in schools are part of this integration of children's services movement, to improve children's life chances in the widest sense.

The practical outcomes of the Every Child Matters agenda in schools and other agencies means policymakers initially concentrating on the outcomes in relation to inspection. The permeation of the more fundamental aspects of the agenda will take longer. The formal, hidden, experienced and observed curriculum will need to incorporate health, safety, enjoyment and achievement if the final outcome for all school leavers is to be able to make a positive contribution to society and to achieve economic well-being. This is not just about sharing a vision for children and young people, but having the very practical and operational strategies to put the vision into action. All those reading this book have their own particular role to play.

References

Bartlett, S and Burton, D (2003) *Education studies: essential issues*. London: Sage.

Campbell, A and Fairbairn, G (2005) *Working with support in the classroom*. London: Paul Chapman.

Children Act 2004. London: TSO. Available at **www.opsi.gov.uk/acts/acts2004/20040031.htm** (accessed 7 April 2006).

Coyne, A (2005) *Why workforce planning?*. Presentation from 'Growing the New Primary Care Workforce'. Liverpool: Liverpool University Press.

DfEE (1988) The National Literacy Strategy. London: Department for Education and Employment

DfEE (1999) The National Numeracy Strategy. London: Department for Education and Employment

DfES (2003) *Every Child Matters*. London: TSO/ Department for Education and Skills.

DfES (2004) *Every Child Matters: Change for Children*. London: HMSO/Department for Education and Skills

DfES (2005) Children's Workforce Strategy. London: Department for Education and Skills.

Dryden, G and Vos, J (2002) *The learning revolution*. Stafford: Network Educational Press.

EiC/DfES (2003) *Learning mentor training*. London: Excellence in Cities/Department for Education and Skills and Liverpool Excellence Partnership.

Goddard, G (2005) The changing role of the teaching assistant. Presentation at the TA Conference, Stafford, March 2005.

Greenhalgh, P (2002) *Reaching out to all learners*. Stafford: Network Educational Press.

Hall, W (2005) Making the most of the teaching assistant for special educational needs, in Campbell, A and Fairbairn, G (eds) *Working with support in the classroom*. London: Paul Chapman.

Hughes, P (2005) Learning mentors in primary classrooms and schools, in Campbell, A and Fairbairn, G (eds) *Working with support in the classroom*. London: Paul Chapman.

Laming, S (2003) *The Victoria Climbié Inquiry Report*. London: DfES.

Maslow, A (1962) *Towards a psychology of being*. New York: Nostrand.

Matheson, D (2004) *An Introduction to the study of education*. London: Fulton.

NHS Institute (2005) *Managing the human dimensions of change*. Warwick: National Health Service Institute for Innovation and Improvement.

OFSTED (2005) *Inspecting schools – inspection report template*. London: Office for Standards in Education.

Pariser, E (2000) The community school: developing the approach of 'relational education', in *A coalition for self-learning: creating learning communities*. Available at **www.creatinglearningcommunities.org/ book/schools/pariser.htm** (accessed 20 April 2006).

Purkis, S (1993) *Using school buildings*. London: English Heritage.

Ward, S (2004) *Education studies: a student's guide*. London: RoutledgeFalmer.

Part 2

Learning and teaching

Chapter 7

Schools and classrooms

Chapter 8

The child, family and society:

Early Years in context

Chapter 9

Polarisations in English

Chapter 10

Mathematics for the future

Chapter 11

Science and society

Chapter 12

Technology and education:

debates, contexts and computers

Chapter 13

The nature of higher education

Chapter 7

Schools and classrooms

Denis Hayes

Introduction

When most people think of schools and classrooms they have a mental image of places where pupils sit around tables in light and airy spaces with teachers supervising proceedings, and one or more assistants helping out with specific learning needs. In the mind's eye, schools are orderly, well-equipped and designed. The curriculum is planned. Older pupils might be taking tests and grappling with the question papers; knitted brows and thoughtful looks, pens clicking across the page, eyes glancing anxiously at the clock. Younger children might be working, playing, dancing, singing and chattering excitedly. Computers and printers hum and emit their odour of technology. Teachers might be marking books, discussing pupil progress, drinking coffee, moaning about the government and swapping ideas. Indeed, most schools are happy, industrious places and an integral part of the community. But it has not always been this way. This chapter briefly chronicles the long and turbulent history of schools and classrooms within the UK, including the role of the church, the growth of state involvement, and the influences that have helped to shape educational provision today. The lessons of history are important. If they are ignored, we will learn very little and simply repeat the same mistakes over and over again.

The growth of formal education

The formal education of pupils in Britain has its roots deep in history and is inextricably linked to the growth and mission of the Christian church. For a long time national education was unknown; there were no colleges, universities or centres for academic learning available for the general public, or 'the masses' as they were described. There were no schools and no paid teachers of the kind with which we are familiar today. For the small number of children from wealthy backgrounds who had access to schooling, some received an education rooted in literature and Latin. This was known as 'grammar' education, from which the term 'grammar school' would emerge. Over time, the grammar schools insisted that pupils were literate at the point of entry, so elementary education in which reading and writing were key components became essential for the wealthy few.

Unfortunately, political turbulence during the sixteenth- and seventeenth centuries meant that systematic education almost ceased to exist for the vast majority of the population. Most people were too concerned with eking out a living to worry about such niceties as being able to read and write, even if they could afford the time to master them. As the industrial revolution swept through the country in the eighteenth century, the plight of children working in factories and mines became a serious political and social issue. Pioneers such as Robert Raikes, who founded the Sunday School movement in 1780, Charles Gordon, who built 'ragged schools' to educate and provide sustenance for the destitute, and Charles of Bala, in Wales, were determined to provide an education for these child labourers. The Quaker Joseph Lancaster and, a little later, the priest Andrew Bell promoted a system of elementary schooling in which more experienced and capable pupils ('monitors') would help to teach the younger and less able scholars. This 'monitorial' system required a very small number of teachers thus reducing the cost of schooling considerably and became the means of providing mass education for working class children.

The first publicly funded schools that we would recognise as such were only established as recently as the mid-nineteenth century to give a basic education to children from poor families. Throughout this time, control of education gradually switched from the church to the state, though provision was uneven and there was intensive and sometimes acrimonious debate about whether church or state should have the greater influence over the way that education was organised and managed, and the content of the curriculum (Chadwick, 1997). One of the key political figures determined to extend state provision of education in the first half of the nineteenth century was James Kay-Shuttleworth. He not only founded training colleges for teachers but also encouraged newly-founded Board Schools (funded from taxation) and voluntary schools to widen the curriculum beyond reading, writing and arithmetic (the so-called three Rs). As the nineteenth century progressed it became increasingly clear that government intervention would be needed if education was to become universally available. However, there was genuine anxiety expressed by many sections of society about the adverse impact on the economy of removing children from the workplace and sending them to school each day. Employers were anxious about labour shortage, and poor parents, often with large families to feed, were worried about the loss of earnings, a situation reflected in impoverished nations today.

A feature of schooling during the mid- to late nineteenth century was the 'payment by results' system that was introduced in 1861 and persisted until its abolition in1895. With 'payment by results', the government gave a grant to a school based on assessment of each child's academic ability and their attendance. Teachers felt obliged to introduce rote learning and to drill the pupils to absorb factual knowledge, though the process did not, of course, guarantee understanding. After the abolition of 'payment by results', the curriculum was extended in many schools to include a wider range of subjects and teaching approaches. It is interesting to note the similarity with schools today, where teachers are expected to ensure that pupils meet the necessary 'standards', the same term that was used in the 1800s, as assessed through tests and examinations.

Similar advances in educational provision were being made in other areas of the UK during the nineteenth and early twentieth centuries. Thus, between 1846 and 1848, the Welsh Education Committee and the Cambrian Society were formed, which evolved into national schools in Wales. The 1867 report of the Royal Commission on Education led to the Education Act of 1872 that resulted in improvements in education for every child in Scotland. In the period running up to the setting up of the state of Northern Ireland in 1920, education became one of the areas of tension between Ulster unionism and Irish nationalism. Before partition, the overwhelming majority of Irish schools were under denominational control even though they were financed chiefly from public funds (Harris, 1993).

Meanwhile, in the face of considerable opposition, and as a means of guaranteeing education free of charge for all pupils, W.E. Forster introduced the important 1870 Elementary Education Act in England. At that time, the government's obligation was principally to 'fill the gaps' where voluntary provision did not exist. Reforms were slow in being implemented and even at the commencement of the twentieth century schooling was inconsistent and attendance spasmodic. Paradoxically, however, there were more 3-and 4-year-old children attending school at the end of the 1800s than there were almost one hundred years later! With singing, handwork, games and dancing, the infant curriculum at the turn of the new century was surprisingly innovative.

Pause for thought | gender issues in schooling

Miller and Davey (2005) have argued that too little emphasis was placed on the role of women and girls in nineteenth century society. They have claimed that debates about citizenship and liberal democracies which underpinned much theory about schools are too patriarchal. To what extent is the modern day secondary school operated from what may be broadly described as a male perspective? Is the situation different in primary schools where the vast majority of staff are female? What, if any, are the implications for pupils and their learning?

Secondary and further education also has its roots in the mid-1800s. Increasing concern that Britain's lack of competitiveness in the world was widely perceived as a skills shortage, with the result that there was increasing emphasis placed on vocational education and training. At the same time, the much-debated Education Act of 1902 ushered in three key changes:

- **education came under county council control;**
- **money from local rates was made available to voluntary schools;**
- **councils were empowered to fund secondary education.**

These changes were revolutionary for two main reasons: public funds were made available for education for the first time, and secondary education was formally established. Indeed, the year 1902 can rightly be described as the birthday of secondary education. Important, too, was the fact that voluntary schooling that had dominated the nineteenth century was struggling to cope with the increasing demands for education. Without state financial intervention the school system would have collapsed.

In 1918 the school leaving age was raised to 14 years. A few years later the influential Hadow Report published in 1926 gave official sanction to the principle that the elementary phase of education in England should formally conclude for all children at age 11 (to be known as the 'primary' phase) followed by separate provision of secondary schooling. There were many important Education Acts over the following years, notably the highly influential Butler Act of 1944 which introduced the following statutory requirements that have, with minor changes, remained in force to the present day:

- **the appointment of a Minister for Education in England and Wales;**
- **local authority funding for secondary as well as primary schools;**
- **raising the school leaving age in stages from 14 years to 15 years to 16 years;**
- **the requirement for schools to hold an act of worship;**
- **free medical (including dental) care for all pupils;**
- **education provision for pupils with special learning needs;**
- **payment for all teachers according to a nationally agreed scale;**
- **the prevention of schools from debarring or dismissing a female teacher when she gets married.**

> *Pause for thought* | contrasting 'then' and 'now'
>
> Look again at the summary of reforms drawn from the Education Act of 1944. Consider the similarities and differences between the conditions for teachers in 1944 and today. Are there any surprises? Note that female teachers did not receive equal pay until 1955 and, until the 1970s, teachers' pay was similar to that received by manual workers. Was the post-war period the 'golden age' that it is sometimes described as?

In the years between 1944 and the early 1980s there was a series of curriculum developments, including a major extension of so-called 'sandwich' courses (periods of study in the middle of regular employment) and the establishment of a Schools Council. A major school rebuilding programme was undertaken and the comprehensive (all-ability, non-selective) secondary schools made their appearance. A limited number of more academic pupils was able to gain free places in a grammar school if they passed an examination at the age of 11 years (the so-called 'eleven-plus'). This policy led to divisions of pupils across the country and was the subject of intense political debate that has continued to the present time. Pupils who did not sit or failed the examination could only gain access to a secondary modern school, and later on, to the newly-founded technical schools for children of average ability who were considered more suited to practical rather than academic work. In 1965, an additional external examination (the Certificate of Secondary Education or CSE) was introduced for pupils in the middle ability range for whom the traditional Ordinary level examination (O level, introduced in 1953) was too demanding. After fierce debate throughout the 1970s and 1980s, the O level and CSE examinations were combined in 1986 to create a new national secondary examination known as the General Certificate of Secondary Education (GCSE) in England (equivalent to the TGAU or Tystysgrif Gyffredin Addysg Uwchradd in Wales and the Standard Grade in Scotland). The GCSE is usually taken by secondary school pupils at age 16, though more able children may sit the examination earlier.

Introduction of a National Curriculum

Only a generation ago, primary teachers had great liberty in making decisions about what to teach and how to teach it. Secondary teachers were governed more strictly by syllabuses and national examinations but were not normally under pressure to adopt specific teaching approaches. In fact, the freedom that teachers enjoyed to organise learning in a way that suited classroom circumstances was considered to be an essential element of their professional autonomy (Silcock, 2002; Hurst and Reding, 2006).

By the mid-1970s there had been very few studies about the aims of education from the teacher perspective (though see Ashton et al., 1975). There was also a dearth of research about 'school effectiveness', which in more recent times has been separated from the concept of 'school improvement' (Kelly, 2003; MacGilchrist and Buttress, 2004; Harris and Bennett, 2005). The famous (some would say, infamous) Ruskin College speech by the then Prime Minister, James Callaghan, in 1976 was yet to unleash what was grandly titled 'The Great Debate' about the future of education. There was an increasing political awareness, however, about the large amount of public money that was being spent on education and the need for rigorous accountability. The mood of the education world was conducive to a close scrutiny of the purpose of education and a move towards radical change.

One of the most significant events that resulted from this wide-ranging review of educational provision was the 1988 Education Reform Act (ERA) from which emerged a National Curriculum (NC) that would operate in all state-maintained schools and many private ones in England, Wales and Northern Ireland (through the Department of Education in Northern Ireland or DENI). The NC was designed to provide a minimum educational entitlement for pupils of compulsory school age, to ensure that the curriculum of each school was balanced and broadly based, and to promote the spiritual, moral, cultural, mental and physical opportunities, responsibilities and experiences of adult life. Prior to 1988, schools had been able to make their own decisions about curriculum provision at a local rather than a national level but the NC curtailed this freedom. Educational provision was divided into four key stages:

- **Key Stage 1 (KS1) for pupils aged 5 to 7 years;**
- **Key Stage 2 (KS2) for pupils aged 7 to 11 years;**
- **Key Stage 3 (KS3) for pupils aged 11 to 14 years;**
- **Key Stage 4 (KS4) for pupils aged 14 to 16 years.**

Since its introduction in 1989 there has been a number of versions of the NC. Additionally, there has been considerable emphasis placed on the teaching of English (focus on literacy) and mathematics (focus on numeracy). In 1999, a Foundation Stage curriculum was published for children aged four and five in nursery and reception classes. After the turn of the new century, the lower end of secondary education (KS3) became the focus of attention, as it was perceived that standards of attainment levelled out once pupils left primary school. Consequently, a national strategy was introduced to raise standards of teaching and learning across the curriculum for all 11- to 14-year-olds.

Another significant dimension of the NC was the introduction of pupil assessments by means of national tests at the end of each key stage. KS1 pupils take the 'end of key stage' tests at age seven, KS2 pupils at age 11, and KS3 pupils at age 14. There are other optional tests available to primary pupils at the end of other school years but, unlike the end of key stage tests, the results of the optional tests are not published. KS4 is assessed by levels of pupil achievement at GCSE. Having completed GCSEs, pupils have a choice of whether to continue with further education at school or college or to seek a job, though the government tries to encourage students to remain in full-time education after the age of 16.

Political intervention

One of the particular characteristics of the English education system in recent years has been what is seen by some educationalists as an over-simplification of complex educational issues in political debate (e.g. Carr and Hartnett, 1996; Richards, 2001; Alexander, 2004). The UK government has opened national policy decisions to critical scrutiny through extensive forms of consultation, though there is widespread scepticism about the usefulness of the process. Education priorities have moved a considerable way from the time of the Taylor Report in the mid-1970s when a key characteristic of teachers' professionalism was deemed to be their freedom to design and teach unhindered by external pressures (Taylor et al, 1974). Astonishingly, and at the time, surveys of teachers concluded that they believed that politicians were the least influential people in school life! Today, the situation is almost the exact opposite, as political priorities are imposed, promoted, scrutinised and complied with.

The government's insistence that schools and teacher training institutions follow its educational agenda (DfES/TTA, 2002) has resulted in a situation where failure to comply with its demands invites sanctions for the schools and colleges concerned. Every institution, from those providing childcare for the under-fives to the largest higher education establishment, has its education provision closely monitored by the Office for Standards in Education (OFSTED). A poor inspection outcome results in the worst cases in school or college closure. Success in reaching the required targets for examination success, on the other hand, results in increased resources, public accolades and the possibility of salary enhancements for staff. A system has gradually emerged in which the government, rather than the school staff, has most influence over the curriculum to be taught, the teaching methods to be employed and the assessment criteria to measure success.

Research box

curriculum provision in state-controlled education

Halpin et al (2004) have researched educational standards in schools designated within Education Action Zones (EAZ) to which additional government resources have been allocated together with finance from private investment and links with the voluntary sector. EAZs were charged with raising educational standards and combating social exclusion and economic disadvantage by introducing innovative approaches to education, including new forms of curriculum provision. The research team found that innovations ranged from additional use of learning support assistants and volunteer reading mentors, to one-to-one counselling, activities to combat truancy and variations in staff deployment. Some schools innovated by increasing the resources spent on support for the basic skills; other schools did precisely the opposite, including 'a few teachers who explicitly justified their involvement in these schemes in terms that stressed the need to ameliorate what they saw as shortcomings in the prescribed curriculum'. The research illustrated the difficulties of developing an innovative, responsive and inclusive curriculum within a highly regulated state system with high stakes testing.

The government's desire to exercise tight control, not only over *what* is taught but *how* it is taught, has created a situation in which teacher professionalism is being transformed from one of autonomy to one of compliance (Hayes, 2001). It is difficult for schools today to avoid being sucked into an attitude of deference that threatens to stifle initiative and restrict professional autonomy by refusing to trust teachers to act in pupils' best interest. Frowe (2005) reasoned that while the amount of money invested in education necessitates accountability and monitoring of practice, 'the over-regulation of the profession is corrosive of many of its most valuable elements'. The attempt to telescope all teaching and learning situations into a single model flies in the face of reason. Circumstances from school to school and class to class are so diverse that it is difficult to justify a policy that is so utilitarian that it takes little account of the immediate choices and decisions that all teachers have to make every working day. As Wrigley (2003) noted: 'Improvement by command from above results in the problematic implementation of macro initiatives by teachers who feel unable to question or even fine-tune them.'

Education provision today

There are four types of mainstream school operating within the education system in England and Wales today.

- *Community schools* **(formerly known as county schools). The vast majority of schools fall into this category. The local education authority (LEA) employs staff, owns the school land and buildings and determines the arrangements for admitting pupils.**
- *Foundation schools* **(formerly grant-aided schools). The governing body employs staff and has primary responsibility for admissions. The school land and buildings are owned by the governing body or a charitable foundation.**
- *Voluntary aided schools*. **Most of these schools are church schools. In similar fashion to foundation schools, the governing body employs staff and has responsibility for admissions. The school land and buildings are owned by a charitable foundation.**
- *Voluntary controlled schools*. **These schools are almost always church schools and the same conditions apply as pertain in aided schools, except for the important provisos that the LEA employs the staff and has responsibility for admissions.**

Statutory schooling lasts for 11 years between the ages of five and 16. Children are legally required to start attending school at the start of the term after their fifth birthday, on 31 August, 31 December or 31 March, though in practice children often start earlier than this owing to the widespread provision of nursery education. Pupils are required to stay in school until the last Friday in June of the school year in which they reach the age of 16. During this time children must receive an appropriate full-time education suited to their age, ability, aptitude and special educational needs. Most pupils transfer from primary to secondary school at the age of 11. Students who remain in education after the age of 16 are described as being in the post-compulsory stage of education.

The late twentieth and twenty-first centuries have seen great changes take place in the way that education is organised and monitored. The KS2 primary curriculum has become more subject-focused with the introduction of lessons of fixed duration located within a pre-determined timetable. Secondary education has also undergone a transformation, including the founding of specialist and 'beacon' schools (those with proven academic excellence; primary schools are also able to claim 'beacon' status) and of more private involvement in the state sector.

The Key Stage 3 curriculum now consists of English, mathematics, design and technology, ICT, history, geography, modern foreign language, art and design, music, PE and citizenship. Other areas of the curriculum that must be taught are religious education (RE), sex and relationships, and careers' education (from Year 9). All schools must teach RE according to the locally agreed syllabus, unless they are designated as voluntary-aided or faith schools. However, a detailed critique of KS3 in the 14–19 White Paper (DfES, 2005) noted that the design of the curriculum had encountered significant problems. Some programmes of study were considered incoherent and some material was repeated in different subjects. The heavily prescribed curriculum left schools with little space to assist struggling pupils or to extend gifted students. Consequently, science, history, geography and design and technology are now receiving extra attention, with an emphasis on real-life issues. The KS3 strategy is properly referred to as the Secondary National Strategy, as some of its work extends to KS4.

A vocational GCSE was introduced in 2000 to encourage students to take a work-related route at school and includes courses such as engineering, applied business, and leisure and tourism. From September 2004 the word 'vocational' was dropped to show that the vocational side of learning is equivalent in status to the traditional academic side. Some private schools have encouraged their pupils to progress straight to A level (disregarding GCSE) or to take the international baccalaureate diploma.

The appropriateness and relevance of testing and examinations continues to be actively debated among educationalists, in particular the suitability of formal tests for young children and the need for a public (national) examination for all pupils at the age of 16. In the primary sector, there has been a rediscovery of the significance of play in the education of younger children (Broadhead, 2004; Moyles, 2005) and creativity in learning (Fisher and Williams, 2004; Jeffrey and Craft, 2004). A decision about using so-called 'synthetic phonics' (a system based on teaching children letter sounds so that they recognise the different components within a word) as the core strategy in teaching reading to be employed in schools was made by the government early in 2006.

The present education system obliges schools to ensure that pupils and students attain the highest possible scores on national tests and have introduced the concept of 'individualised learning' to provide a bespoke curriculum for pupils. In late 2005 the Department for Education and Skills (DfES) introduced a new system called 'pupil achievement tracker' (PAT) that allows schools and LEAs to import and analyse their own pupil performance data against national performance data. There are four areas of analysis available: school level analysis; pupil level value added; target setting; question level analysis.

Research box

vocational learning for 14- to 16-year-olds

In their study of the effectiveness of the Increased Flexibility for 14- to 16-year-olds Programme (IFP) to provide vocational learning opportunities at Key Stage 4 for those young people who would benefit from them, Golden et al. (2005) found that around 90 per cent of young people who had been involved in the first cohort of IFP had continued into further education or training post-16. 42 per cent of young people said that their participation in vocational learning had influenced their decision about their post-16 education futures. It is clear that motivation for learning was a key factor affecting the young people's view of education and its significance in their lives.

Summary and conclusions

For the past hundred years or so governments of every persuasion have taken a deep interest in educational provision, not least because of the considerable national expenditure involved. This close attention on the best way to educate pupils reflects the fact that it has invested increasingly large political as well as financial capital in the process, with two broad consequences, one positive, the other less so. The positive consequence has been an improvement in the continuity and coherence of educational provision across England and Wales. The adverse consequence has been constraints on teachers' ability to exercise professional judgement about what is appropriate for their pupils. In particular, there is anxiety among many teachers about the way in which the climate of testing and inspecting has developed at the expense of attending to the social needs of children and young people. School leaders and practitioners at every phase of education constantly grapple with implementing the latest government initiative while ensuring that educational standards are maintained.

In reality, there is a difference between the 'specified' curriculum (formal programme of work) and the 'operational' curriculum (classroom practice) found in schools. The hiatus between 'specified' and 'operational' largely depends on the experience and confidence of the teachers concerned, though the support of school leaders (headteachers, heads of departments, curriculum leaders) is crucial for staff that wish to employ more imaginative and creative teaching approaches. Regardless of government edicts or externally imposed requirements, each educator's personal framework of values is of crucial significance in determining the choices and decisions about the curriculum and its implementation. Learning is not only about delivering subject knowledge, it is about the attitudes and behaviours fostered by teachers. Winning hearts and minds has been the challenge and inspiration for every teacher since schooling began and will, hopefully, always remain at the heart of education.

References

Alexander, R (2004) Still no pedagogy? Principle, pragmatism and compliance in primary education. *Cambridge Journal of Education*, 34(1): 7–33.

Ashton, P, Davies, F and Kneen, P (1975) *Aims into practice in the primary school: a guide for teachers*. London: University of London Press.

Broadhead, P (2004) *Early years play and learning*. London: Routledge.

Carr, W and Hartnett, A (1996) *Education and the struggle for democracy*. Maidenhead: Open University Press.

Chadwick, P (1997) *Shifting alliances: church and state in English education*. London: Cassell.

DfES (2005) 14–19 *Education and Skills*. London: Department for Education and Skills.

DfES/TTA (2002) *Qualifying to teach*. London: Teacher Training Agency.

Fisher, R and Williams, M (eds) (2004) *Unlocking creativity: teaching across the curriculum*. London: David Fulton.

Frowe, I (2005) Professional trust. *British Journal of Educational Studies*, 53(1): 34–53.

Golden, S, O'Donnell, L, Benton, T and Rudd, P (2005) *Evaluation of increased flexibility for 14- to 16-year-olds programme: outcomes for the first cohort* (DfES Research Report 668). London: Department for Education and Skills.

Halpin, D, Dickson, M, Power, S, Whitty, G and Gewirtz, S (2004) Curriculum innovation within an evaluative state: issues of risk and regulation. *The Curriculum Journal*, 15(3): 197–206.

Harris, A and Bennett, N (eds) (2005) *School effectiveness and school improvement: alternative perspectives*. London: Continuum.

Harris, M (1993) *The Catholic Church and the foundation of the Northern Irish State*. Cork: Cork University Press.

Hayes, D (2001) Professional status and an emerging culture of conformity amongst teachers in England. *Education 3–13*, 29(1): 43–9.

Hurst, B and Reding, G (2006), *Professionalism in teaching*. Upper Saddle River, NJ: Pearson.

Jeffrey, B and Craft, A (2004) Teaching creatively and teaching for creativity: distinctions and relationships. *Educational Studies*, 30(1): 77–87.

Kelly, T (2003) *Benchmarking for school improvement: a practical guide for comparing and achieving effectiveness*. London: Routledge.

MacGilchrist, B and Buttress, M (2004) *Transforming learning and teaching*. London: Paul Chapman.

Miller, P and Davey, I (2005) Family formation, schooling and the patriarchal state, in McCulloch, G (ed) *The RoutledgeFalmer reader in history of education*. London: RoutledgeFalmer.

Moyles, J (ed) (2005) *The excellence of play*. Maidenhead: Open University Press.

Richards, C (ed) (2001) *Changing English primary education*. Stoke on Trent: Trentham.

Silcock, P (2002) Under construction or facing demolition? Contrasting views on English teacher professionalism from across a professional association. *Teacher Development*, 6(2): 137–55.

Taylor, PH, Reid, WA, Holley, BJ and Exon, G (1974) *Purpose, power and constraint in the primary school curriculum*. Basingstoke: Macmillan Education/Schools Council.

Wrigley, T (2003) Is school effectiveness anti-democratic? *British Journal of Educational Studies*, 51(2): 89–112.

Chapter *8*

The child, family and society: Early Years in context

Wendy Bignold

Introduction

Early Years education is considered here in the broadest sense and from birth to age five. It looks at how 'education', or learning, takes place as part of socialisation before formal schooling even begins and it examines the ways in which young children develop a sense of themselves and of those around them and the role that the family, gender and society have in this process. The chapter concludes by considering the role and demands made of Early Years practitioners operating in an increasingly complex world.

Developing a sense of self

From the moment they are born, young children begin to learn about themselves, the people around them and the world in which they live. While the statutory age for starting school is fixed at five, formal education in nursery or reception classes can begin as young as three or four. A young child's sense of self has a significant impact on his or her relationship with other people and with all subsequent learning (Dowling, 2000).The importance of a strong self-identity or self-image cannot be underestimated. This is recognised in the Early Years curriculum in England:

> *Gaining knowledge and understanding of their own culture and community helps children develop a sense of belonging and strong self-image. Each child has a culture defined by their community and more uniquely by their family. ... A positive self-image and high self-esteem gives children the conveyance and security to make the most of opportunities, to communicate effectively and to explore the world around them.* (QCA, 2000, p29)

If young children are to explore the world around them, making sense of it and engaging with it, then a secure knowledge of who they are and a sense of their own worth will give them the confidence to do this. There are essentially two elements to self-image:

- **self-concept or becoming aware of who you are;**
- **self-knowledge or recognising your own strengths and weaknesses.**

From birth onwards, young children build a picture of themselves based on other people's responses to them and particularly the response of significant adults around them (e.g. mother, father, siblings, carer). Babies recognise that they matter when they smile at a face that smiles back at them. Having one or more stable relationships with an adult provides a sense of continuity for a young child to develop a concept of himself or herself within. The development of self-concept has been written about at length. Bee and Boyd (2004) have identified two main stages:

- **a subjective stage, which takes place during a child's first year when a baby is learning that he or she matters and can make things happen (e.g. can move an object);**
- **an objective stage, when, as a toddler, a child learns that he or she has a name, is a boy or girl, is big or small, and so on.**

As children get older they also become more knowledgeable of what they can and cannot do and how this relates to other children and adults. They begin to recognise what they need help and support with. When they are acknowledged, praised, respected or rejected, this contributes to the regard they have for themselves. The two components of self-image (concept and knowledge) become more complex as children grow older and have a wider range of experiences to draw upon.

The family

Young children are heavily reliant on adults or older children to help them make sense of the world around them. Because of a lack of experience and understanding, they are easily influenced by others. For the majority of babies, the immediate environment includes their families. Parents have now been acknowledged as children's first educators, (e.g. Barber, 1996; Glauert et al, 2003). Children look to those people who are familiar to them and who they feel an attachment to, for information and security. The views of family members, or other key adults, are hugely influential. The different ways in which family members behave towards a child will help that child to develop an understating of who he or she is and how he or she relates to others. This informal education, which takes place within the family or care unit, is called primary socialisation. With primary socialisation, values, morals, prejudices, stereotypes and attitudes are all passed from one generation to the next.

Siblings, particularly older siblings, are hugely influential in primary socialisation. It is well known that a younger sibling will copy an older sibling's behaviour thereby adopting the values and attitudes of older children. A young child learns that not everything he or she does will be approved of and that certain types of behaviour are not acceptable and will have to be modified. It is only as children grow older and start to become independent of their families that they may adopt values and attitudes of their own.

> *Pause for thought* | primary socialisation
>
> *...the significance of family relationships for their [children's] well-being and sense of identity is now increasingly being taken into account by researchers and professionals working with children.* (Gabriel, 2004, p71)
>
> Reflect upon your own childhood. Consider the many things that you were socialised into by your family such as mealtime conventions or religious worship. To what extent has this early education influenced you in your life so far and impacted on your sense of identity? Reflect upon the different roles played by families in educating young children. Are there other institutions which could do these roles more effectively?

The process of gender socialisation begins at birth. The first words which announce a baby's arrival are usually 'It's a girl!' or 'It's a boy!' This is generally reinforced by family and friends in the toys and clothes which are given as presents. By the age of two, children can usually identify themselves as girls or boys (Dowling, 2005). They have a working, if not yet fully formed, definition of their own gender identities and the gender identities of others. A child of this age may think that anyone with short hair is a boy, for example. It takes a little longer to learn that gender is a constant. That is, that people stay the same even when they change their appearance, when they wear different clothes, or change the length of their hair. By the age of four, most children are developing a stronger gender identity based on their personal name and how they belong to a wider community of family and friends (Linden, 1993). This is the process of socialisation where attitudes and reactions of those around them help children recognise and understand accepted values and behaviour of the group to which they belong. This can be both positive and negative depending on the stereotypes held by key family members and strongly held beliefs may lead to the imposition of restrictions. Comments such as 'You're only a girl, so you can't' or 'Big boys don't cry' influence behaviour in young children. It is suggested by Gelder (2004) that young children are praised by close adults when they display gender-appropriate behaviour. The importance of the family to primary socialisation is paramount.

The role of society

Secondary socialisation involves the development of a child's understanding of social expectations, rules and so on. This occurs outside of the family in the community and wider society through key groups such as:

- **the media;**
- **the government;**
- **the influence of peers;**
- **Early Years practitioners.**

Values held by certain groups in society and social conventions are learned by young children through the process of secondary socialisation.

The media

Boys and girls are expected to play in very different ways. This can be seen in the gender-biased adverts for toys on television. Manufacturers now target very young children before they can even speak and so the media impacts on children's play from an early age (Burke, 2005). In socio-dramatic play, pretend activities are often based on domestic scenarios, such as putting baby to bed, shopping or cooking. Thematic fantasy play is based on fictional narrative and imaginary events such as acting out the plots of television programmes. Stone (1981) has suggested dramatic play functions as an 'anticipating socialisation' device. In other words, as a way of children preparing themselves for the roles they may adopt as adults. Stone claimed that in western societies socio-dramatic play involving domestic themes is more characteristic of girls than it is of boys and that boys are more likely than girls to act out thematic fantasies with the result that 'the dramatic play of children in our society may function more to prepare little girls for adulthood than little boys'.

> *Pause for thought* | the media
>
> The media play an increasingly important part in secondary socialisation as children are bombarded with images, both visual and verbal, through television, radio, books, newspapers and now computers (Marsh, 2005). Watch a set of adverts in between children's TV programmes. What do they promote? Consider what messages they are giving children about:
>
> - personality traits and characteristics of boys and girls;
> - gender roles within the family;
> - gender professions.
>
> Think how these images might influence young children as they develop a sense of themselves and of others around them. Are stereotypes evident? Do you agree or disagree with the stereotypes they generally promote? Do you think current social trends linked to gender or other influences are damaging the individual or the family?

Young children's early sense of others can be positive or negative and may develop into prejudices or stereotypes. What is important is where these categories are used and to what purpose they are put. Stereotypes are dangerous when they provide a false and misleading picture of what people are actually like. Continuing with the example of gender, the Sex Discrimination Act (1975) introduced legalisation which made it unlawful to discriminate against someone on grounds of gender. It was recognised as a significant issue in society which required government legislation in order to combat it. However, over 30 years on, it remains an issue in society and one which Early Years practitioners need to be aware of so that they may combat Early Years prejudices.

The government

With a government committed to offering good quality and affordable childcare for every parent who wants it, Early Years provision for the under fives has developed rapidly in the past 10 years (HMT, 2004). In the late 1990s, the government recommended that there should be a fully integrated approach to Early Years education and care or 'educare' (Whalley, 2001) which resulted in the publication of the National Childcare Strategy (DfES, 1998). Subsequent public initiatives have seen an increase in multi-agency provision for young children. These have come under various headings including Centres of Excellence and SureStart. All have offered services to children under the age of 5 and to their families. The emphasis is on 'one-stop provision' offering a variety of education, health and welfare services on one site. The government has also committed itself to providing 3500 Children's Centres by 2010 (Ball and Vincent, 2005). Such government initiatives now recognise the key role that parents and families have in young children's early learning. These have been set out in the Early Years Framework (DfES, 2002), which indicated that:

- **parents and families are central to the well-being of young children;**
- **relationships with other people (both adults and children) are of crucial importance in the lives of young children;**
- **a relationship with a key person at home or in an Early Years setting other than a home is essential to young children's well-being;**
- **babies and young children are social beings and competent learners from birth.**

If there is such a comprehensive provision of 'educare' underpinned by the principles from the Early Years Framework, this must surely have a positive influence on young children's socialisation. However, there have remained many barriers to access of provision for different groups of families. This lack of access has reduced the impact of publicly funded Early Years services in secondary socialisation.

Research box

issues of access

Government childcare funding is targeted mainly at the most economically disadvantaged areas in the country. The Daycare Trust (2004) investigated the impact of this policy on those families living outside these areas and highlighted childcare gaps for other disadvantaged parents and children. Although cost is a huge barrier to parents accessing childcare for under fives there were other key barriers too. These included:

- inflexibility of provision in terms of 'opening hours';
- information on childcare generally being inaccessible in a suitable form or in minority languages, so many parents from ethnically diverse groups were not aware of what provision was available;
- a lack of childcare workers from black and other minority ethnic groups, so diverse communities were not reflected in the staff of the settings;
- a monocultural curriculum or the lack of a truly multicultural curriculum over and above tokenism;
- poor transport facilities to get children and families to the settings;
- a lack of trust of childcare workers.

Peer influence

Relationships with other children outside the family often begin with children of a similar age (e.g. through parent and toddler groups). These relationships can develop through different stages of play:

- **parallel play or playing alongside another child independently;**
- **co-coordinated play or play involving interaction with another child;**
- **co-operative play or play positively engaging with another child.**

As children are developing a sense of self and a recognition of their gender identity, they may start selecting toys to play with that they see same-sex peers playing with. Young children are particularly influenced by older peers around them and so may be influenced in their choice of toys by those who are already aware of stereotyped gender-specific behaviour. In this way young children may also be influenced by peers in their early attitudes towards individuals and groups as well as to themselves.

Pause for thought | peer pressure

Ramsey (1991) has identified four categories which encompass children's social status and behaviour. These are described as follows:

- popular children – have lots of 'friends' who often want to play with them or be near them;
- rejected children – want to play with peers or be near them but are often refused this, have backs turned on them or may even be pushed away;
- neglected children – do not try to interact with others and their company is not sought by peers;
- controversial children – may be popular with peers but are often in trouble for aggressive behaviour or breaking rules.

Consider how the social skills of children in each category might influence their sense of self. While practitioners cannot make friendships happen or make a child popular with peers (Peters, 2003), how might they help a child to develop positive social skills and so a more positive self-identity?

Early Years practitioners

Early Years practitioners play two key roles in secondary socialisation:

- **to pass on their own values and attitudes;**
- **to provide a curriculum for children to learn from.**

Being in a position to pass their own values and attitudes on to the children they work with, it is crucial that practitioners have identified their own prejudices and stereotypes so that they are aware of them. They need to learn to deal with them in positive ways (Siraj-Blatchford, 2001). This is important to ensure that they do not adversely influence young children or their families. Only once Early Years practitioners have acknowledged their own prejudices can they help young children to overcome their own through planned and unplanned experiences (Bignold, 2005). Early Years practitioners are also responsible for the curriculum or experiences that the children will have while in the setting. The experiences and opportunities available to children and the images they see, or don't see, through resources, influence them in the way in which they view themselves and relate to others. Learning social conventions through the planned routines of the setting is one example of this. This is a key element to the Early Years provision in other countries, such as the Reggio Emilia centres in Italy, acclaimed as one of the best Early Years education systems in the world. In Reggio Emilia centres, mealtimes play a key part in every child's day. Mealtime conventions, such as eating manners, are 'taught' to children through the act of socialising around the dinner table. Children are encouraged to engage in this social experience as soon as they are able to sit up. The practitioners encourage the children to become independent as this has a positive impact on their self-worth and self-esteem. They are 'helped to value their own competencies', whatever these might be (Rinaldi, 2005).

Pause for thought | recognising your own attitudes and prejudices

We all hold stereotypes and prejudices about groups and individuals whether we would like to admit it or not. This is because we have all been through the process of socialisation. For some of us, our attitudes and prejudices will be very similar to our parents, 'or carers', for others, they will have changed and been influenced strongly by peers and partners or by experiences as we have grown up. The important thing is to recognise them so that we may combat them and not influence others with them. Consider your own attitudes, stereotypes and prejudices. What are they? Can you recognise where they have come from? How might you combat them or overcome them?

Nature *vs* nurture

A child's identity and sense of self is not just a product of primary and secondary socialisation or nurture. Nature, involving genetically inherent characteristics, also plays its part. While there has been much debate over the differing effects and contributions of nature versus nurture and which is most influential on a child's development, it is now generally accepted that both are influential (Griffiths, 2005). Two key theories of why boys and girls and men and women are different, for example, included:

- **biological determination;**
- **feminism.**

Biological determinism argues that boys and girls are predisposed towards acquiring certain knowledge and skills, and to presenting certain behaviours because of inherent genetic biological differences (nature). One complication for Early Years practitioners is that these inherent sex differences create differences in learning between boys and girls. This requires a variety of learning styles to be catered for in order to provide equality of opportunity. Feminism presents a different perspective on gender difference. It argues that boys and girls are naturally the same but that they are conditioned by parents, peers and society (nurture). Girls are conditioned to be submissive and to be dominated by boys. This conditioning is 'institutional in the way that racism is institutional' (Epstein, 1998). This clearly has implications for Early Years practitioners too.

The impact of socialisation and other influences on young children

In recent times, gender has been identified as an issue for Early Years practitioners in three different arenas (Gaine, 1999):

- **in equal opportunities concerns;**
- **in the interplay between race and class;**
- **in levels of achievement.**

The 1970s saw concern over equal opportunities in relation to gender. There were concerns about girls' experiences within male-dominated structures. This supported the idea that girls' choices in relation to activities and the Early Years curriculum were a result of opting for choices less popular with boys and so not dominated by them. It was argued that this prohibited girls from having equal access to provision. In the 1980s there was renewed interest in issues of gender, class and ethnicity and how these related to each other and to children's identities. This began to recognise the complexity of these issues. There was concern that equity and social justice should be facilitated. The 1990s to the present day has seen an emphasis on achievement. Education has been dominated by analysis of performance data in relation to gender. Boys' underachievement in literacy has been of particular concern and has regularly been picked up by the media as newsworthy. According to Siraj-Blatchford (2001):

> *Recently we have heard a good deal in educational debates about (working class) boys' underachievement. The results from the school league-tables suggest some boys do underachieve in basic literacy.* (p100)

Siraj-Blatchford does warn Early Years practitioners of not making general assumptions about all boys underachieving. These assumptions would be stereotypes in themselves and children should always be treated as individuals. Indeed, as many gender studies have demonstrated, there can be as much variation within any one gender as there is between them.

The three broad areas of concern identified above highlight the general ways in which gender impacts on young children:

- **in access to provision;**
- **in self-identity and self-esteem based on stereotyped expectation behaviour;**
- **in achievement or underachievement in the Early Years or later in life possibly affected by prejudices held by others.**

These are recognised in the Early Years curriculum where practitioners are required to meet the needs of both boys and girls equally. If equal opportunities to access the curriculum are to be provided then different activities or resources may be needed to meet the requirements and interests of both groups. There is a number of strategies which Early Years practitioners can implement in order to reduce negative effects on gender and to combat prejudices. These can be categorised into four broad areas:

- **training;**
- **provision;**
- **resources;**
- **employment.**

Practitioners should receive appropriate training to enable them to meet the needs of both boys and girls. This includes confronting stereotypes as part of basic childcare training (Penn, 1998). Provision in Early Years settings should be examined to ensure that a variety of learning styles is catered for. Girls are more likely to request help with an activity and to work cooperatively than boys. Girls often have longer concentration spans than boys who tend to become bored more quickly. Practitioners should be trained to cater for these differences in their provision. Boys are more likely to receive negative comments from an adult in a setting than girls and so, not surprisingly then, more adult talk is in communication with boys than with girls. This can give the message that boys are more important than girls even if they are 'seen' as more 'disruptive'. Resources can go some way to encouraging boys or girls to choose activities that they may not normally select. Boys and girls tend to adopt gender-stereotyped behaviour from an early age. Reading and writing activities may be seen by boys as female activities while maths, science, IT and PE-related activities tend to be rated as 'masculine'. Exciting resources which engage and motivate both gender groups and individuals can have some impact on what children choose to do, as can practitioner expectations. Employment and a lack of male role models in the Early Years continue to be key issues which need both local and national commitment if progress is to be made. Various estimates put the number of men who work with young children between 1 and 3 per cent:

> *Design of courses as well as the gendered nature of the profession (It's women's work) are to blame as well as low pay and lack of career opportunities.* (Abbott and Pugh, 1998, p157)

Men working directly with young children provide a way of challenging gender-stereotyped roles as well as being beneficial to children and encouraging greater involvement of fathers in their children's Early Years education. This must be seen as a priority for all providers of Early Years services.

Summary and conclusions

This chapter has considered how young children develop a sense of self and of others. It has identified the role of the family, peers, the media and the government in primary and secondary socialisation. It has taken gender as a particular illustration of the socialisation process. Issues relating to gender have been analysed in terms of how they impact on young children and how Early Years practitioners might overcome them. There are other significant influences on children's identity, and these include social class or poverty, race or ethnicity (including culture, language and religion) and disability (of the child or family member).

Research has shown that even by the age of about 22 months, there are differences in children's learning as a result of family and other influences. These influences may impact on young children in ways which are based on stereotyped expectation, behaviour and achievement or underachievement in the Early Years or later in life, possibly affected by prejudices held by others.

With common trends come common solutions. Having a diverse workforce in the Early Years, for example, can provide a positive role model for the wide variety of children who see themselves reflected in the staff who care for them. It can also help other children to overcome their own stereotypes as they get to know individuals from backgrounds different from their own. In order to be successful it requires a whole-setting approach underpinned by government support and initiatives. However, it is the family and the Early Years practitioner who will have the greatest impact on a young child's sense of self and subsequently his or her relationship with society.

References

Abbott, L and Pugh, G (eds) (1998) *Training to work in the Early Years*. Buckingham: Open University Press.

Ball, S and Vincent, C (2005) The childcare champion? *British Educational Research Journal*, 31(5): 557–570.

Barber, M (1996) *The learning game*. London: Victor Gallancz.

Bee, H and Boyd, D (2004) *The developing child*. Boston, MA: Pearson Press.

Bignold, W (2005) Valuing diversity: the role of support workers in the Early Years, in Campbell, A and Fairburn, G (eds) *Working with support in the classroom*. London: Paul Chapman.

Burke, D (2005) Two year olds branded by advertising. *Ecologist*, 35(7): 17.

Daycare Trust (2004) *Talking about childcare*. London: Daycare Trust.

DfES (1998) *National Childcare Strategy. London*: Department for Education and Skills.

DfES (2002) *Birth to Three Matters: An Introduction to the Framework*. London: Department for Education and Skills.

Dowling, M (2005) *Young children's personal, social and emotional development*. London: Paul Chapman.

Epstein, D (ed) (1998) *Failing boys? Issues in gender and achievement*. Buckingham: Open University Press.

Gabriel, N (2004) Being a child today, in Willan, J, Parker-Rees, R and Savage, J (eds) *Early childhood studies*. Exeter: Learning Matters.

Gaine, C (1999) *Gender, 'race' and class in schooling: a new introduction*. London: Falmer.

Gelder, U (2004) The importance of equal opportunities in the early years, in Willan, J, Parker-Rees, R and Savage, J (eds) *Early childhood ctudies*. Exeter: Learning Matters.

Glauert, E, Heal, C and Cook, J (2003) Knowledge and understanding of the world, in Riley, J (ed) *Learning in the early years: a guide to teachers of children 3–7*. London: Paul Chapman.

Griffiths, L (2005) Becoming a person, in Willan, J, Parker-Rees, R and Savage, J (eds) *Early childhood ctudies*. Exeter: Learning Matters.

Her Majesty's Treasury (2004) *Choice for parents, the best start for children: a ten year strategy for children*. London: Her Majesty's Treasury. Available at **www.hm-treasury.gov.uk/media/426/F1/pbr04childcare_480upd050105.pdf** (accessed 7 April 2006).

Linden, J (1993) *Child development from birth to eight*. London: National Children's Bureau.

Marsh, J (2005) Digikids: young children, popular culture and media, in Yelland, N (ed) *Critical Issues in Early Childhood Education*. Maidenhead: Open University Press.

Penn, H (1998) Facing some difficulties, in Abbott, L and Pugh, G (eds) *Training to work in the Early Years*. Buckingham: Open University Press.

Peters, S (2003) Children's experiences of friendship during the transition to school. *Early Years*, 23(1): 45–53.

QCA (2000) *Curriculum Guidance for the Foundation Stage*. London: Qualifications and Curriculum Authority.

Ramsey, P (1991) *Making friends in school*. London: Teachers College Press.

Rinaldi, C (2005) *In dialogue with Reggio Emilia*. Abingdon: Routledge.

Sex Discrimination Act 1975. London: HMSO. Available at **www.pfc.org.uk/legal/sda.htm** (accessed 7 April 2006).

Siraj-Blatchford, I (2001) Diversity and learning in the Early Years, in Pugh, G (ed) *Contemporary issues in the Early Years – working collaboratively for children*. London: Paul Chapman.

Stone, Judith (1981) *International Year of the Child: the continuing challenge*. (Report of the UK Association for the International Year of the Child.) London: International Year of the Child Trust.

Whalley, M (2001) *Involving parents in their children's learning*. London: Paul Chapman.

Chapter 9

Polarisations in English

Ruth Hewitt and Elizabeth Hopkins

Introduction

Considering the fact that English is no real newcomer to the school curriculum, it is quite remarkable that it has been an almost constant subject of controversy and debate. Strong views and polarisations have characterised the history of English teaching that continue to the present day. It has been argued, for example, that even as recently as the 1980s, the dominant ideology of English teaching has involved too much concentration on personal responses and creative aspects of English to the detriment of others. The fact that this balance underwent a massive shift back in the other direction with the introduction of a National Literacy Strategy in schools in England and Wales in the 1990s is typical of the pendulum-like nature of developments in English in schools. This chapter explores both the history of English as a curriculum subject and the dilemmas facing educationalists today. Teaching English is doubtlessly too important a topic to be distracted by opposing factions or beliefs. However, a close look at some of the apparent dichotomies, both past and present, will give an insight into how English got to where it is today, as well as giving greater knowledge on which to base decisions about where English should go in the future.

The concept of English as a subject

Do changes in English teaching priorities go round in cycles reflecting the prominent educational, cultural or political mood of the day? Or would it be more accurate to say that disparate aspects of the subject can be seen as belonging to a continuum over which the pendulum swings slowly backwards and forwards over time, with more emphasis being given at different points to some knowledge, understanding and skills rather than others? The very nature of English as a curriculum subject has always been complex and variable and this, in turn, has affected issues of how to teach it.

Before the eighteenth century, the teaching of oral expression, written expression, logic, grammar and literacy were well-established educational elements in English. However, by the nineteenth century, comprehension and interpretation had gained in prominence. The thinking skills needed for the comprehension and interpretation of texts, that would probably be the domain of English Literature teaching today, had gained in importance at the expense of oral expression and logic, although literacy and grammar were still taught. By the early 1900s, the English curriculum was made up of standard English and grammatical correctness, emphasising an instrumental or utilitarian approach to what was needed for adults to play a useful role in society. As was indicated by the Board of Education (1910): 'pure English is not merely an accomplishment, but an index to and a formative influence over character'. However, during the First World War the high level of illiteracy amongst conscripts caused concern to the government. As a result of this, the government set up an enquiry that led to the Newbolt Report (Board of Education, 1921) which emphasised literary values with the intention of making available the supposed civilising and humanising values of the public school to all people, whatever their class. A 'liberal education' would emerge as a feature of all schools, at the heart of which would be the nation's greatest literature. In this move, the twentieth-century swing from language to literature had begun again. This trend continued with 'a series of sustained attempts on the part of literature specialists to eradicate the study of language or grammar', (Mittins, 1964).

During the 1960s, attempts were made by Dixon (1967) to reconcile these two separate ideas by proposing that the main purpose of English teaching was to help pupils build their own 'representational world' *through* the use of language. Dixon also propounded the idea that a study of literature enabled an exploration of human nature and situations and therefore led people to look at themselves and possibly develop and grow through this self-awareness. As Dixon himself indicated: 'in ordering and composing situations that in some way symbolise life as we know it, we bring order and composure to our inner selves'. This model of English teaching, therefore, included literature that was closer to children's interests and experiences. It also focused on the acquisition of language skills through the study of literature. This is in contrast to the position today in Key Stages 1, 2 and 3 in which the acquisition of literary understanding is achieved through the study of language. Being narrower in focus than the English National Curriculum, which remains the statutory instrument in England and Wales, the 'literacy' in question in the National Literacy Strategy may initially have had a slightly larger frame of reference but hotly debated issues still remain as to how to reconcile a greater concentration on knowledge about language with the maintenance of a love of and creative engagement with texts (Willinsky, 1994). A concern that primary-aged pupils' work at Key Stages 1 and 2 has moved too far away from whole texts and personal responses to them has been partially responsible for the recent introduction of the Excellence and Enjoyment strand of the Primary National Strategy.

The nature of English taught in the school curriculum has obviously been an issue of ideological debate long before the present era and this has always been influenced by the political context in which English has found itself. There have clearly been different emphases and priorities in English at different times in its history. But has it really changed in its fundamentals?

Research box

multitextuality and multimodality

It could be argued that the nature of English really does need to change more drastically in the present day if it is to reflect the advances in the types of texts that people now encounter in their daily lives (see Foucault, 1988; Robinson, 2000). How far English as a curriculum subject should ever reflect current culture is, however, debatable. If it is to do so at all, aspects of current ways of reading, writing and engaging with texts need to be considered (see Meek, 1991; Andrews, 2001). According to Sefton-Green and Nixon (2003), it has become a truism that 'most texts enjoyed by children are screen-based', which seems to imply that the concentration on print-based fiction and information texts in schools is increasingly out of touch with the experiences that modern children bring to the classroom. This also points to the growing role of visual and graphical forms of communication. Modern texts are also changing in a qualitative way in that they are often multimodal in nature, drawing on more than one medium at the same time and utilising several different text types at once (see Goodman and Graddol, 1996). For example, computer games tend to incorporate a cinematic point of view, written and spoken texts and music (possibly even with lyrical content). Also, the distinctions between speech and writing are becoming ever more blurred with the increasing visual representation in SMS Messaging, in particular, of what would, before new computer technology, have been essentially oral acts – spontaneous conversations between two or more people. Should English as a subject, therefore, become 'Textual Studies' and concern itself with reflecting modern culture and modern texts, embracing new technologies and the resultant modern ways of reading those texts, rather than restricting itself predominantly to books in general and to the literary canon in particular?

Rationales for the teaching of English

Having looked briefly at the history of English in schools, it would be appropriate to consider the five rationales or models for English outlined in the influential Cox Report which considered the place of English in the curriculum in the late 1980s (DES, 1989), and to use these to consider whether an emphasis on different rationales or models of English teaching has prevailed at different times. Cox's five rationales or models are presented as follows:

- **Adult needs** – this focuses on communication outside the school and emphasises the responsibility of English teachers to prepare children and young adults for the language-demands of adult life, including the workplace, in a fast changing world. Is this the view that prevailed in the early 1900s?
- **Cross-curricular** – this focuses on the school and emphasises the need for all teachers to have a responsibility to help children and young adults with the language-demands of different subjects in the school curriculum. Is this the view that prevails in the Primary National Strategy today?
- **Cultural analysis** – this focuses on values and society and emphasises the role of English in helping children and young adults towards a critical understanding of the cultural environment and the world in which they live. Children and young adults should know about the processes by which meanings are conveyed and about the ways in which print and other media convey messages. This view may never have been prominent in the past but should it be in the future?
- **Cultural heritage** – this focuses on the identification of prominent and influential literature and emphasises the responsibility of schools to lead children and young adults to an appreciation of those works that have been widely regarded as amongst the finest in the language. Is this the view embodied in all versions of the National Curriculum, particularly the literary canon drawn on for the list of texts to be read and studied at Key Stages 3 and 4?
- **Personal growth** – this focuses on the child and young adult and emphasises the relationship between language and learning and the role of literature in developing imaginative and aesthetic lives. This view rose to prominence in the late 1960s and continued for the next twenty years or so. Is it still the most important rationale for English teachers trained during this period?

As can perhaps be seen, the past, present and future shifts in priorities in English seem to rest upon the relative balance of these rationales for the teaching of the subject and all are important. But when it comes to deciding what the bulk of English curriculum time should be spent on and what should be at the heart of the curriculum there might well be differences of emphasis between individuals, and this could potentially cause problems. Cox, for example, was quite clear that the cross-curricular needs of learners should be met by *all* teachers. If this were to really take place, then the case for English or literacy lessons to predominantly address these needs would become diminished. Goodwyn and Findlay (1997) found in repeated questionnaires that personal growth was overwhelmingly given as students' and teachers' most important rationale for the teaching of English. If 'literacy' in a primary school context, however, focuses mainly on the basic skills needed by pupils to access the rest of their learning across the curriculum, then this has the effect of making English a service subject and not concerned to any great extent with the development of personal and social knowledge and understanding, nor with the 'love' of literature cited as being so dear to many English teachers' hearts (Goodwyn, 2003). This could be a case of teachers and policy-makers being poles apart in what they consider to be the most important aspects of the subject.

Pause for thought | Cox's five rationales or models

Having considered the five rationales or models presented by Cox (DES, 1989), place these into:

- your rank order of their importance as rationales for the teaching of English;
- your rank order of the strength of their influence on current classroom practice as you understand or remember it.

Share your own views with friends, colleagues and lecturers and try to draw some conclusions.

The fact that 'literacy across the curriculum' is one of the strands of the National Literacy Strategy for Key Stage 3 confirms that finding a definitive role for the place of English teaching in schools has never been easy to resolve. Bullock suggested that 'all teachers are teachers of English', and in his lengthy report, *A Language for Life* (DES, 1975), went far beyond the scope of what could be covered in the curriculum slot designated as English. His comment that 'explicit instruction out of context' is 'of little value' could, surely, not be disagreed with by many educationalists and yet the challenge for schools is in how to avoid doing this. Hopefully, if a school gets it 'right', whatever that means, the result is a shared understanding between all staff of the role of language in pupils' learning and how work in different subjects can contribute to and benefit from the development of pupils' ability to communicate effectively. But, as English language is both a subject and a medium of learning for others, it is always going to be difficult to negotiate and enhance this relationship.

Pause for thought | literacy across the curriculum

Educational institutions are charged with a responsibility to ensure that English is studied in its own right as well providing a medium of learning for others and to manage this relationship so that the knowledge, understanding and literacy skills of children and young adults can be effectively developed.

- How does an educational institution go about achieving a holistic approach to the teaching of literacy?
- Where and when should specific speaking, listening, reading and writing skills, knowledge and understanding, be explicitly taught and, significantly, assessed?
- How can an institution ensure all aspects of literacy are covered effectively?
- What problems, if any, could occur when trying to ensure that literacy is taught across the curriculum?
- What benefits, if any, accrue when a literacy policy works well?

Language, literature, culture and the great naming debate

One of the longer-lasting causes of the polarisations in focus in English lies in the fact that the subject can include the study of language, literature or culture. One possible solution to this could be to create a separate subject in the secondary curriculum entitled 'Language'. This could concern itself with language study and appreciation and encompass links with other languages such as French, German or Spanish already being studied by pupils. Socio-linguistic, critical linguistic and discourse-oriented models of language could open up a world of exploration to pupils of all ages and abilities. Topics such as *Language and Power*, *Language and Identity*, *Language and Gender* and the study of spoken texts, currently restricted to pupils studying AS and A2 English Language, could be incorporated as well as more obvious areas such as grammar, syntax and morphology. If pupils were encouraged to know more about other 'Englishes' and other languages, this would surely be beneficial as a way of gaining insights into their own version of English, and maybe a greater tolerance of different languages, cultures and societies would also result. It would undoubtedly be educationally detrimental, however, if connections between language understanding and language use – in other words the links between the ability to read, understand and talk about texts and the ability to write them – were broken. Language study should not just take place in a separate part of the curriculum to that in which the study of texts produced in that language is carried out. Study of a broader range of spoken and written texts could be included within a wider remit for the subject English. In this way the highly popular 'newcomers' to the curriculum, such as media studies, film studies, communications or even ICT, might be encompassed within the umbrella of 'English', and parallels between texts and ways of analysing them might more easily be drawn. Knowledge, understanding and skills gained from the study of one type of text could surely then be made more easily transferable to another. But what would this do for the study of our literary culture? Could experience of the English Literary Heritage be better placed within a citizenship-type curricular area, alongside the study of our democratic background and values, our cultural heritage and our society in general? If several different curricular areas, such as those outlined earlier, covered various strands of what is currently taught in English, would this imply an acceptance of their equal value as aspects of English? And if so, would this be appropriate? Are they equally important?

Before we leave this topic of naming, there is also, of course, the issue of 'literacy' itself. The fact that 'literacy' has replaced 'English' in most primary schools signifies to many educationalists the current emphasis of curricular content on language skills and technical accuracy in reading and writing as opposed to the engagement with literature and creativity implied in the broader term (or as Cox would put it, cross-curricular needs as opposed to personal growth). For these people the naming of the subject has become politically and ideologically charged.

Pause for thought | 'that which we call a rose by any other name would smell as sweet'

What should English be called? Consider the suggestions below in turn and think about their potential benefits and drawbacks:

- cultural studies;
- culture;
- English Language;
- English Literature;
- English studies;
- language;
- literacy;
- literary studies;
- literature;
- textual studies.

Is there another name that would more effectively encompass the scope of English as a subject or do you think the subject should be split into various parts? What is your preferred term or set of terms? Justify and explain your own choices.

English in higher education

Changes in the nature of English degrees and the growth of new varieties have been significant indicators of the underlying currents within English teaching in general. During the 1970s and 1980s, the emergence of a whole plethora of critical and theoretical approaches to literature took place replacing the previously predominant literary criticism based on the methods established by F.R. Leavis, where the study of literature was 'an exercise in value judgement' (Hardman, 2001). In addition, the study of language that had grown and found strong voices in figures such as Chomsky began to offer insights not only into language itself but also into the understanding of the human mind and human society. This impinged on the study of literature directly through the concept of stylistics and indirectly through the role of linguistics as one major source of the structuralist movement. The growth of socio-linguistics led to a focus on the development of children's knowledge about language through the close study and critical analysis of language as it was actually used, as opposed to focusing on how it should be used. It embraced an understanding and critical awareness of all forms of language and media texts and aimed to contribute to young people's literacy demands by providing them with tools for understanding the modern world. Other innovations in the study of language also had their impact on English in higher education. The growth of Cultural Studies, Communication and Media departments in universities led to a significant reconsideration of what constituted a text and of what could or could not be counted as 'English'. English became perceived as a cultural or social semiotic study (Peim, 2000). Today, the wide variety in what can be studied as part of an 'English' degree has been noted by the Higher Education Funding Council for England amongst others. In their Subject Overview Report, HEFCE (1995) commented on the diversity of provision in that 'different emphasis can be given to knowledge of literature, skills in the use of English and the exploration of the cultural contexts of English and its uses'. There is, clearly, an acceptance of diversity in English curricula at this level of education that, unfortunately, no longer seems to be matched in others.

Cross-phase discontinuity

One of the consequences of the movements in Higher Education in the 1980s was a breakdown in the shared purpose that had long existed between universities and schools. There had been very little difference between English Literature teaching at universities and by sixth form teachers in terms of pedagogical practice and the same texts tended to be selected from a shared canon with similar terms and methods of textual analysis applied to them. For the reasons outlined earlier, this common culture does not exist as it did today.

A discontinuity in English teaching between various phases of education is present in other ways too. The National Literacy Strategy was first introduced to primary schools in the late 1990s but it did not appear in secondary schools until 2000. There is currently quite a substantial number of sixth form students who choose to study English Language, either in a joint AS and A2 format with English Literature or as a subject on its own. An emphasis on knowledge about language is therefore increasingly embedded in English teaching at Key Stages 1, 2, 3 and 5 and in many university degree courses, as we have already seen. Yet this is not the case at Key Stage 4 where there is still a strong focus on, and time commitment to, analysis of figurative language and literary written texts in both English Language and English Literature GCSE courses.

So, what of the future? Will Key Stage 4 syllabuses change in line with this general trend towards knowledge about language just in time to see a reverse swing of the pendulum in other key stages, with a return to the primacy of literature for its own sake and a fostering of 'creativity' and personal growth? If there is one thing we may have learned from a look at the past, it is that we should not be surprised if this were to be the case.

Pause for thought | the future of English

The Qualifications and Curriculum Authority's *English 21* survey asked teachers, students, parents and employers, as well as writers, academics, librarians and publishers, about what English as a curriculum subject might look like by 2015 (QCA, 2005). The survey invited responses on a diverse range of topics related to how English lessons 'might need to change to embrace new thinking, priorities and technologies'. Reflect on some of the questions drawn from *English 21* below in the light of your own experience and consider your views on the future literacy needs of the population:

- What place should there be for creativity and imagination in English?
- How much time should be spent on teaching knowledge about language or allowing pupils to explore the way in which our language works?
- How can English in the future reflect the types of texts pupils will be familiar with and come across in their daily lives?
- What acknowledgement should be made of American or Australian English or of the place of English in the world as a result of the dominance of American culture in particular?
- What elements of English are essential and which should be offered as optional GCSE, A level or degree subjects?
- What sort of testing or assessment arrangements will be most appropriate for the knowledge, understanding and skills being taught?

Summary and conclusions

In looking at the history of English as a curriculum subject there have been cycles in the relative emphasis given to language or literature. These cycles can be traced from the early twentieth-century preoccupation with standards of technical accuracy and reading skills and the opinion that English Literature was a second class subject, to the mid-twentieth century prevalence of ideas about personal growth and the importance of personal responses to literature, to the late-twentieth century rebirth of a concentration on knowledge about language. On past experience this cyclical nature of change could continue well into the future. In more recent times, there have been additional elements in English to consider. New types of texts have sprung to life as a result of advances in ICT and there have been increased study and awareness of spoken texts. These could either be thrown into the English melting pot, which would involve yet more jostling for position and priority in an already crammed curriculum area, or left as the domain of other, newer, curriculum subjects, leading to the redundancy of English itself.

The rationales or models for English teaching, as expressed by Cox, seem just as relevant to the English debate today as they did in the 1980s, but policy-makers and practitioners do not seem to be any closer to reaching a consensus as to which should be considered most important, or on reconciling a position in which these various rationales or models can happily co-exist. It would be an interesting exercise, for example, for English educators to actually pinpoint which aspects of work covered in their lessons directly address the enhancement of personal growth, as opposed to preparing pupils for their literacy needs as adults, or to consider how much time they give to the five different rationales or models in their schemes of work. It could well be that the way they feel about the subject is not matched by the realities of the lessons that they teach. It could also be the case that learning about language through literature and learning about literature through language are not really the poles apart that they might seem to be. They are certainly not mutually exclusive, either in theory or in practice.

English teachers remain the constant in the sea of change caused by politicians and the new curricula and syllabuses they introduce. Whether through laziness (e.g. simply not wanting to change the lesson plans they devised 20 years ago), recalcitrance (e.g. disagreeing with the principles behind an initiative) or ignorance (e.g. too little knowledge of grammar or ICT), teachers rarely swing from one extreme to the other. It is to be hoped that, in the case of the many reflective practitioners, a reasoned central standpoint will be taken, making use of the best new changes, but not losing sight of the same old effective ones.

References

Andrews, R (2001) *Teaching and learning English: a guide to recent research and its applications*. London: Continuum.

Board of Education (1910) *Circular 753*. London: HMSO.

Board of Education (1921) *The Teaching of English in England* (the Newbolt Report). London: HMSO.

DES (1975) *A Language for Life: Report of the Committee of Inquiry appointed by the Secretary of State for Education and Science* (the Bullock Report). London: Department for Education and Science/HMSO.

DES (1989) *English for Ages 5–16* (the Cox Report). London: Department for Education and Science/HMSO.

Dixon, J (1967) *Growth through English*. Oxford: Oxford University Press.

Foucault, M (1988) What is an author?, in Lodge, D (ed) *Modern criticism and theory*. London: Longman.

Goodman, S and Graddol, D (1996) *Redesigning English: new texts, new identities*. London: Routledge.

Goodwyn, A (2003) We teach English not literacy: 'growth' pedagogy under siege in England, in Doecke, B, Homer, D and Nixon, H (eds) *English teachers at work*. South Australia: Wakefield Press.

Goodwyn, A and Findlay, F (1997) *English teachers' theories of good English teaching and their theories in action*. Paper given at the BERA conference York, 1998

Hardman, F (2001) What do we mean by Secondary English teaching?, in Williamson, J, Fleming, M, Hardman, F and Stevens, D (eds) *Meeting the standards in Secondary English*. London: RoutledgeFalmer.

HEFCE (1995) *Subject Overview Report – English*. Bristol: Higher Education Funding Council for England.

Meek, M (1991) *On being literate*. London: Bodley Head.

Mittins, WH (1964) *The teaching of English in schools*, in Quirk, R and Smith, AH (eds) *The teaching of English*. Oxford: Oxford University Press.

Peim, N (2000) The cultural politics of English teaching, in Davison, J and Moss, J (eds) *Issues in English teaching*. London: Routledge.

Poulson, L (1995) *Research, policy and practice in literacy and language education*. Exeter: University of Exeter.

QCA (2005) *English 21*. London: Qualifications and Curriculum Authority.

Robinson, M (2000) What is(n't) this subject called English?, in Davison, J and Moss, J (eds) *Issues in English teaching*. London: Routledge.

Sefton-Green, J and Nixon, H (2003) The challenge of popular culture, digital technologies and curriculum change, in Doecke, B, Homer, D and Nixon, H (eds) *English teachers at work*. South Australia: Wakefield Press.

Willinsky, J (1994) Introducing the new literacy, in Stierer, B and Maybin, J (eds) *Language, literacy and learning in educational practice*. Clevedon: Open University Press.

Chapter *10*

Mathematics for the future

Mark Patmore

Introduction

There is increasing concern about the state of mathematics education in this country. It is generally recognised that mathematics is vital. It matters to individuals and to society as a whole, it underpins research and development in the sciences, technology and ICT, and it is essential for the future economic prosperity of this country. Additionally, it provides a set of key skills to enable individuals to reach their full potential in terms of life and work. Getting the teaching and learning of mathematics right is therefore a major education priority, yet the country is struggling to recruit or retain the number of mathematics teachers required. A large number of pupils is being taught in classes by teachers with no mathematics qualification. It is clear that a vicious circle is being established – a poor supply of mathematics teachers now will result in an even greater shortage in the future. Additionally there is debate, but no agreement, about what mathematics should be taught. This chapter is intended to challenge you to think about the nature of the mathematics we need to study now and about mathematics teaching. Some of you may have negative feelings towards mathematics, others may be more positive. However, the issues arising in mathematics education have to be recognised and faced by all and not just by those who have a vested interest in the subject.

Concerns for mathematics

The frequently raised question 'Where will the next generation of mathematicians and mathematics teachers come from?' is a serious one indeed. It may seem alarmist but it illustrates that many people engaged in education, industry and commerce feel that there are serious problems and issues associated with the teaching and learning of mathematics in the UK and with the future supply of the mathematicians needed in the twenty-first century.

There is now clear evidence of a fall in the number of students taking A level mathematics and further mathematics, as reported each year when the A level results are published in the daily press and elsewhere. At GCSE, press comments focus on the steady rise in the number of students gaining grades A* to C on papers that are perceived to be both getting easier and on which the marks required for 'acceptable grades' are getting lower. The Confederation of British Industry (CBI) and other similar bodies have also expressed concern about the mathematical capabilities and competences of 16- to 18-year-olds who are starting employment, and university departments of mathematics, science and engineering have all expressed concern over the content and lack of rigour of the A level mathematics courses. At university, these concerns are supported by the evidence of deteriorating performance on the same tests set year on year to each new group of first year undergraduates. Indeed, some university departments now require their undergraduates to attend additional classes in order to acquire the knowledge and skills deemed to be lacking, while others have extended their courses from three years' to four years' duration with consequent financial implications for their undergraduates. Importantly, press reports frequently refer to a decline in the number and quality of students entering highly numerate university courses, to a lack of qualified mathematics teachers, to a shortage in the number of high-quality IT specialists, to a shortage of mathematicians in industry and commerce, and so on. Contrary to popular opinion, the mathematical demands of the workplace have not been, and will not, be reduced by the introduction of calculators and computers. Instead, these tools have enabled people to introduce new and more efficient techniques and working patterns which in turn call for new levels of mathematical and statistical understanding.

> *Pause for thought* | perceptions of mathematics
>
> Together with a group of friends or colleagues, think back to when you last studied mathematics. This might have been at secondary school or as part of some work-related experience. You might be studying mathematics right now as part of your degree programme! Should mathematics be part of the formal school curriculum at all? Why do you think mathematics appears to be in decline as a subject area? What do you think could be done to 'turn mathematics around' and make it more popular? Does mathematics matter?

Many would argue that there is too little attention paid to mathematics, that mathematics education is deeply inadequate and misconceived, and that current attitudes and current practice need to be changed, both within the compulsory school sector and beyond – improving, for example, the provision for older students and adult learners, and reducing the mismatch between school and the demands of university. Anderson (2002) wrote:

> *The continuing health of mathematics as a subject depends not only on recruiting students for advanced study but also of creating a wider understanding of why mathematics should be financially supported.* (p31)

It is of course only fair to point out that some, including both academics and journalists, would argue that mathematics is an over-admired and over-privileged subject. Perhaps such views are commonly held by those whose qualifications are within the field of the arts rather than in the sciences, and it must be of concern that the subject has no or few friends at court – very few politicians have either a scientific or mathematical qualification. So while politicians proclaim the importance of the knowledge society and of a skilled workforce, it seems that the reality is different. There is a risk that the most privileged parents, aware of the demands of society and work, will ensure that their children are well prepared and prepared. The independent schools, whose share in A level mathematics is already a higher proportion than their A level share overall, might increase this share still further and the less privileged will be left with qualifications that place them at a disadvantage. This cannot be good for the country or for the individual.

Research box

international comparisons

Comparisons in the mathematical performance of children and young adults between countries are often made, with the UK frequently depicted as performing less well than its 'competitor' nations (e.g. IEA, 1995; BSA, 1997; Kaiser et al., 1999; PISA, 2000). It is worth reflecting on the fact that in the Pacific-rim countries of Japan, Hong Kong, Korea and Taiwan, the time devoted to mathematics in the school curriculum is considerably more than in the UK and probably more than in many other western countries. The question 'Should the school curriculum be adjusted to give mathematics more time?' is one that surely would not receive a favourable response from the teachers of many other subjects! That said, the *School Matters* effectiveness study of Mortimore et al (1988) showed that the school effect had a significantly greater influence on progress in mathematics over time than did the impact of family background. In comparison, the study showed that for reading the school effect was much less though still greater than that of home. According to Hanson (2004), reasons why children in other countries perform better at mathematics than children in the UK (at least as far as the tests employed demonstrated) include a healthier and more positive attitude towards mathematics at school, a recognition of the importance of a general education, which includes mathematics, and certain culture-specific organisational features (e.g. teaching and learning strategies, classroom layout, setting by ability, and so on).

Mathematics under the microscope

In recent years, school mathematics has been affected by changes imposed by central government. While the introduction of the Mathematics National Curriculum in 1989 resulted in reforms to the teaching and assessment of the subject, changes had, of course, been taking place before then. In the

1970s, for example, published reports stated that there was an apparent lack of basic computational skills in many children, increasing mathematical demands made on adults and a lack of qualified mathematics teachers. The government's response was to set up an inquiry chaired by Sir William Cockcroft into the teaching of mathematics. Many of the recommendations in what is commonly referred to as the Cockcroft Report (DES, 1982) were implemented in the Mathematics National Curriculum that followed and in the examinations taken at the end of formal schooling. The teaching and learning of mathematics in primary and secondary schools and the examination system itself have been under the microscope ever since. As recently as 2002, the government set up an independent inquiry chaired by Professor Adrian Smith into post-14 mathematics education. The Smith Report, *Making Mathematics Count* (DfES, 2004a), made recommendations to further amend the curriculum, qualifications and pedagogy for those aged 14 and over in schools, colleges and higher education institutions to enable those students to acquire the mathematical knowledge, understanding and skills necessary to meet the requirements of employers and further and higher education today. So 22 years after the Cockcroft Report, the issues and concerns surrounding mathematics education were still very much evident. So how can the issues and concerns be addressed, if at all? Clearly, how mathematics is taught, as well as what mathematics is taught, must be considered together.

What mathematics?

The opening words of the government's response to the Smith Report (DfES, 2004b) appeared to acknowledge the nature of the problem facing the status and purpose of mathematics in today's fast-changing world:

> *It is difficult to overstate the importance of mathematics in today's world, both for the individual and for the economy. The acquisition of mathematical skills is essential for progression in education and employment. At the same time a sufficient supply of mathematical skills is critical if we are to maintain our economic competitiveness.* (p5)

However, further reading of the response shows that the need to ensure that a 'sufficient supply of mathematical skills' (i.e. a highly qualified workforce) is ignored and indicates that the focus should be concentrated instead on the 'needs of all learners'. This is a familiar line taken by successive governments over the years, effectively thinking that a reduction in the level of intellectual challenge will result in more students being prepared to engage with the subject. The fallacy in this line of reasoning can be seen in the decline in the number of A level mathematics candidates following the revisions to A level mathematics courses made in an attempt to make the subject more attractive and more accessible. In 2005, there were about 60,000 entries for A level mathematics, 11 per cent fewer than in 2001 and 21 per cent fewer than in 1991. The latest change to the Key Stage 4 mathematics curriculum, the introduction of a two-tier GCSE, has been subject to the same line of reasoning and will, in terms of producing a mathematically qualified section of the population, almost certainly fail and exacerbate the situation, focusing as it does on raising the number of grade C passes at the expense of providing challenge to the higher-achieving candidates—politically good for league tables but not for the take-up of the subject at A level, with the consequent implications for universities and employers. One consequence of what is sometimes described as the 'dumbing down' of mathematics is illustrated by Tall (1995):

> *Thus it is that fractions prove difficult for some and impossible for many and so have no place in a democratic curriculum on a ladder which all will climb. But the more successful students, who would find such things cognitively simpler, may be denied adequate exposure to the topic to give it meaning.* (p29)

One solution put forward to the problem of addressing the lack of skills for most, while maintaining the possibility of challenge for some, is the introduction of functional mathematics, success at which will be required for the award of a grade C at GCSE together with a new examination called 'further mathematics for the more able'.

Pause for thought | mathematics in school

Spend a few minutes reflecting on the following questions. Try to ignore any thoughts about the demands of the end of Key Stage tests (primary or secondary) or GCSE and A level requirements.

- What mathematics should be taught in schools and who should make the decisions?
- Who should teach mathematics in schools and how should they be trained?
- How should mathematics be assessed and for what purpose?
- Should what is taught focus on employment and the world of work and the mathematics needed in society, or focus on more theoretical aspects?

As you reflect upon the final question, perhaps you should also like to think about the mathematical demands of different subjects and occupations (e.g. teaching, nursing, the legal profession, plumbing, electrical work, and so on).

Any discussion about the nature of school mathematics up to GCSE can be held at a number of different levels. Clearly mathematics in school is concerned with number, shape, algebra, measurement, data handling and so on, and while these give the subject its particular 'flavour', they have applications in other areas of study. While the subject content of school mathematics is identifiable and distinctive, what is much less clear is that it also requires specific forms of learning. Skemp (1971), for example, a mathematician and psychologist, investigated how mathematical concepts are formed. Skemp distinguished between two forms of teaching and learning: that which results in relational understanding and that which results in instrumental understanding. Skemp described instrumental understanding as involving memorisation and the routine application of procedures and formulas (e.g. focusing on what to do and how to get answers). In contrast, Skemp described relational understanding as involving meaning (e.g. being able to explain reason and use multiple representations to arrive at solutions). It is obvious that these approaches exist in other contexts and in other subjects. Indeed, one could suggest that instrumental understanding could lead to better examination and test results overall, while relational understanding offered better preparation for work and adult life.

Mathematics for public understanding

Most people, if stopped in the street and asked to look back at their own mathematical experiences in school, would probably identify Skemp's notions of understanding, although in many cases instrumental understanding would probably be more familiar than relational. Many people, for example, may remember the rule for dividing fractions but have no idea why it works. If the same people were then asked what they thought mathematics was, it would be a 'safe bet' that the majority of the answers would include descriptions such as 'hard' or only for the 'bright' or 'boring' or would list actual topics that had been imprinted on their minds such as Pythagoras's theorem or quadratic equations. Probably very few would list the skills and qualities that are developed through the study of mathematics or how it benefited them in later life. It is also very likely that their responses would reflect the fact that school mathematics has the potential to engender unhelpful attitudes and feelings such as 'anxiety', 'helplessness' and 'apathy'. The development of positive attitudes and values are valid objectives for mathematics education in their own right, together with other desirable qualities such as confidence, independence, imagination, cooperation, while not forgetting that the recognition of the simple fact that knowing mathematics can be personally satisfying and empowering. One challenge clearly is to think how positives can be developed and experienced by all and the impact of negatives reduced.

The perception that mathematics is a difficult and minority subject needs to be changed into one in which the acquisition of mathematical knowledge, understanding and skills is valued and seen as necessary. For example, encouraging positive attitudes towards mathematics could include:

- **seeing mathematics as an essential element of communication;**
- **recognising that mathematics is a powerful tool;**
- **developing an appreciation of relationships within mathematics;**
- **developing an awareness of the fascination of mathematics;**

- **recognising that mathematics can encourage and develop imagination, initiative and flexibility of mind;**
- **developing the skills of working in a systematic way;**
- **developing the skills of working both independently and cooperatively;**
- **developing confidence in one's mathematical abilities;**
- **developing the skills of critical reasoning.**

This list recognises that some social development – the ability to work cooperatively for example – can and should take place within mathematics lessons or in a separate mathematical context. The list also acknowledges that the development of critical reasoning is important, allowing children and young adults to enhance their ability to understand the world around them and build their confidence. Compare the list above with the implicit list provided within the following quotation:

> *[Thus the aim is primarily] to ensure that children leave school literate, numerate and with a modicum of scientific knowledge, it should not extend beyond these three core subjects, nor attempt to do more than set minimum standards in basic knowledge and technique.* (Lawlor, 1988, p5)

This quotation suggests that, for example, Skemp's instrumental understanding is all-important. It also implies that numeracy and not mathematics is the aim. Note that if the aims of mathematics teaching are to embrace both independent and cooperative working and communication, a change to the traditional role of the teacher may be required. A view from America is useful here. According to the National Research Council (1989):

> *Teachers' roles should include those of consultant, moderator and interlocutor, not just presenter and authority. Classroom activities must encourage students to express their approaches, both orally and in writing. Students must engage in Mathematics as a human activity; they must learn to work cooperatively in small teams to solve problems as well as to argue convincingly for their approach amid conflicting ideas and strategies.* (p61)

The challenges must be to ensure that a sufficient supply of mathematical skills is generated while the needs of the more able are met, at the same time allowing all to have an opportunity to develop the transferable skills necessary for future employment.

Mathematics or numeracy?

The word numeracy has appeared earlier in this chapter but is not, other than in educational circles, a commonly used term. Indeed, every time numeracy is typed into a document, computer spell checkers indicate that the word should be replaced by numeric or innumeracy. So what is numeracy and can it be defined?

In the Cockcroft Report (DES, 1982) it was suggested that being numerate implied the possession of two attributes: an 'at homeness' with number (the ability to make use of mathematical skills in order to cope with the practical mathematics of everyday life) and an ability to have some appreciation of information presented in mathematical terms (such as in graphs, charts, tables or equations). The essential elements of being numerate, as set out by Cockcroft, are still considered important today. Tout (1997), for example, has suggested:

> *We believe that numeracy is about making meaning in mathematics and being critical about maths. ... it is about using mathematics in all its guises – space and shape, measurement, data and statistics, algebra and, of course, number – to make sense of the real world, and using mathematics critically and being critical of maths itself. It acknowledges that numeracy is a social activity. This is why we can say that numeracy is not less than maths but more.* (p13)

Tout's definition, through the phrase 'to make sense of' and 'using mathematics', suggests the need to work within a mathematics curriculum and extend it through context and application rather than producing a curriculum for numeracy. However, the current plans for numeracy, in the guise of functional mathematics, exclude all but the simplest forms of algebra and geometry and a large part of statistics, especially those elements that allow for the critical interpretation of data even at a fairly simple level. In some official circles, numeracy is seen to be synonymous with mathematics. In particular, this extends to the National Numeracy Strategy, which provides a structure or guide for teachers and is subtitled 'The framework for teaching mathematics'. On the other hand, if numeracy is taken to mean arithmetic and number sense, and if the assumptions that numeracy and mathematics are the same and that this is all that is needed by all students, then we are in fact doing our students, and by implication our future society, a major disservice.

There is, of course, a paradox here, because if we look at the mathematical activities in adults' working lives, we may only find traces of school mathematics and so conclude that the mathematical demands of adult life are insignificant. If we accept that there is little mathematics used in the workplace, then the mathematical knowledge of the school curriculum becomes less relevant and important and so a downward and negative spiral ensues – what is taught becomes less important to working practices as working practices show less evidence of making use of what is taught in school. If mathematics is reduced to simple arithmetic then most children will be able to learn what they need by the time they begin secondary school, in which case mathematics can be dispensed with. If that happens, so we dispense with any serious appreciation of science, engineering, statistics, and so on.

A further paradox also arises. If we acknowledge that many pupils have a lack of mathematical confidence and experience feelings of alienation towards the subject of mathematics but we seek to alleviate the problem, we run the risk of divorcing the subject from its roots in science and technology, leading to mathematics being disconnected from what is genuinely useful.

An additional factor emerges from the nature of mathematics itself. Mathematics consists primarily of human mathematical problem-posing and solving. It is part of human culture and the mathematics of each culture serves its own unique purposes and is equally valuable. Consequently, school mathematics should acknowledge the diverse cultural and historical origins and purposes and the contributions made to mathematics by all, including women and people from other countries. But does it? Additionally, if the focus moves towards numeracy and mathematics for the workplace, how can the acknowledgement of the universal origins be achieved?

Numeracy and literacy: a winning combination

We would probably all agree that being literate at some level is a basic skill that no one can afford to be without. But the importance of being numerate, particularly towards employment, has, until recently, not been fully recognised. The Department for Education and Skills (DfES, 2003), in their *The Skills for Life Survey*, produced a national profile of adult literacy and numeracy and assessed the impact different levels of skill had on people's lives. The survey found that:

> *Those with level 2 or above numeracy (i.e. GCSE grade C or above) earned an average of … £8,200 more than those with entry level or lower numeracy and that lower levels of literacy and numeracy can lead to social exclusion, denying people the opportunity to get the most out of what is available to the rest of society.* (p77)

Indeed, Bynner and Parsons (1997) have listed four interrelated numeracy and literacy categories, each of which has a profound bearing on an individual's employment and earning potential:

- **poor numeracy and poor literacy;**
- **poor numeracy and competent literacy;**
- **competent numeracy and poor literacy;**
- **competent numeracy and competent literacy.**

Research has shown that men and women showing the lowest levels of full-time labour market participation tend to be those with poor numeracy skills rather than poor literacy. Men with poor numeracy skills tend to be those most prone to unemployment. Women with competent numeracy and poor literacy skills tend to be almost twice as likely as those with poor numeracy and competent literacy to be in full time employment. These conclusions may come as something of a surprise, as literacy has always had a higher profile than numeracy or mathematics. It is clear that what is to be taught in schools is vital. So, should we teach mathematics or should we teach numeracy? Are they the same or is one a subset of the other? Should we focus on mathematics or numeracy for employment or for the love of mathematics or both? Comparing literacy and numeracy again, most people do not forget how to read, to follow written instructions, or even how to add up simple numbers, but the ability to work out, for example, percentages, unless practised, becomes relegated to 'something I did at school'. But even if agreement can be found about what should be taught, the problems of underperformance and underachievement in mathematics needs to be addressed; particularly so with girls and sections of the population from ethnic minority backgrounds or for those for whom English is not their first language. What does seem to be a self-evident truth is that the acquisition of any mathematical skills is only worthwhile if children and young adults have the personal, social and moral education to make some sense of the world in which they live and thus know how to make use of those skills.

Pause for thought | mathematics, culture and underachievement

Consider this quotation from Zaslavsky (1981):

> It is the content and methodology of the mathematics curriculum that provides one of the most effective means for the rulers of our society to maintain class divisions. (p15)

With reference to the points drawn from Costello (1991) and Ernest (1991) presented below, to what extent do you believe this to be true?

- Mathematics is generally taught in a narrow context with little concern for its historical and cultural setting.
- Mathematics is presented as absolutist and the product of white middle-class males with decontextualised, abstract and formal mathematics most prized.
- Gender-biased texts reflect and presuppose the male-dominated cultural context.
- The mathematics curriculum in Britain is racist in the sense of discriminating against the needs, values and best interests of certain ethnic groups.
- IQ and other tests or means of assessment are culturally biased.
- Mathematics is used politically to promote certain values or social developments.
- School mathematics is remote from the experiences of many pupils and their own culture.
- Mathematics reflects a particular culture or society in a way that can be reasonably and productively understood.
- A lack of positive female and ethnic minority role models in mathematics serves to reinforce stereotypes.

Summary and conclusions

There are many issues to be addressed when debating what is required of mathematics education for the twenty-first century. Pupils certainly need some basic mathematics as part of their life skills 'package' (or should this be considered numeracy?) and employers will increasingly require not only mathematical knowledge and understanding but also transferable skills such as the ability to apply mathematics in context, to reason logically and to be organised and systematic. How this combination of outcomes is to be achieved remains somewhat problematic.

References

Anderson, J (2002) Being mathematically educated in the twenty-first century, in Haggarty, L (ed) *Teaching mathematics in secondary schools: a reader*. London: RoutledgeFalmer.

BSA (1997) *International Numeracy Survey: a comparison of the basic skills of adults, 16–60, in seven countries*. London: Basic Skills Agency.

Bynner, J and Parsons, S (1997) *Does numeracy matter?* London: Basic Skills Agency.

Costello, J (1991) *Teaching and learning mathematics 11–16*. London: Routledge.

DES (1982) *Mathematics Counts: Report of the Committee of Inquiry into the Teaching of Mathematics in Schools under the chairmanship of Dr WH Cockroft* (the Cockroft Report). London: HMSO/Department for Education and Science.

DfES (2003) *The Skills for Life Survey: a national needs and impact survey of literacy, numeracy and ICT skills.* London: HMSO/Department for Education and Skills.

DfES (2004a) *Making Mathematics Count: Report of Professor Adrian Smith's inquiry into post-14 mathematics education* (the Smith Report). London: HMSO/Department for Education and Skills.

DfES (2004b) *The response to Professor Adrian Smith's inquiry into post-14 mathematics education.* London: HMSO/Department for Education and Skills.

Ernest, P (1991) *The philosophy of mathematics education.* London: The Falmer Press.

Hanson, M (2004) Learning and mathematics, in Ward, S (ed) *Education studies: a student's guide.* London: RoutledgeFalmer.

IEA (International Association for the Evaluation of Educational Achievement) (1995) *Third international maths and science study.* Available at **isc.bc.edu/** (accessed 7 April 2006) (includes reports from subsequent years).

Kaiser, G, Luna, E and Huntley, I (eds) (1999) *International comparisons in mathematics education.* London: Falmer.

Lawlor, S (1988) *Correct core.* London: Centre for Policy Studies.

Letwin, O (1988) *Aims of schooling.* London: Centre for Policy Studies.

Mortimore, P, Sammons, P, Stoll, L, Lewis, D and Ecob, R (1988) *School matters.* Wells: Open Books.

National Research Council (1989) *Everybody Counts. Report to the nation on the future of mathematics education.* Washington, DC: National Academy Press.

PISA (2000) Knowledge and skills for life. Available at **www.pisa.oecd.org** (accessed 7 April 2006) (includes reports from subsequent years).

Skemp, R (1971) *Psychology of learning mathematics.* Harmondsworth: Penguin Books.

Tall, D (1995) Can all children climb the same curriculum ladder?, in Mond, D (ed) *The mathematical ability of school leavers.* Gresham Special Lecture. London: Gresham College.

Tout, D (1997) *Some reflections on adult numeracy.* Proceedings of the Third International Conference of Adults Learning Maths – a Research Forum (ALM-3). London: Goldsmiths College.

Zaslavsky, C (1981) Mathematics education: the fraud of 'Back to Basics' and the socialist counter-example. *Science and Nature*, 4: 15–27.

Chapter *11*

Science and society

Richard Walton

Introduction

Modern society is largely defined by the products of science and its applications. Consequently, an understanding of science is now regarded as essential for the educated individual. Whether applying scientific ideas as an expert or making decisions as a layman, there is an increasing need for the public to have at least a minimum level of scientific literacy. Yet why should science be given such a preferred position in the curriculum that it is treated as a compulsory double subject at school with all pupils conscripted to its cause? Science education, that is to say the teaching and learning of science, has become one of the great influences upon the wider world of education. In part, this is because it has stimulated some of the most innovative research of recent decades, but also because it is seen as underpinning the economic and technological future of the nation. This chapter touches upon science's historical roots, to consider what it is about the nature of science that makes it stand out, not only as such a remarkably successful human enterprise, but also what differentiates it from other competing subjects. It also discusses the many challenges and opportunities currently faced by those at the chalk face.

What is science?

From the time of Aristotle during the fourth century BC, an attempt has been made to draw a distinction between scientific knowledge and technical skill. In doing so, Aristotle identified scientific knowledge (*episteme*) as a means of providing truths that can be demonstrated about the world as opposed to technical skill (*techne*) which was regarded as the ability to create new materials and artefacts. This distinction provided a relatively clear and simple view of the nature of science and its purpose. The Aristotelian view that the world can be systematically examined and understood strongly influenced the development of science, first of all in the Muslim world and then in Christian Europe. In the thirteenth century, Robert Grosseteste and Roger Bacon drew upon Aristotelian ideas to construct a scientific method through which knowledge was generated by an inductive–deductive pattern of scientific enquiry. The process of induction and deduction has always been seen as central to the way in which scientific knowledge is built up. *Induction* begins with making observations and leads the scientist to construct explanatory principles from them. By contrast, *deduction* takes the process in reverse. Beginning with general principles, the scientist is able to predict specific instances that may then be observed. The importance of practical observation in science education was stressed in the seventeenth century by Jan Comenius.

So, from the earliest days, the teaching of science has not simply been a matter of remembering and recalling facts, it has also included the need to teach and make full use of various skills, including observation and how to make reasoned judgements. Science education, therefore, focuses upon at least three elements:

- *knowledge* – science has a canon of facts and principles which forms the basis to our shared understanding of how the world works;
- *practical skills* – the skills of observation need to be learned through engagement with apparatus and equipment;
- *evaluatory frameworks* – scientific ideas are built up using logical processes by which evidence is evaluated, predictions made and hypotheses tested, often using the application of mathematics.

Science is, in simple terms, an intellectual, practical, creative and social endeavour that seeks to help us better understand and make sense of the world in which we live. In more recent years there has been a recognition that scientific understanding is not simply a one-way process. Science and its associated technologies have the power to interact with and change our surroundings and this requires children and young adults to acquire an awareness of humankind's ecological impact (Walton, 2000). Similarly, it is increasingly the case that the wider role played by science in shaping our attitudes as members of society is being recognised through the inclusion of *citizenship* as an element in the school science curriculum (Ratcliffe and Grace, 2003).

The place of science as an element in a compulsory core curriculum has long been argued along with significant discussion of the reasons why it important for the general public to have greater levels of scientific understanding (White, 1982). Millar (1996) has argued that the school science curriculum should aim for public understanding in which the notion of understanding includes science content, science methods of enquiry and science as a social enterprise. The point has also been made by Wellington (1990) and Walton (2002) that not all science is learned in the formal environments of schools and classrooms but that informal sources (e.g. television, museums and science centres) have an increasingly important role to play as the pace of scientific and technological change increases.

Pause for thought | justifying science

According to Millar (1996), the five arguments that justify the place of science in the curriculum are:

- cultural – science is a major achievement of our shared culture and it is as important to know about science as it is about the arts;
- economic – science forms the basis to many careers such as engineering, medicine and research;
- democratic – many decisions that must be made by the general public (e.g. whether to eat GM foods, use nuclear power or have our children vaccinated) are informed by scientific ideas;
- utilitarian – the application of science is useful to people living in a technologically-based society;
- social – it is important to maintain links between science and wider culture to prevent alienation of the individual.

What do you think about Millar's views? Is Newton as important a cultural figure as Shakespeare? It is really the job of schools to ensure that a supply of scientifically trained individuals is maintained? Can the public really make scientifically informed choices in complex situations? What do you regard as the most useful scientific knowledge or technical skills? Is there already a division between the scientific and technical haves and have-nots?

Science education and cognitive development

In her seminal work arising from the Children's Learning in Science Project (CLISP) at Leeds University, Driver (1983) was led to the philosophical position that one could not apply simple induction to the methods adopted by children in learning science. This is because the prior understandings that form a child's personal interpretation of phenomena may run counter to the accepted scientific view. These alternative explanatory frameworks are neither capricious nor transitory but, as Driver's mapping showed, are tenacious and follow consistent patterns of development. For Driver this meant that when constructing new explanatory frameworks in science, children have to be challenged to overcome what they believe and understand to be true. Driver interpreted this shift in pupils' thinking as being akin to the paradigm shift put forward by Kuhn when scientific thought undergoes a revolution taking it from one pattern of orthodoxy to another (Kuhn, 1996). Driver's work removed from science education the myth of the *tabula rasa* where the minds of the young are empty slates or vessels waiting to be filled with knowledge. Her central theme was that new knowledge must be *constructed* and that this personal and social process of construction is strongly rooted in the use of language and appropriately structured tasks. In part, the findings of CLISP only served to confirm what one might expect, that as children grow older and mature intellectually so too does their capacity to understand increasingly more abstract ideas.

Research box

Vygotsky and the ZPD

Vygotsky (1934) drew a distinction between *spontaneous* concepts, which arise through a child's everyday practical activity and social interaction, and *scientific* concepts, which are the product of systematic instruction. As children grow, and 'the development of scientific concepts outstrips the development of spontaneous concepts' this transition places greater emphasis upon the intervention of the teacher in promoting learning through instruction (Sutherland, 1992). Central to Vygotsky's approach was the notion of the zone of proximal development or ZPD:

> *The zone of proximal development of the child is the distance between his actual development, determined with the help of independently solved tasks, and the level of the potential development of the child determined with the help of tasks solved by the child under the guidance of adults and in cooperation with more intelligent partners.* (Van der Veer and Valsiner, 1991, p337)

Children can, therefore, learn how to progress in their scientific knowledge and understanding through the intervention of the teacher or through working with more experienced peers.

The notion that through exposure to appropriately structured tasks a child may be helped to advance in terms of cognitive development has been one of the major outcomes of the work of Shayer and Adey (1981). Their Cognitive Acceleration in Science Education project (CASE), based at King's College London, has played an important role in British science education, and the influence of Shayer and Adey's work has extended into other subject areas and to the broader realm of standardised assessment and testing. Interestingly, Shayer and Adey recently repeated their original study only to find a general deterioration in the performance of British school children when compared to that of their predecessors a generation earlier. At present, it is not clear what causative factors are responsible for this decline (Crace, 2006).

Recent insights into science education and cognitive development have tended to move away from a simple constructivist model for science education into more complex fields of enquiry (Solomon, 1994; Osborne, 1996; Ogborn, 1997; Jenkins, 2000). Lave and Wenger (1991), for example, have employed the notion of 'situated cognition' to indicate the importance of the *context* in which learning takes place, while Engeström (1991) has explored Lave and Wenger's own notion of 'legitimate peripheral participation' even further. By contrast, Sharp and Kuerbis (2006) have drawn upon recent evidence from cognitive neuroscience to maintain that children's mental models of certain scientific phenomena are formed through a process of chaotic thought.

Science in primary and secondary schools

The primary classroom has long operated as an environment in which subject integration is often the norm. Indeed, the boundaries between subject areas have usefully been blurred where class teachers have decided to organise pupils' work around themes or through project activity. Also, the training of primary teachers generally continues to encourage a broad and balanced view, not just of science, but of the curriculum as a whole, which at its very best can present the pupil with a highly coherent educational experience. Science, however, poses a particular problem in that many primary teachers either lack confidence in teaching scientific ideas (Harlen and Holroyd, 1997) or that the faulty transmission of scientific ideas from teacher to pupil takes place because primary teachers themselves retain significant misconceptions and alternative explanatory frameworks (Jarvis et al., 2003). These can be addressed by more effective training and mentoring in science during the pre- and post-service training of primary teachers (Sharp, 2004; Hudson, 2005). In secondary schools science is essentially taught in isolation.

The fact that there are very different environments in which science is taught in primary and secondary schools raises problems of it own. Speering and Rennie (1996) have suggested that, rather than being an entirely positive experience, the transition from primary to secondary school can be a time of unfulfilled expectation for pupils who often move from a stimulating child-centred environment in the primary school to the less motivating 'teacher-centred, blackboard-directed learning' of the secondary school. Of course, recent years have seen the development of a National Curriculum in schools in English and Wales. The introduction of a common core of science ought to have addressed some of the problems of continuity and progression faced by children as they move through the school system and particularly at the transition from primary to secondary. Gorwood (1991) suggested that the difficulty of transition was not entirely solved by the introduction of the National Curriculum since primary and secondary teachers do not always communicate with each other effectively. This view is consonant with the more general findings of Galton et al. (1999), who stated:

> The most striking evidence of a drop in pupil performance emerges in OFSTED's data around the time of transfer from primary to secondary schooling with a steep rise between the end of Key Stage 2 (KS2) and the early stages of Year 7 in the proportions of schools where pupil attainment was judged to be 'unsatisfactory' — a figure of 50% of all secondary schools is reported. (p13)

Clearly, difficulties of transition are not restricted to science alone but science does have the particular problem of pupils often facing disappointment on entry to secondary schools, where their high expectations of secondary science classes are not realised when faced with the often pedestrian way in which secondary science is sometimes presented when compared with the more motivating experience of science teaching at primary level.

Science teaching in secondary schools has long been dominated by its division into three subject disciplines, physics, chemistry and biology, with the implication that these subjects are supported by a working knowledge of mathematics. Science teaching in many secondary schools is built around an infrastructure of laboratories and departmental organisation that supports this way of arranging the curriculum. Such subject divisions seem to reflect the natural organisation of the world. Physics reveals the fundamental forces and relationships between bodies; chemistry applies these to the interactions between atoms and molecules; biology studies the complex relationships between living organisms. Critics of this separate subject model see science as an integrated discipline in which interpenetrating subject areas should be taught in a coordinated, thematic manner. This, it is felt, more accurately reflects the way in which science is met in the world. But, as Atkin and Black (2003) have pointed out, there is no simple middle ground between advocacy of a separate subject approach and that of integrated science. This has led to a situation in which the content of science has been structured in three different ways in secondary schools today:

- **as separate subjects with physics, chemistry and biology taught by separate specialist teachers (may lead to individually certificated awards in each of the subject areas);**
- **as coordinated subjects with physics, chemistry and biology taught as part of a scheme in which linking themes are developed and teaching expertise shared (certification is likely to be a double award in coordinated science).**
- **as an integrated subject called science all delivered by perhaps one individual (certification is likely to be a double award in science).**

There are advantages to delivering science as an integrated subject. By not tying science teachers to separate subject disciplines, schools have greater flexibility in deploying their staff and timetabling and resourcing of science is made easier, particularly for smaller schools where a limited pool of science staff may not support separate subject work. However, such an approach only highlights the problem that much physics teaching in particular is delivered by non-specialists. This is due to the relatively small numbers of physicists entering the teaching profession when compared to those with backgrounds in chemistry and the life sciences.

Within the National Curriculum, the end of Key Stage 4 marks the end of compulsory education. It is the point at which young people first gain the qualifications in public examinations that they will carry with them throughout their lives. In this regard science education must fulfil a double purpose: preparation for further study and also preparation for the world of work. It used to be that curriculum content was decided in a top-down manner. Universities decided what was required for matriculation and this, in turn, determined the content of A levels taken at age 18. A level requirements then determined the content of O level examinations at age 16. This was a system driven by the need to provide a single academic route from school to university. This produced a system in which A level examinations were regarded as the 'gold standard' for education as high quality, intellectually demanding, objective tests. The difficulty was that a system designed to produce an academic elite was ill-suited to a system of mass education with important vocational needs. Science education from nursery to university is perhaps more complicated than ever before and still undergoing change.

Science, education and the world of work

There is a growing crisis in the supply of scientists (Roberts, 2002). Many reasons have been given for this state of affairs. Some relate to the nature of the subject disciplines themselves, with the physical sciences in particular perceived as being more difficult than others because of the knowledge base required, some to the need to show proficiency in mathematics and some to the abstract nature of many scientific concepts which makes study intellectually demanding. In addition to this is the belief that scientific careers do not provide the high levels of remuneration that are enjoyed by those working in other fields such as law or finance. It has also been the case that the public image of the scientist has generally been associated with character types that young people do not find particularly attractive. The media still portray stereotypical views of scientists as *gauche,* rather socially inept individuals: the 'boffins' of yesteryear transmuted into the 'nerds' of today. There has also been a tendency to portray science as a white, male and middle class pursuit, a state of affairs which has served to exclude on grounds of gender, class and race (Bevins et al., 2003). On the other hand, and with the rise of new subjects such as information technology, media production, sports science and the paramedical disciplines, which bring together a wide range of cross-curricular elements, the cultural divide that was once held to exist between the sciences and the arts is now no longer so prevalent. And, even if fewer people are moving into the traditional pure sciences, this is offset by people moving into a wider range of careers that require some level of scientific literacy.

In order to address the need to provide more scientists, increasing efforts are being made to supplement the experience gained in the classroom through curriculum enrichment activities giving pupils access to science and applications in industrial and other 'real-world' contexts (Parvin et al., 1997), although Osborne (2000) casts doubt upon the efficacy of placing so much emphasis upon providing 'pre-professional training' when so few pupils actually progress to take up science-based careers. Despite Osborne's reservations, significant central government and regional development investment has been placed into providing networks to support and supplement the science curriculum.

Recent years have seen the rise of the 'public understanding of science movement' (Gregory and Miller, 1998). In part this is a response to the duty laid upon scientists to communicate their work more effectively but it is also a response to a perceived need for improved scientific literacy. This has led to the development of government policy to support programmes of informal science education. Informal programmes mean that significant science learning can take place outside the physical environment of the school classroom and outside the structure of the formal curriculum. However, Jeffs and Smith (2005) have emphasised the point that both formal and informal education are not mutually exclusive terms in that they reflect a 'shared concern for learning' on the part of formal and informal educators. The motivational effect of learning in informal settings such as zoos, museums or hands-on science centres, or through curriculum enrichment activities such as competitions, drama and role-play is so strong that, increasingly, activities such as these that were once thought to be peripheral to the science curriculum are now seen as part of the mainstream (Walton, 1997).

Summary and conclusions

Science plays a central role in the school curriculum. It provides the groundwork of knowledge, skills and attitudes that enable individuals not only to understand the world around them but also to play a full part as members of an increasingly technological society. The growth of science since the mid-twentieth century has been driven in part by the economic and strategic necessity to provide a technically literate workforce. However, increasingly in recent years, the emphasis has shifted towards a view of scientific literacy that places greater emphasis upon the individual's need to make informed choices within a democratic society. This has produced a concomitant shift away from the uncritical acceptance of the authority of the scientist as expert. The public is now expected to enter into more informed debate and, in so doing, draw upon some understanding of the nature of the scientific enterprise, including its content and its methods.

Alongside this growth in science, parallel developments in science education have been at the forefront of promoting change in teaching and learning. The influence of constructivist approaches to pedagogy, for example, has extended far beyond the boundaries of the school science curriculum. This has had for some the unsettling effect of removing the old certainties that science seemed to provide by questioning the objectivity of scientific knowledge itself, a situation which may in turn challenge the authority of the science teacher.

The future of science education seems to present the prospect of a more complex relationship between the intrinsic need to provide a critically aware and scientifically informed public, and the extrinsic factors that require pupils to be adequately prepared for the world of work. This will be a challenge for science teachers, not only to be able to develop their own skills not only as scientists but also as teachers, counsellors and advisers, and which will require them to acquire many more of the 'soft skills' that were previously the province of the informal educator.

References

Atkin, JM and Black, P (2003) *Inside science education reform: a history of curricular and policy change.* Buckingham: Open University Press.

Bevins, S, Harrison, W and Jordan J (2003) *Ethnicity and underachievement in science and mathematics education.* A Report to the Royal Society. Sheffield Hallam University: Centre for Science Education.

Crace, J (2006) Children are less able than they used to be, *Guardian*, 24 January.

Driver, R (1983) *The pupil as scientist?* Milton Keynes: Open University Press.

Engeström, Y (1991) Non scolae sed vitae discimus: towards overcoming the encapsulation of school learning. *Learning and Instruction*, 1: 243–59.

Galton, M, Gray, J and Ruddock, J (1999) The impact of school transitions and transfers on pupil progress and attainment: DfEE Research Report No. 131. London: HMSO.

Gorwood, B (1991) Primary–secondary transfer after the national curriculum. *School Organisation*, 11(3): 283–90.

Gregory, J and Miller, S (1998) *Science in public: communication culture and credibility.* New York: Plenum Trade.

Harlen, W and Holroyd, C (1997) Primary teachers' understanding of concepts of science: impact on confidence and teaching. *International Journal of Science Education*, 19(1): 93–105.

Hudson, P (2005) Identifying mentoring practices for developing effective primary science teaching. *International Journal of Science Education*, 27(14): 1723–39.

Jarvis, T, Pell, A and McKeon, F (2003) Changes in primary teachers' science knowledge and understanding during a two year in-service programme. *Research in Science and Technological Education*, 21(1): 17–42.

Jeffs, T and Smith, MK (2005) *Informal education: conversation, democracy and learning.* Nottingham: Educational Heretics Press.

Jenkins, E (2000) Constructivism in school science education: powerful model or the most dangerous intellectual tendency? *Science and Education*, 9: 599–610.

Kuhn, TS (1996) *The structure of scientific revolutions.* Chicago: University of Chicago Press.

Lave, J and Wenger, E (1991) *Situated learning: legitimate peripheral participation.* Cambridge: Cambridge University Press.

Millar, R (1996) Towards a science curriculum for public understanding. *School Science Review*, 77(280): 7–18.

Ogborn, J (1997) Constructivist metaphors of learning science. *Science and Education*, 6: 121–33.

Osborne, JF (1996) Beyond constructivism. *Science Education*, 80(1): 53–82.

Osborne, J (2000) Science for citizenship, in Monk, M and Osborne, J (eds) *Good practice in science teaching: what research has to say*. Buckingham: Open University Press.

Parvin, J, Key, M and Mapletoft, M (1997) Industry as a resource for teaching science, in Thompson, DL (ed) *Science education in the 21st century*. Aldershot: Arena.

Ratcliffe, M and Grace, M (2003) *Science education for citizenship: teaching socio-scientific issues*. Maidenhead: Open University Press.

Roberts, G (2002) *SET for Success: Report on Sir Gareth Roberts' review of the supply of people with science, technology and mathematics skills*. HM Treasury: HMSO.

Sharp, J (ed) (2004) *Developing primary science*. Exeter: Learning Matters.

Sharp, JG and Kuerbis, P (2006) Children's ideas about the solar system and the chaos in learning science. *Science Education*, 90(1): 124–47.

Shayer, M and Adey, P (1981) *Towards a science of science teaching: cognitive development and curriculum demand*. London: Heinemann.

Solomon, J (1994) The rise and fall of constructivism. *Studies in science education*, 23: 1–19.

Speering, W and Rennie, L (1996) Students' perceptions about science: the impact of transition from primary to secondary school. *Research in Science Education*, 26(3): 283–98.

Sutherland, P (1992) *Cognitive development today: Piaget and his critics*. London: Paul Chapman.

Van der Veer, R and Valsiner, J (1991) *Understanding Vygotsky: a quest for synthesis*. Oxford: Blackwell.

Vygotsky, LS (1934) Thinking and speech, in Rieber, RW and Carton AS (eds) (1987) *The collected works of LS Vygotsky: vol. 1 Problems of general psychology*. New York: Plenum.

Walton, RJ (1997) Improving the image of science, in Thompson, DL (ed) *Science education in the 21st century*. Aldershot: Arena.

Walton, RJ (2000) Heidegger in the hands-on science and technology centre: some philosophical reflections. *Journal of Technology Education*, 12(1): 50–61.

Walton, RJ (2002) *Science teaching and the public understanding of science*. Sheffield: Sheffield Hallam University Press.

Wellington, JJ (1990) Formal and informal learning in science: the role of interactive centres. *Physics Education*, 25: 247–57.

White, J (1982) *The aims of education restated*. London: Routledge and Kegan Paul.

Chapter *12*

Technology and education: debates, contexts and computers

John Potter

Introduction

Technology is part of our material culture. It is used by learners and their teachers in many aspects of their lives. Increasingly, individuals experience and interact with learning through their consumption and production of digital media in particular. This experience changes the ways in which knowledge is produced, shared and accessed in fundamental ways. As a result, the locus of control of learning is shifting between formal and informal structures and sites and a wide range of critical perspectives is needed to understand this. As the capacity and range of technology itself has changed over the years, a number of theoretical positions and their influences on learning, which were once seen as discrete and deterministic, have themselves begun to change. Partly because of the growing accessibility of media production to learners, for example, technology is increasingly written about by authorities in the fields of cultural and media studies. In this chapter, examples of critical viewpoints that are currently shaping the understanding of technology and education are discussed in detail.

Visions of pedagogy with technology

The relationship between pedagogy and technology has been explored by a number of different authors. Twining (2002), for example, has investigated computer use in schools and developed the Computer Practice Framework (CPF) which identified three contexts for studying the use of computers in most educational settings. These are outlined as follows:

- **using computers to develop the skills of IT use itself (the 'IT' category);**
- **using computers as a learning tool to develop learning in areas other than IT (the 'learning tool' category);**
- **using computers in ways not covered in the first two dimensions of use (the 'other' category).**

Twining's work in detail presented 19 different rationales associated with all three contexts, any one of which might drive an initiative, or influence a decision about pedagogy and technology at any one time (Table 12.1).

Table 12.1 Rationales for using computers in education (adapted from Twining, 2002)

Context	Corresponding rationales
The 'IT' category	In order to learn IT skills
The 'learning tool' category	As a tool to achieve traditional teaching and learning goals across the curriculum
	In order to extend and enrich learning across the curriculum
	In order to motivate learners
	As a catalyst for educational change
	Because of the impact of ICT on the nature of knowledge
	In order to fundamentally change teaching and learning
	As a tool to support learners in thinking about their own learning
	In order to provide access to the curriculum for those who might otherwise be excluded from it
The 'other' category	In order to increase productivity in education
	In order to reduce the cost of education
	In order to make education more efficient
	As a substitute for teachers
	In order to reward learners
	As preparation for living in a society that is permeated with technology
	As preparation for work or employment
	In order to support and stimulate the country's economic development
	In order to impress stakeholders (e.g. inspectors, funders, prospective parents or students)
	In order to reduce inequalities between students/pupils with differential access to ICT outside formal education

Twining (2005) later approached the issue of pedagogy with technology by going back to first principles and examining the various rationales which appear to have guided technology's introduction into formal educational sites. His 'dICTatEd' project (Discussing Information and Communications Technology, Aspirations and Targets for Education) aimed to discover whether those learning and working in education do, in fact, have a shared vision.

Loveless (2003) has theorised pedagogy and technology from a teacher–learner-centred perspective. Loveless has argued that problematic issues and key differences in learner experiences with computers arise from the varied ways in which teachers frame their understanding of children's learning itself. Her research is based on many hours of observations of learners and teachers in classrooms. Loveless writes about technology in relation to the curriculum as it is described and structured in schools in England, but without losing a focus on the learner as the centre of activity in the educational settings. For Loveless, there are key properties of the medium of the computer in schools which foster learner agency. These properties include those that allow learners to make and change decisions rapidly or to model a variety of hypotheses before deciding on a solution to a problem. She writes about the ways in which this provisionality alters fundamentally and irreversibly the role of the teacher, from instructor to one of mentor–facilitator. This change is not always easily accomplished and sometimes unrecognised as necessary, particularly where the overall rationale for the use of technology in places of learning is so diffuse.

> *Pause for thought* | using computers in educational settings
>
> Think about your own experiences of using technology and computers in education. Look at the table of rationales provided by Twining (2002). Which rationales best characterise the ways in which you were introduced to using the tools of information technology in your own learning? Were you expected to develop IT skills during hours of de-contextualised 'computer training'? Were these skills then employed in any meaningful sense in other areas of your learning? Has the idea that technology might have a pedagogical framework ever been made explicit to you before? After thinking through some of these issues, it might be useful to contribute to the debate by visiting Twining's own 'dICTaTed' website itself (Twining, 2005).

A variety of other writers has used literacy and our changing understanding of the term as a hook on which to hang a series of interlinked arguments and discussions about pedagogy with technology (Gamble and Easingwood, 2000). Millwood (2000), for example, has proposed a vision of pedagogy with technology based on an emerging new relationship with media. Digital tools make it possible for learners to produce differentiated work in a range of media which take account of viewpoint, needs and interest. This changes our understanding of the role of the teacher in similar ways to the arguments raised by Loveless, moving further in the direction of learner agency. Kempster (2000), from the perspective of a librarian, has written about the movement towards a learner-centred, personalised pedagogy. She takes as a starting point a discussion of the ways in which new technologies, as libraries have done for centuries, provide guidance and facilitation to learners for use on ipsative learning journeys, as well as markers of progress and development.

Some writing and research has been more focused on what happens within specific subject traditions and cultures in schools as a result of the introduction of new technology. John (2005), for example, sees the issues as bound up as much with identity formation and self-perception amongst teachers as it is with any technological matters. John's argument is about how technology influences an identity which a teacher has formed over many years' work teaching a particular subject. Something is lost and something is gained in a process equivalent to trading aspects of identity, surrendering expertise in technology while asserting subject expertise.

Whichever perspective is explored, the relationship between pedagogy and technology is complex, with a number of interdependent factors at play. These include the learner experience, teacher experience and the differing rationales for introducing technology in the first place. This reflects the rhetoric–reality gap of using technology as a force for raising the attainment for learners.

Computers and learning theories

Although the argument has been made that learners need to see technology in school because it is omnipresent in the world of work, a great deal of time and money has been spent (and made) designing age-specific, curriculum- and learner-centred software and other online resources. These are tools which provide, amongst other things, child-friendly versions of office tools, multimedia composition and learning games. This has created a software industry which is concerned with marketing learning solutions for educational settings often predicated on improving standards. The design of educational media, such as software, hardware and, more recently, websites, has often been informed by learning theory.

The earliest programmes in the UK and the United States for the classroom were designed under the paradigm of computer-assisted learning (CAL). This took the form of a variety of archetypes, from simple drill-and-practice titles which were essentially behaviourist, offering rewards for the correct answer, through to software that has been designed with constructivist and social-constructivist theories of learning in mind. One example, perhaps the most famous of educational software tools, Logo, illustrates the link with learning theory explicitly. Logo has been described by its inventor, Seymour Papert, as arising directly from the time he spent working with the early constructivist theorist Jean Piaget. The link between the particular theory of learning in this case is presented as unbroken from source to end product. In using Logo, learners are expected to operate entirely within the parameters of the programming language, controlling and moving graphical objects by means of a series of commands. The programming language allows the learner to construct their own understanding of concepts, initially of shape and space and other mathematical areas. Papert himself emphasised that it was the process, the creation of 'objects to think with', which was the key focus for the development of Logo (Papert, 1993). Crook (1996) later wrote about the ways in which Logo can be understood by different criteria, not only by a solitary learner constructing their own understanding of an aspect of mathematics or programming. Observing learners in the classroom working with Logo and communicating with each other, Crook developed a social-constructivist view of technology in an educational setting. According to Crook, learning was constructed socially in the discourse in the classroom around the onscreen activity, between the learners, in what Vygotsky refered to as the 'zone of proximal development' (Daniels, 2005). Whilst Crook has written about the ways in which social-constructivism can inform our understanding of technology and education, two other branches of intersecting learning theory are also important:

- **activity theory;**
- **the theory of communities of practice.**

Activity theory suggests that our experience of the world is mediated by cultural and social organisation and their related artefacts. For computers and technology in educational settings this means that our understanding of pedagogy and technology is deepened by taking into account the structures which surround its use (Engeström et al., 1999). The theory of communities of practice argues that shared engagement in social practice is the fundamental process by which we learn and form our identity (Wenger, 1999). This suggests that interaction around and through technology in educational settings is key to its development as a learning tool. This concept is extended and developed in relation to earlier theory by writers who see the development of online communities in education as representing a new and important aspect of technology in our learning and in our lives, namely that of communal constructivism (Leask and Younie, 2001). Communal constructivism finds its corollary in the wider theories of education that emphasise the social role in cognition and formation of identity. These theories suggest the world outside the school may be the most significant for the learner (Bruner, 1996). With learners increasingly engaged in online activity, this may be the most significant area of study of thinking and learning with technology.

Pause for thought | computers and theories of learning

Think about your own experience of any task you have recently undertaken at the computer. This could be a piece of formal writing for a particular audience (e.g. an assignment) or a less formal piece of personal relevance (e.g. a blog entry, a forum contribution or a long email, downloading some recommended music). Reflect on the processes you went through and how these relate to your understanding of the principles of activity theory or communities of practice. How did you find what you were looking for? What was most important to you? Was it building on what you already knew or something different? Was it following a particular path dictated by shared understanding and enjoyment? What did the technology make possible that was impossible without it? The extent to which technology is embedded within your life and social practices is far reaching.

Technology-related literacies and cultures

Gaming literacy, media literacy and information literacy, to name only a few, are terms which are being used in technology and education contexts to try to capture a range of responses to the way in which technology is shaping our experience of the world and our understanding of learning.

Theories of how children learn and interact with media culture through, for example, video gaming (online and standalone) have recently begun to inform educational debate. Why do learners devote so much time, concentration and effort to computer games and so little time to the equivalent, traditional educational experiences (Gee, 2004)? Do computer games have something to teach us about the ways in which learners become literate and learn in the twenty-first century? The debate about the use of video games on the computer or elsewhere in formal or informal educational settings is one example of a set of emerging literacies that have entered the debates on technology in education. As technologies converge and computers become televisions, video editing suites, library portals, gaming consoles and communication hubs, it has become possible to see similar convergence and overlap in the academic world, in terms of the theoretical perspectives on offer about education and technology.

Technological and theoretical convergence is being explored further in relation to education under the term media literacy. This is defined by the government's telecommunications regulator, OFCOM, as 'the ability to access, understand and create communications in a variety of contexts' (Buckingham, 2004). The breadth of this definition, encompassing 'creation' alongside the 'access' and 'understanding', extends to both informal and formal settings of education. Technology presents learners with access to the means of media production afforded by powerful, affordable and accessible software and hardware. The 'creation' of media content is the new element in educational settings and it is beginning to be theorised in relation to visual literacy, film theory and semiotics by writers like Burn and Parker (2003).

Information literacy is another of the new literacies. This area of thinking about technology and education embraces the notion of accessibility of information and moves it into areas of verifiability, reliability and educational change. When so much information is available, what is true and reliable? When so much is available, what does this mean for the definition of the curriculum and what is the place of teaching and learning within that definition? According to November (2001), the use of the internet in educational settings has changed the relationship between teacher and learner, empowering the latter, but only if it is explicitly integrated into the world of teaching and learning. November's work has been influential in the UK. November's central argument is that young people are already experiencing the world of readily accessible information in ways that adults barely understand and in ways that, sometimes, teachers fail to equip them for. One of his most famous case studies features the example of a teenage student who was duped by a website written by someone denying the Holocaust. November uses this as a way of alerting teachers and learners to the need to make explicit the skills of information literacy in the curriculum.

Pause for thought | personal use of digital media

Have you experienced the production and distribution of digital media yourself? Do you share digital photos, online music or create your own website or blog? What factors are important to you in considering the content for these new media outlets? In your thinking, consider some of the issues that appear to be important in relation to the readings discussed, including the influence or otherwise of peers. If this particular use of new technology does not apply to you, apply the same pattern of thinking to gathering and disseminating information. Can you always find what you want? Reflect on what the writers describe as the main areas of concern, namely, the establishment of validity and reliability? How do you reference it? What impact does the amount of information available, and the skills needed to search for it, have on your own thinking about learning?

The micro- and macro-politics of shaping the experience of technology

A further factor in thinking about pedagogy and technology is the shaping of the learner (and teacher) experience by political factors. These have influence at the macro-level and the micro-level.

At the micro-level, the school or other setting in which learners and teachers find themselves engaging with technology, factors that influence the popularity of technology include the teacher's own beliefs and technological skill levels. Notwithstanding how the outside world influences thinking, the mind set of teachers and their own input has been shown time and again to be highly significant. If teachers feel that the technology is part of their world-picture, professionally and personally, they will use it in ways that are innovative and which match the experiences and needs of their learners. In an educational setting where, for whatever reason, access is difficult or training opportunities limited, there will be no significant change. The institutional micro-politics have a highly significant impact on the situation in formal settings of education (Preston et al., 2000).

Turning to the macro-level of politics, Selwyn (2002) has pointed out that massive expenditure in the UK in recent years has pursued the vision of raised standards and economic prosperity. Selwyn found a distressing lack of evidence in the form of both quantitative and qualitative work that actually evaluates the impact of technology on teaching and learning. Selwyn has claimed that there is no evidence to suggest that there is a significant impact at pupil level and that large corporations stand to gain most from pursuing a determinist agenda, which seeks a 'quick fix', using computers to raise standards.

Research box

ICT and standards of attainment

In order to investigate the impact of billions of pounds of investment in technology in education in the UK in the past few years, the British Educational Communications and Technology Agency explored the link between the use of networked technologies and raised standards of pupil attainment (BECTA, 2002). The quantitative component of the study found that there were learning gains in some year groups in some subjects, but not all. For example, 'a statistically significant positive association between ICT and higher achievement in National Tests for English was found at Key Stage 2'. The qualitative component of the study looked at the use or otherwise of these technologies in the home and school settings to try to contextualise their use and to look at likely longer-term impact. Findings were mixed. The use of technology as a primary teaching tool is highly controversial.

The digital divide: technology inside and outside formal educational settings

A number of academics and other commentators has begun to argue that there is a genuine digital divide opening up between learner experience in formal settings and informal settings. McFarlane (1997) has argued that the skill sets being developed in traditional curriculum models, largely driven by outmoded forms of assessment, were inappropriate at the time of the approaching new century. McFarlane called for serious consideration of major changes to these systems to incorporate the authentic use of information technology in education:

> *Perhaps the deciding factor will be that those people who will find gainful employment in the next century will be the ones who are flexible, independent learners capable of finding the information they need and applying it to the problem in hand. All these skills have been shown to be enhanced by judicious use of information technology in the classroom. The school leavers who can simply write neatly, spell, and recite their tables will be joining the dole queues.* (p3)

The argument based on economic imperative has been the one which has made the most impact on education spending and has fuelled the technology–standards link. Nevertheless, it points to a wider truth about the gap between what the curriculum and assessment models offer students and what they are experiencing outside school in new ways of thinking and learning.

Heppell (2001) has for a long time been an advocate of major change in educational systems to take account of the possibilities of technology to change the learner experience. He points out in his writing that all change appears initially threatening where it might lead to enhanced learner agency and freedom, citing the ball point pen and the calculator as early examples of technology which were, at first, not welcome in formal educational settings.

Cuthell (2002) conducted a study of the ways in which children and young people work and learn with technology and concluded that those young people were developing strategies and skills well beyond what was measurable in the classroom. Technology has made it possible for young people to assimilate large pieces of information and then reassemble the information in different contexts. In this way they become 'cyber bricoleurs [constituting] a new knowledge community', which is in a constant state of renewal and development. This is not easy to absorb within the larger structures of assessment and league tables which is part of life in formal educational settings in the UK and elsewhere. These structures make change in response to technological innovation difficult to achieve at the speed it is needed. If Cuthell's analysis is correct, young people will be working and learning outside those structures, renewing and reassembling knowledge and ideas in pursuit of their own goals, in their own communities.

Pause for thought | technology, creativity and learner agency

Learner agency has been a focus of the work that Loveless (2002) has contributed to the field of ICT in education, particularly as it relates to creative activity with new technology. She has pointed to work that suggests that there are particular innate qualities of software and hardware tools which render them usable in creative settings in education. Can you think of instances where you and/or others have completed projects that were creative, using technology? What were the features of the technology which made this possible? What were you able to do that you could not do without it? Think about these issues in the light of your reading.

Summary and conclusions

Different contemporary versions of pedagogy with technology have been categorised and explored in this chapter, including those around new media and learning, creativity with digital technology, the socio-political agenda, and learning theory with new technology. Each of these pedagogical frames has been related to an understanding of technology in contemporary contexts and debates about learner agency, knowledge acquisition and collaboration. At the same time, the emergent new literacies of media production, information retrieval and assembly have been shown to propose a changed vision of what it means to be a learner.

It is difficult to imagine how education might remain unchanged by technology. Educational assessment systems and value judgements are all in need of review in the light of learner activity, in its range and freedom and its ability to move between the worlds of formal and informal settings using digital technology. The former settings are likely to become increasingly irrelevant unless some serious acknowledgement is given to the ways in which the world of technology is changing for ever the relationship between how we learn, where we learn and what we learn.

References

BECTA (2002) *ImpaCT2 – the impact of information and communication technologies on pupil learning and attainment.* Coventry: British Educational Technology and Communications Agency.
Bruner, J (1996) *The culture of education.* Cambridge, MA: Harvard University Press.
Buckingham, D (2003) *Media education: literacy, learning and contemporary culture.* Cambridge: Polity.
Buckingham, D (2004) *The media literacy of children and young people.* London: Centre for the Study of Children Youth and Media Institute of Education.

Burn, A and Parker, D (2003) *Analysing media texts*. London: Continuum.

Crook, C (1996) *Computers and the collaborative experience of learning: a psychological perspective (International Library of Psychology)*. London: Routledge.

Cuthell, J (2002) *Virtual learning: the impact of ICT on the way young people work and learn*. London: Ashgate.

Daniels, H (ed) (2005) *An introduction to Vygotsky*. London: Routledge.

Engeström, Y, Miettinen, R and Punamäki, R-L (eds) (1999) *Perspectives on activity theory (Learning in doing: social, cognitive and computational perspectives)*. Cambridge: Cambridge University Press.

Gamble, N and Easingwood, N (eds) (2000) *ICT and literacy: information and communications technology, media, reading and writing*. London: Continuum.

Gee, JP (2004) *What video games have to teach us about learning and literacy*. New York: Palgrave MacMillan.

Heppell, S (2001) Preface to Loveless, A and Ellis, V (eds) *ICT, pedagogy and the curriculum: subject to change*. London: RoutledgeFalmer.

John, P (2005) The sacred and the profane: subject sub-culture, pedagogical practice and teachers' perceptions of the classroom uses of ICT. *Educational Review*, 57(4): 471–490.

Kempster, G (2000) Skills for life: new meanings and values for literacies, in Gamble, N and Easingwood, N (eds) *ICT and literacy: information and communications technology, media, reading and writing*. London: Continuum.

Leask, M and Younie, S (2001) Communal constructivist theory: information and communications technology pedagogy and internationalisation of the curriculum. *Journal of Information Technology for Teacher Education*, 10(1 & 2): 117–134.

Loveless, A (2002) *Literature review in creativity, new technologies and learning*. Bristol: NESTA Futurelab.

Loveless, A (2003) *The role of ICT*. London: Continuum.

McFarlane, A (1997) *Information technology and authentic learning*. London: Routledge.

Millwood, R (2000) A new relationship with media?, in Gamble, N and Easingwood, N (eds) *ICT and literacy: information and communications technology, media, reading and writing*. London: Continuum.

November, A (2001) *Empowering students with technology*. Arlington Heights, IL: Skylight.

Papert, S (1993) *Mindstorms*. Hemel Hempstead: Harvester Wheatsheaf.

Preston, C, Cox, M and Cox, K (2000) *Teachers as innovators: an evaluation of the motivation of teachers to use Information and Communications Technologies*. London: Mirandanet /TTA.

Selwyn, N (2002) *Telling tales on technology – qualitative studies of technology and education*. London: Ashgate.

Twining, P (2002) Conceptualising computer use in education: introducing the Computer Practice Framework (CPF). *British Educational Research Journal*, 28(1): 95–110.

Twining, P (2005) dICTatEd – discussing ICT, aspirations and targets for education. Available at **www.med8.info/dictated** (accessed 7 April 2006).

Wenger, E (1999) *Communities of practice: learning, meaning and identity. (Learning in doing: social, cognitive and computational perspectives.)* Cambridge: Cambridge University Press.

Chapter *13*

The nature of higher education

Stephen Ward

Introduction

University education in the UK used to be for an intellectual elite but policies for expansion and widening participation are leading to a mass higher education system. The university is now said to be a business in the higher education market and higher tuition fees mean that students might become more like customers than students. Unlike schools, universities have traditionally enjoyed autonomy from government controls and academic freedom for their staff. This chapter examines higher education in universities and colleges, and its role in UK society today. It looks at the ways in which universities have traditionally defined knowledge, what counts as knowledge, and how this has changed with more government control. In particular, it examines the ways in which market forces have affected what universities do and the ways in which they are run. The terms 'university' and 'university knowledge' will be used as shorthand for the various higher education institutions and the courses operating therein.

What is higher education?

Higher education (HE) is a level of study that begins after A Levels or their equivalents. It is taught in higher education institutions (HEIs) such as universities and colleges. A basic hierarchy of awards at different levels, with the usual length of full-time study includes:

- **the one-year Certificate in Higher Education (CertHE);**
- **the two-year Diploma in Higher Education (DipHE);**
- **the two-year Foundation Degree (FdA);**
- **the three-year Bachelor of Arts (BA) and Science (BSc) degrees;**
- **the one-year Master of Arts (MA) and Science(MSc) degrees;**
- **the three- or four-year Doctorate (PhD).**

There are also vocationally oriented degrees with specialist professional titles such as Bachelor of Education (BEd) or Masters in Business Administration (MBA). Higher education is sometimes confused with further education (FE), which is the term used to refer to education after the statutory school leaving age of 16 but at a lower level than higher education. This is complicated by the fact that Further Education Colleges often teach higher education degree and diploma courses. These are validated and awarded by a university or other body. It is unusual for further education courses to be taught in a university or college of higher education.

Pause for thought | why do a degree?

Higher education is an expensive business. Many people give up jobs and earning money in the short term to pay university fees. What are their reasons for doing this? Is it to have a better career and to earn more money later, or is it about education for its own sake? What made you decide to go into higher education and do a degree? Was it because your friends and family expected you to do it? Was it because of your own drive to better yourself or advance your career prospects?

Ancient and medieval origins of universities

The Academy of Plato founded in 387 BC in ancient Greece might be said to have been the first university. Plato was a pupil of Socrates who was committed to a philosophy of rational argument that was contrary to the culture of the times. Found by the Court of Athens to be guilty of neglecting the established gods and corrupting the young, Socrates was sentenced to death and chose to accept execution rather than recant his commitment to rational truth. Socrates's principles are fundamental in the modern university: the fearless pursuit of truth in the face of irrational belief and bigotry.

The term 'university' is derived from the Latin *universitas*, meaning 'a community'. So the original notion was of a universal kinship of scholars. China had universities in the seventh century. The Al Azhar Islamic University began in Cairo from 1000 AD. In Europe, the first universities were in Bologna and Paris in the twelfth century for the teaching of Roman Catholic theology. As Haddad (2000) explained, the medieval European universities were internationally linked. The lack of national frontiers in the medieval period, and the use of Latin as a *lingua franca*, allowed academics to interact freely across geographical areas and there was recognition of awards across institutions. The early universities were exclusively male institutions. Teachers were known as 'Masters' and wore hoods and gowns, and degrees were awarded 'with honours'. These medieval traditions continue in university life today and most strongly at Oxford and Cambridge, which, established in the thirteenth century, were the first universities in England. While they still have the highest reputation built on long history and tradition, Oxford's students did not always live up to expectations:

> Trevelyan describes the early days as 'riotous, lawless and licentious'. The typical student, he says, was 'miserably poor; he often learnt very little for want of books and tutoring, and left without taking a degree….. Some of these old Oxonians, apparently, were as young as 14, but took easily to the tavern and the brothel. They even had a tendency to roam the countryside in robber bands. (Ellis, 1995, p54)

Things rapidly improved with the founding of the college system and the two universities went on to supply the nation's political and administrative leaders for centuries.

The Renaissance drew universities away from the control of the church, with tutors increasingly recruited from civil society, and with the fermentation of new ideas. The seventeenth century saw the formation of nation states, border controls and the use of national languages in education. The result was that universities lost their universal, borderless quality and became enclosed within national systems. The European Union's Socrates Scheme now funds students and staff to make links between European universities. However, van der Wende and Huisman (2004) have pointed out that attempts to develop a common university curriculum across Europe have been frustrated by government resistance and closed doors.

It would be a mistake, though, to see the medieval period as a golden age of academic freedom. The knowledge the universities were allowed to share was determined by the church. The Sorbonne in Paris, for example, was based upon a contract between the college and the crown to teach theology, and church control over university knowledge remained powerful even throughout the Renaissance. Universities developed the idea of nation through scholarship. There was no original research, and privileges were only guaranteed as long as the teachings of the Roman Catholic Church were not questioned. Universities were still supporting the church in 1633 in Galileo's trial for heresy, with the sentence against him read publicly in every university. The role of the university at this time, then, was restricted to preserving and deepening the officially recognised knowledge of the church, or 'revealed' rather than 'verifiable' knowledge.

The modern university

The modern university began with the Enlightenment and the industrial revolution of the late eighteenth- and early nineteenth centuries when the entrepreneurial society turned to the university for scientific knowledge and trained professionals to fulfil the needs of the economy. The University of

Berlin became the prototype for the modern university, a national institution with academic freedom to pursue truth. Its principles were based on the philosophy of Immanuel Kant and the humanist ideals of its founder Wilhelm Humboldt. Kant differentiated between knowledge that should be controlled by the state, such as law and medicine, and the pure academic truth of philosophy. In creating the University of Berlin, Humboldt's ingenuity was to resolve the conflict between the state and the academics. He emphasised that the state needed a common cultural identity and that the role of the university was to reinforce this through the advancement of culture, reason, learning and teaching. So the Humboldt university model provided the highly educated professionals required by industry in exchange for freedom and autonomy in the knowledge it produced. Neave (2000) showed that the university contributed to a definition of the nation state itself in the form of the transmission of national culture and particular knowledge traditions:

> *In von Humboldt's notion of academic freedom, the state itself served as a 'buffer organ' against outside pressures, not least of which was the utilitarianism associated with the rising industrial classes.* (p35)

Towards the end of the nineteenth century the university evolved into a research facility because industrial production began to need scientific knowledge and academics trained in experimental methods. It is the nineteenth-century Humboldt University model on which the civic universities of the UK were based:

- **the state funds the university;**
- **the university has autonomy to define and codify knowledge and its staff have the freedom to pursue truth and engage in a critique of the *status quo*;**
- **the university provides skilled professionals and the new knowledge and research required by industry;**
- **the university contributes to the definition of the nation state through the knowledge and culture which it defines.**

> *Pause for thought* | academic freedom
>
> The model of the Humboldt university is an attractive one for academics as they have complete freedom to determine what counts as knowledge and what should be learned. In contrast, the school curriculum is heavily controlled by the state. What are the advantages and disadvantages of university staff having unrestricted academic freedom? Do you agree with the Humboldt university model, or should governments have more control and accountability for tax-payers' money? Should students have the right to decide what is taught at university?

The university and the state in the UK

In Britain, the relationship between universities and the state has been ambiguous. Kogan and Hanney (2000) have detailed the various influences and directions which have been in place since the nineteenth century. Compared with most other countries, and compared to other sectors of the state, UK universities have had a high level of autonomy for much of the twentieth century. They enjoyed legal status and freedom in:

- **their mission;**
- **their finances;**
- **employment of staff;**
- **student admissions;**
- **the content of courses;**
- **deciding on what counts as knowledge.**

Neave (1988) has suggested that the universities of continental Europe became firmly embedded into national bureaucracies over this period, whereas in Britain 'the status of universities as a property-owning corporation of scholars ... was preserved'. The philosopher John Stuart Mill argued that government intervention in universities should be limited in order to avoid the evil of adding to government power. Mill's formulation leads to the notion of a 'facilitatory state which would provide resources to universities whose freedom would be enjoyed within an area of negotiation largely controlled by the universities themselves', (Kogan and Hanney, 2000).

The binary system in the UK

The first part of the twentieth century saw the development of the 'red-brick' universities in urban centres of Britain such as Liverpool, Birmingham, Bristol, Leeds and Glasgow to respond to the local needs for knowledge and technology. All universities were well funded by the government but remained free from state control. In many ways, this was an ideal higher education system, except that it was for a small elite with only about five per cent of each school cohort progressing to university, much less than most of Europe and the United States. The Robbins Report, published in 1963, recommended an immediate expansion of higher education with new universities to be built and Colleges of Advance Technology to be given university status. This led in the 1960s to the development of the so-called 'plate-glass' universities such as Warwick, Bath, Lancaster, Essex and York, all with royal charters to award degrees.

At the same time, higher education began in other colleges of technology and colleges of education which, like schools, were mostly run by the local education authorities (LEAs). Their degrees were awarded by other universities. During the 1970s many of the colleges were merged to form large polytechnics and the Council for National Academic Awards (CNAA), a national body for the approval and awarding of degrees in the colleges and polytechnics, was founded.

These developments gave Britain a 'binary system' of higher education: universities with a royal charter, and polytechnics and colleges whose degrees were awarded by the CNAA and which were funded by the LEAs. Anthony Crosland, the Labour Education Minister at the time, had proposed the system in the 1960s with the ambition of creating separate branches of higher education to serve different purposes, with the universities to provide 'academic' education and the polytechnics to provide more 'vocational' and technical higher education over which the state would have more direct control.

Pause for thought | academic and vocational higher education

The 'binary' higher education system was designed to create universities providing 'academic' degrees, and polytechnics providing 'vocational' studies. Kogan and Hanney (2000) pointed out that this was in contradiction to the Labour government's policy for schools, which was to move to a 'unitary' system of secondary education with all comprehensive schools and the abolition of grammar schools. Do you agree with the principle of there being two types of university: those which teach purely 'academic' subjects such as philosophy or the arts, sciences and humanities, and those which teach 'vocational' subjects such as teaching and nursing?

The heads of the polytechnics resisted being treated like schools, with their finances controlled by the LEAs, and fought for financial independence. This was granted by the Secretary of State for Education in 1989 with the incorporation of polytechnics as independent institutions, although the request for the title of 'polytechnic universities' was refused. However, things were to change rapidly: the binary system was soon abolished when all the polytechnics were given full university status in 1992. Britain suddenly had a single higher education system of universities, with some colleges of higher education, many of which later attained university title as 'teaching universities'.

Universities in the twenty-first century: mass higher education in the market place

Although most HEIs are now referred to as 'universities', the hierarchy of university status continues, with the ancient universities of Oxford and Cambridge, and Durham and the London Universities, at the top. These and other elite universities identify themselves as 'the Russell Group' because their vice chancellors regularly meet together in the colonial surroundings of the Russell Hotel in London. The hierarchy of institutions is now formalised through league tables of university quality and student satisfaction surveys in which, interestingly, the traditional high status universities were not always rated highly by their students. Just as companies rate their products through satisfaction surveys, the state now tests market opinion in the same way. So, while not directly controlling the knowledge taught in universities, the state controls universities through the market.

The market is the massively increased numbers of students in higher education, which has risen from 5 per cent of the university-going age cohort in the early 1960s to some 40 per cent now, with a target of 50 per cent by the year 2010. This is sometimes depicted as a government target. In fact, it is a target for the whole of the European Union and was determined at the EU Lisbon agreement in 2001 to equip Europe to compete in global markets. Coulby (2005) has noted four features of the knowledge economy:

- *accessibility* of knowledge, information and data through increased technology;
- *superabundance* of information;
- *marketisation* of knowledge bought and sold as a commodity;
- *internationalisation* of knowledge which is readily developed and exchanged over continents.

Mass higher education, then, is seen as one of the mechanisms for Europe's survival in the race for prosperity and knowledge at a time when countries like China are opening a new university every few months. The debate about universities has now moved away from academic autonomy to who pays, and this has created its own problems:

- increased state funding for universities as a result of mass higher education means higher taxation;
- political parties who propose higher taxation do not get elected;
- high-tax economies tend to be less successful.

Pause for thought | higher education and the economy

Successive governments and the European Union argue that economies need more higher education, although Wolf (2002) provides evidence that economies across the world do not necessarily benefit from higher education in the sense of increasing production or raising a country's position in the international economic league tables. Do you agree with expanding higher education to a wider audience or does it just lead to the prospect of unemployed and disaffected graduates? Does the economy need so many graduates?

With the onset of mass higher education, the state was no longer able to fund universities as it had done for the elite universities of the past. So funding needed to come from elsewhere. In the late 1990s, the Dearing Report on higher education (NCIHE, 1997) recommended the introduction of substantial tuition fees payable by individual students, together with a system of student loans, repayable on employment. This was accepted after fierce political controversy, to be followed by further increases in student fees. There is every indication that tuition fees will continue to rise as the demand for high quality higher education increases. Tuition fees transfer the funding of higher education from the state to the individual and form part of the UK government's attempts to reduce the control of the state and to allow the market to control development and quality. The argument for market-driven higher education is that:

- **students have a choice of university;**
- **students pay their fees for a degree which will secure them more remunerative employment;**
- **universities have to compete for students;**
- **increased competition raises quality in higher education;**
- **the state can reduce its financial commitment and keep taxes low;**
- **low-tax economies are more successful;**
- **businesses and employers will have more resources to pay high salaries to well-educated graduates.**

This 'virtuous' circle is reinforced by Wolf (2002), who showed that the introduction of tuition fees in other countries has not deterred university entrants, and by the argument which outlines that graduates' earnings over a lifetime exceed those of non-graduates (the implication being that graduates can afford to pay for it).

Pause for thought | who pays for university degrees?

Some people argue that higher education should be free. Others argue that graduates benefit from their degrees and should contribute financially to their own education. What are the economic arguments for and against these positions? Should there be a special case for those graduates who go on to perform particular public functions (e.g. teachers, doctors, dentists) or should all graduates be treated the same? See Stevens (2004) for further discussion of the politics of university fees.

Widening participation and the world of work

Despite all the efforts to increase the number of places in universities from the 1960s, those taking up the opportunity remain predominantly from the middle classes. The extreme end of this is the way in which the Universities of Oxford and Cambridge have taken relatively high proportions of students from public schools and then supplied government and businesses with its leaders. This has been depicted by Ellis (1995) as 'the Oxbridge conspiracy'.

The higher education system of progression from school at 18 also worked against those who were already in employment and were not successful in school education. In order to allow working class people to penetrate higher education, UK governments have instituted a policy of 'widening participation' designed to extend access beyond the middle class. This is expressed through a variety of strategies:

- **the Open University began in the 1960s to allow part-time degree study by correspondence;**
- **access courses began in the 1980s as a bridging year to higher education for mature people without formal entry qualifications;**
- **foundation degrees began in the late 1990s for those in work to study on a part-time basis while continuing in employment;**
- **links between universities and secondary schools have been developed to raise working class pupils' awareness of the possibilities of higher education;**
- **the setting up of the Office for Fair Access to Higher Education (OFFA) to ensure equality of entry to universities.**

As well as widening the social class of students, governments have also moved to ensure that the university curriculum is directly linked to students' employability. To this end, the Quality Assurance

Agency was established in the 1990s with a remit to approve and improve teaching and learning in higher education. A kind of government inspection agency, it did not have the remit to approve curriculum content in degree courses – governments are not allowed to interfere in academic autonomy. It was designed to ensure that students were taught properly and that their studies equipped them with 'transferable skills' which could be used in employment.

Postmodern higher education: the university in ruins

The case for marketised mass higher education has its critics. Some argue that mass higher education has had a 'dumbing-down' effect: the value of a degree has been devalued and standards in universities have fallen. Others raise more serious academic concerns about marketisation and the decline of the state. In the 'modern' university, the state played a strong role in funding and, by holding onto its autonomy, the university was able to define the cultural identity of the nation. With marketisation and privatisation in the 'postmodern' world, the state is weakened (Green, 1997).

One impact of marketisation on the university curriculum is that more and more students, rather than academics, make decisions about degrees and their content. As a result, popular degree subjects such as Media Studies, Sports Science, Drama, Dance, Commercial Music, Football, Golf and Astrology thrive, while traditional subjects close down because they are no longer economically viable. Recently, some universities have closed down departments such as Mathematics and Chemistry, which were found to be 'uneconomic' to run. The government has found itself unable to prevent these closures, firstly because it was unable to control the university curriculum directly and secondly because it was unable to find additional funding simply to subsidise a university department not 'paying its way'. Readings (1996) has argued that on this basis the very foundations of the traditional western university are crumbling in postmodern chaos. The 'hollowing out' of the nation state through global capitalism and trans-national corporations has led to the ruin of the modernist university:

> *The modern university was conceived by Humboldt as one of the primary apparatuses through which this production of national subjects was to take place in modernity, and the decline of the nation-state raises serious questions about the nature of the contemporary function of the university.* (p46)

The 'commodification' of knowledge as information to be bought and sold, and the 'proletarianisation' of the student population, mean that the university ceases to reflect the state culture becoming nothing more than an economic instrument, like an airline. Decisions about which subjects are taught are similar to decisions about which routes to fly and decisions about which subjects to study are similar to decisions about what people will pay to get there. A Vice Chancellor becomes the Chief Executive of a private company. Higher education is no longer to be the exclusive preserve of universities and colleges. Recent changes to HE provision make it possible for private organisations such as Microsoft to award HE qualifications; and provision exists for even schools to offer higher education level courses.

Research box

the infantilisation of higher education and the decline of the intellectual

Furedi (2004) has argued that the government control of universities has become stronger through academic auditing by the Quality Assurance Agency (QAA). Academics from different universities are employed by the QAA in policing subject quality. This makes it appear that the universities retain autonomy, but Furedi has suggested that this process has converted academics into 'professionals' who serve as inquisitors on behalf of the QAA and others who act on behalf of the university. This leads to the denigration of intellectual life, a diminished level of individual freedom and a decline in the search for 'objective truth'. According to Furedi, intellectuals should influence the politics of the real world; instead they are trapped as professionals in the institutional bureaucracy of the university:

Professionalism promotes values and forms of behaviour that may well be inconsistent with those of the intellectual. Activities such as offering a critique of the status quo, acting as the conscience of society, or pursuing the truth regardless of the consequences are not what the job of a professional is all about. (p39)

The shifting balance between state control and control by the institution results in the diminishing of the academic freedom and the independence of university knowledge.

Barnett (2000) has also noted the university disappearing as a tangible entity that defines and codifies knowledge:

The contemporary university is dissolving into the wider world ... The postmodern university is a distributed university ... It is a multinational concern, stretching out to and accommodating its manifold audiences. It [is] ... no longer a site of knowledge, but, rather a site of knowledge possibilities ... The university is no longer to be understood in terms of the category of knowledge but rather in terms of shifting and proliferating processes of knowing. (pp20–21)

Barnett makes another point about the university curriculum. It is not simply that subjects are determined by the market, but that the nature of university knowledge has changed from the pursuit of truth to the teaching of 'performative skills'. Students' learning in a subject is now depicted in terms of the skills they will learn to equip them 'to perform' in the world of employment. History graduates, for example, are no longer historians, but those with the transferable skills for industry. As Barnett has suggested: 'as an institution with rules of its own that governed what it is to know, the university is no more'. Of course, it is the world that is changing around the university. Barnett has argued that we are in a world of 'fragility' and that the university must acknowledge uncertainty, unpredictability, challengeability and contestability. Scholarship should take on a worldly role, there should not just be self-indulgent private debates between academics. The postmodern university should help people to live without fear in an uncertain world. Delanty (2001) has argued a new role for the university in the context of cultural and epistemological changes in society with the democratisation of knowledge:

Given that the university is no longer the crucial institution in society for the reproduction of instrumental/technical knowledge and is also no longer the codifier of a now fragmented national culture, it can ally itself to civil society. No longer the privileged site of particular kinds of knowledge, it can become a key institution in a society that is coming to depend more and more on knowledge ... (p6)

Research box

the university in the twenty-first century

Despite the concerns raised by Barnett (2000), the possibilities for the future of the university in which it may be able to retain its modernist role are endless if only it would wake up to this. Although there is an overwhelming call for skills, he has argued, wider society calls for knowledge, breadth, critical reason and freedom:

society is hesitantly intimating that it needs the universities to live up to their rhetoric of guardians of reason. The university seems intent on constructing itself in narrower frames of self-understanding. A trick is being missed. (p34)

In *The ignorance explosion*, Lukasiewicz (1994) has suggested that the proliferation of knowledge is text-based and that there is more of it than can be comprehended. Knowledge production far exceeds knowledge comprehension and the relationship between academics and their audience has broken down. There is, then, a new illiteracy. Students are reduced to having data-handling skills and the human mind is reduced to processing data. The paradox becomes that knowledge production creates ignorance. Increase in academic fields also increases illiteracy and produces the need for academic literacy courses. We are ignorant of the world we have created. It is an unknowable world.

Summary and conclusions

The chapter has outlined the changes that have taken place in higher education with the move from the 'modern' to the 'postmodern' university in relation to changes in the market place. Higher education continues to be in a state of rapid and perhaps irreversible flux, with more to come as the student population increases and successive governments enable the influence of the market on education to continue and develop. Debates on the future of higher education will no doubt focus around several key questions:

- **How do market forces affect the nature and status of university knowledge?**
- **How does higher education relate to the economy and should it be academically or more vocationally inclined?**
- **Does the expansion, massification, commodification and infantilisation of higher education lead to 'dumbing down'?**
- **Does mass higher education lead to improvements in the national economy and the global economy?**
- **Do changes to higher education as a whole necessarily lead to loss of academic freedom and the decline of the intellectual?**

However, such questions, and the inevitable debates that will follow, mask one of the virtues of higher education, the development and self-realisation of the individual through academic study. That this is now open to more people must itself be a matter for celebration.

References

Barnett, R (2000) *Realising the university in an age of supercomplexity*. Buckingham: Society for Research into Higher Education/Open University Press.

Coulby, D (2005) The knowledge economy: technology and characteristics, in Coulby, D and Zamabeta, E (eds) *World yearbook of education: globalisation and nationalism in education*. London: RoutledgeFalmer.

Delanty, G (2001) *Challenging knowledge: the university in the knowledge society*. Buckingham: Society for Research into Higher Education/Open University Press.

Ellis, W (1995) *The Oxbridge conspiracy: how the ancient universities have kept their stranglehold on the establishment*. London: Michael Joseph.

Furedi, F (2004) *Where have all the intellectuals gone? Confronting 21st century philistinism*. London: Continuum.

Green, A (1997) *Education, globalisation and the nation state*, London: Macmillan.

Haddad, G (2000) University and society: responsibilities, contracts, partnerships, in Neave, G (ed) *The universities' responsibilities to society*. International Perspectives Series. Oxford: Pergamon Press.

Kogan, M and Hanney, S (2000) *Reforming higher education*. London: Jessica Kingsley.

Lukasiewicz, J-F (1994) *The ignorance explosion*. Ottawa: Carleton University Press.

Neave, G (1988) On being economical with university autonomy: being an account of the retrospective joys of a written constitution, in Tight, M (ed) *Academic freedom and responsibility*. Buckingham: Society for Research into Higher Education/Open University Press.

Neave, G (2000) Universities' responsibilities to society: an historical exploration of an enduring issue, in Neave, G (ed) *The universities' responsibilities to society*. International Perspectives Series. Oxford: Pergamon Press.

NCIHE (National Committee of Inquiry into Higher Education) (1997) *Education in the Learning Society: Report of the National Committee* (the Dearing Report). London: HMSO.

Readings, B (1996) *The university in ruins*. Cambridge, MA: Harvard University Press.

Robbins, Lord (1963) *Higher Education: Report of the Committee on Higher Education appointed by the Prime Minister ... 1961–1963* (the Robbins Report), Cmnd 2154. London: HMSO.

Stevens, R (2004) *University to uni: the politics of higher education in England since 1944*. London: Politico's.

Van der Wende, M and Huisman, J (2004) Europe, in Huisman, J and van der Wende, M (eds) *On cooperation and competition: national and European policies for the internationalisation of higher education*. Bonne: Lemmens Verlags and Mediengesellschaft.

Wolf, A (2002) *Does education matter? Myths about education and economic growth*. Harmondsworth: Penguin.

Part 3

Themes in education

Chapter 14

Lifelong learning

Chapter 15

Leadership in education

Chapter 16

Race and education

Chapter 17

From special needs to inclusive education

Chapter 18

Faith in education: what place for faith communities in schools?

Chapter 19

Education for citizenship and democracy

Chapter 20

Comparative education

Chapter 21

Globalisation and global education

Chapter *14*

Lifelong learning

Steve Bartlett and Diana Burton

Introduction

This chapter looks at the meaning of lifelong learning and outlines the influence on it of economic development, advances in information and communication technology and globalisation. The importance of lifelong learning within current education policy is discussed. Some consideration is given to whether lifelong learning really is essential in ensuring the future economic and social development of society or if this term is simply part of the rhetoric that is used in maintaining the social compliance of the workforce.

What is lifelong learning?

Lifelong learning is a comparatively new term that has often been used to describe the formal learning that takes place after the compulsory phases of education. It includes what has variously been described as adult education, continuing education, continuing vocational education, continuing professional development and recurrent education (Kogan, 2000). However lifelong learning needs to be seen as something much wider than this. Learning is something we do all of the time. We learn from birth, through childhood, at school, in the workplace. We learn continually as our lives change through one phase to another, from childhood, through adolescence and into adulthood. The learning process takes many forms and there is a multitude of theories attempting to explain how it happens but, certainly, it takes place throughout our lives. Thus we are all engaged in lifelong learning.

We learn during our normal social interaction, so, for example, a football fan will continually discover new information about developments in the sport through going to matches, watching TV, reading newspapers and talking to friends and colleagues about the game. Sometimes we make a deliberate effort to become involved in formal learning situations such as when we decide to take evening classes in cooking or a foreign language. Here there is a conscious attempt to 'better oneself as a person' or perhaps we may enjoy the social activity involved in being part of the class. We may take a particular course of learning in order to gain a specific qualification to help our career and employment prospects. Here the learning is undertaken for clear economic gain. Edwards (2000) has suggested that the concept of lifelong learning 'could provide a framework, like health, for considering learning from the cradle (or earlier) to the grave'.

Some ideologies of lifelong learning

All aspects of education can be seen as ideologically shaped in some way and this is also the case when analysing the meanings and policies that shape developments in lifelong learning (Bartlett et al., 2001). For instance, a progressive or learner-centred view of lifelong learning sees the needs and wishes of the learners as foremost. Learning is viewed in its broadest sense, being both informal as well as formal, and as happening in all areas of life. Lifelong learning is part of attaining self-fulfilment, and individuals should explore life in their own way following their own interests. Thus a learner-centred approach to lifelong learning covers all kinds of learning and may actually stress the informal and unintentional. An important element of this process is the involvement of learners and their willingness to go further in their learning. Much of this learning, though personally rewarding to learners, may or may not benefit them or the wider society economically. Qualifications are not considered as the primary driver since the inner satisfaction and achievement of the learner does not necessarily have to be proved to, or measured by, others. Followers of this ideological approach may prefer the term 'lifelong education' to lifelong learning, where the latter has come to signify a narrower vocational purpose (Edwards, 2000; Crowther, 2004).

Alternatively, an instrumental approach considers how lifelong learning can bring tangible benefits to the individual and also the wider society (Bartlett, 2003). Here the learning is not an end in itself but is done for the economic benefits it brings. This view looks at how certain forms of learning may enhance employability and add to productivity. As such it is concerned with learning outcomes that are often linked to some form of qualification. An instrumentalist standpoint sees lifelong learning as usually taking place after the compulsory phase of education has been passed through by the learner. This learning is closely associated with the career development of the individual and the updating of the skills and capabilities of the workforce as a whole. There is a tendency here to emphasise a planned approach to learning that is monitored and accredited. The two ideologies of lifelong learning presented here can, of course, co-exist. Many accounts of lifelong learning use aspects of both of these ideological approaches, perhaps emphasising one and then the other, at different times.

How we learn

In small-scale communities, especially those that are relatively self-sufficient and dependent for survival upon their own skills of, for example, herding, hunting or farming, learning often takes place in the family and small group setting. Individuals learn all the knowledge and skills they will need from living and working closely with older members of the community. They in their turn will pass this knowledge on when they become adults. The learning is informal and practical and involves all members of the group. This learning is a lifelong process. See early anthropological texts, such as Mead (1942) for interesting functional accounts of small-scale societies and the learning processes in which members take part.

In larger-scale societies where individuals earn a living from paid labour, more formal education systems develop. As the economies within these societies develop and they become more affluent, the education systems themselves become more complex and the length of time spent in formal education is extended. It is easy when living in such societies to assume that formal education is where we do our learning and to forget the concept of lifelong learning.

Pause for thought | the site of learning

Consider the two main phases of compulsory education, primary and secondary. What are the main things you learned at each stage that have remained with you? How will they help you (or not) live your adult life? Are education institutions such as schools the best places to learn such things?

The increasing pace of change

If we learn throughout our lives, why has the term lifelong learning become so significant in recent years? Over the past 50 years, perhaps since the birth of our grandparents' generation, there has been rapid and continuous change in our society that has affected all areas of our lives. Patterns of employment, housing conditions, healthcare, leisure activities, individual mobility and forms of transport have all changed. If we examine forms of information and communication technology (ICT) used in the home we can see the extent of these changes. Forty-five years ago, few households had a TV. Those sets that existed were black and white with only one channel. Twenty years ago, very few households had a personal computer (PC) and these were large and very slow. Ten years ago, few houses had internet access. If they did it was often through a shared phone landline. Broadband did not yet exist. Video recorders will have appeared in every home and disappeared again over a 20-year period. Your children in their time will probably wonder how anyone could have lived their lives using tape technology.

These advances and developments are taking place in all areas of our lives. We have only to walk through modern multinational chain stores and retail outlets to see how commodities that service every part of our lives are continually being updated or replaced as they become redundant. This rapid and accelerating pace of change can be seen as a result of a combination of developments in economic production, ICT and globalisation. These are very much interlinked forces and their rapidity and diversity create a huge range of choice within our lives generally and for learners in particular.

Development of economic production

Methods of production have changed rapidly over a comparatively short time from labour-intensive methods to mass production to a level of automation that now requires few people, if any, in the actual making process. Goods can be produced more quickly and cheaply than previously. A greater variety of products is made in larger numbers than ever before and consequently the standard of living for the majority of people has risen.

Development of ICT

While the development of factories employing early mass production techniques revolutionised industry, the invention of modern computer and robotic-driven systems has produced a further revolutionary leap forward. ICT now plays an important part in all areas of our lives. This has meant that new skills and knowledge are required by us all, both in our daily lives and at work. At the same time many of the old working skills have become rarer and even obsolete, given that they are no longer in demand as part of the production process (e.g. panel beaters or shipbuilders). The technology is advancing so quickly that it becomes very difficult to keep up, and the need for workers to be able to update becomes more important than the skills they currently possess. One of the key factors in creating such rapid change is the revolution in communications. It is now possible to access information and communicate instantly and at any time via the internet and the world wide web. It is as though the earth has shrunk and time has been compressed into smaller units (Edwards, 2000). This can be seen as an important part of the globalisation process.

Development of globalisation

Burbules and Torres (2000) have proposed that globalisation can be seen as having a range of meanings. If by globalisation one means movement of people, ideas and products around the world, then it has always existed. From the earliest times there have always been migrations of people. There have been voyages of discovery, wars of conquest and the development of trade overland and by sea. What has changed is the speed and ease by which labour and goods can now be transported in response to fluctuations in supply and demand around the world. Thus markets have been able to expand until we have what can be termed a global economy.

While there are many benefits to be derived from globalisation, such as greater choice of goods at lower prices resulting from market forces, there are also many potential problems. While competition may benefit the wealthier parts of the globe, those who are poor and forced to sell their labour and economic assets cheaply remain disadvantaged. There is the distinct possibility that the market will result in the dominance of the culture of the rich at the expense of the rest, i.e. the McDonaldization of the world as western, predominantly American, tastes spread and the demand for their products increases globally whilst smaller cultures and languages are lost (Ritzer, 2000).

Beck (1992) has concluded that these forces of the market, modern technology and globalisation are creating changes in the very nature of society, an evolution from modernity to reflexive modernity. This reflexive modernity is characterised by an increased lack of certainty in our lives and consequently individuals have to make constant decisions about how they act in their daily lives. Their choices concern how they work, what they spend their money on and personal relationships with family, friends and others. We will benefit, or not, according to the decisions we make, and so each choice involves an element of risk. Beck sees us as living now in a 'risk society' where rapid changes in our social environment mean that we can no longer be sure of our social structures, such as the family, work or even the government itself, since they are in a state of constant flux. Market forces, which are beyond individual or state control, are seen to have increasing power; in tandem with this is the stronger emphasis on individualisation. Beck notes a growing variation in the ability of individuals to manage their positions in this risk society. Some sections of the population benefit from greater choice, wealthier lifestyles and the latest technology. For others, those who do not have the marketable skills required for regular employment, this increasing choice brings the risk of them losing out even more, resulting in widening social division. These divisions occur within countries but can also be seen as happening globally with great differences between the wealthy and poor areas of the world.

Research box

the third way

The impact of global markets and the profound social changes that have accompanied them has led many social commentators such as Giddens (1998, 2000) to suggest that the policies of the traditional left with their emphasis on state control are no longer feasible. However, while there appears little doubt as to the power of the global market and the inability of governments to maintain total control over their own economies, Giddens has made the point that we should not assume that governments now have nothing to offer against the forces of globalisation. He posited a complex two-way interaction between the global and the local. While nations are influenced by global forces, governments can operate to promote, protect and support where appropriate. Rather than withering away under the growth of the global market, governments can play an active part in helping their people respond. Thus Giddens proposed a third way that lies between the old forms of state socialism and the tyranny of totally free markets. It involves the state promoting competitiveness and efficiency while encouraging inclusion by ensuring the provision of services such as education, health and social security. These structures will provide individuals with the support they need to operate freely in the global 'knowledge' economy. Governments also have an important part to play in the development of the civil society that gives individuals identity, security and belonging in an increasingly uncertain world.

For government, this third way ideology has been manifested in the desire to provide vital services such as health and education for every individual, the creation of opportunity for all to succeed in life whilst at the same time stressing the duty of everyone to play their part in society. There is a strong emphasis on social justice and the rights and responsibilities of each citizen (Lawton, 2005). The language of partnership is used to describe the relationship between government and citizen. It is this third way ideology that has come to influence the thinking of a number of world governments.

Lifelong learning and the response of government

The Fryer Report (NAGCELL, 1997), drawing on the discourse reflected by Beck and Giddens, adhered to the view that the UK is going through a period of profound social change that characterises it as a risk society.

Pause for thought | analysis of change

The Fryer Report has identified 12 key aspects of the changes taking place within our society:

- accelerating change in many dimensions of life, from work to the family, driven in part by powerful and often remote global forces;
- increasing diversity and fragmentation of experiences and institutions and a greater willingness to tolerate, even celebrate, such features of the modern world;
- changing identities, loyalties and aspirations;
- much greater emphasis upon consumption and its pleasures, including too some democratisation of inventiveness and creativity;
- more focus upon choice, lifestyle and individuality;
- the increasing variety and pluralism of popular culture;
- the pervasive and growing role of information and knowledge in many arenas of economic, social, political and working life;
- the growing importance of communications and information technology to many aspects of our lives;
- the development of new dimensions of political participation, in the realms of constitutional reform and active citizenship;
- the emergence of new agendas in politics, concerned with issues as diverse as race and gender equality, disability rights, the environment, food and transport;
- widening of key social divisions, experienced in fields of income, employment, housing, health and education, including access to information;
- evidence of the growth of social exclusion, despair and even a sense of hopelessness, resulting from the impact of multiple deprivations.

Take each of the above points in turn and reflect upon their accuracy. Consider media reports, your personal experiences and those of your peers in relation to the 12 points. Identify what actual evidence exists for each of these changes.

Fryer's report noted changes in employment through the introduction of new work practices, the application of new technologies, the production and delivery of new products and services, and the reduced size of workplaces. These changes have significant effects upon the type of worker required and the report suggests that in the future there will be diminishing opportunities for unskilled and semi-skilled employment, and those with only 'one industry' or task-specific skills will be increasingly at risk. Today therefore we are in the midst of changes in the time, location and forms which work takes.

After coming to power in 1997, the Labour government published its Green Paper, *The Learning Age: a renaissance for new Britain* (DfEE, 1998) in response to the Fryer Report. It saw the greatest challenge for the country as the need to equip people with new skills, knowledge and understanding. To remain competitive in this new world many of our traditional social and economic institutions needed to be modernised and reformed.

The Green Paper described lifelong learning and the creation of a learning culture as a key part of the wider process whereby individuals work together, with the help of government, in forging a better and more inclusive society. Lifelong learning is thus important on two levels. On the individual level, if people are not to be excluded from society they will need to upskill to maintain their employability. At a national level, if our economy is to compete in the new global market we need to maintain a 'flexible' labour force that is adaptable and able to respond immediately. Lifelong learning is portrayed as of central importance within a transformed, globalised economy (Taylor, 2005).

Lifelong learning and education policy

Arnove (2003) has suggested that the development of a global economy and the increasing interconnectedness of societies pose common problems for education systems around the world. The government placed education as a central plank in its policy agenda of modernisation, with the concept of lifelong learning as an important element within that policy. Taylor (2005) felt that government policy on lifelong learning can be divorced neither from its general education policy nor from its broader human capital approach to education, within an ideology of 'marketised welfarism'. The government felt a need to build on the existing strengths of the education system but also to overcome the spiral of disadvantage whereby 'alienation from, or failure within, the education system is passed on from generation to generation' (DfEE, 1998). Thus the importance of education, both in the compulsory years and throughout life, has been stressed. The theme that runs through government policy is the developing of human capital in order to compete in the knowledge economy.

It is worth considering some of the significant developments that have been taking place in education and how they relate to encouraging an ethos of lifelong learning.

- **The development of quality assurance measures aimed at monitoring performance in all phases of education, such as testing of pupils, compiling league tables of performance and regular inspection of all educational institutions, has been designed to raise the currency of educational qualifications.**
- **Nursery provision has been expanded rapidly on the premise that a good start is more likely to lead to a positive view of learning throughout the compulsory phases of education and beyond.**
- **In primary education, the emphasis on 'essential basic skills' is manifest through the literacy and numeracy strategies (consolidated in the National Primary Strategy, Excellence and Enjoyment) and a focus on the use of ICT .**
- **At secondary level, the emphasis has remained on basic skills but in addition there are attempts to raise standards with initiatives to increase parental choice of school and competition between schools, thus specialist schools and academies have been established and there are proposals to allow schools and parents to establish independent trust schools.**
- **The National Curriculum was reformed for all pupils, becoming more flexible and relevant to vocational needs of pupils at Key Stage 4 particularly.**
- **Citizenship has been introduced into the curriculum to help address rapid social change and the potential fragmentation of established communities. While lifelong learning does apply to all stages of education, post-compulsory and adult learning are the phases that most clearly fit under its banner.**
- **The reforms in post-16 education have seen a dramatic increase in the number of pupils who now stay on in education after 16. Vocational 'A' levels were introduced and GNVQs accorded parity of esteem, on paper at least.**
- **The number of students taking first degrees in higher education has increased with the expansion of HE. The aim is that by 2010, 50 per cent of young people in the 18–30 age group will take part in higher education. The development of foundation degrees has emphasised a vocational application of HE.**
- **A range of measures has been introduced to improve education and training opportunities in the workplace. There are programmes to develop the basic literacy, numeracy and ICT skills of those in low paid jobs, the long-term unemployed and young offenders. The need to update older workers in modern ICT skills and other new forms of working is also recognised. Those on welfare benefits are provided with suitable skills training after an assessment of their needs. Financial support is also available for the low paid.**

Policies of lifelong learning do not just involve the domain of education and training. They are part of wider social policies that are aimed at inclusion, such as Excellence in Cities, which was aimed at reinvigorating whole areas that were run down and had disadvantaged populations. There is an overlap between social, economic and education policy in what supporters of the third way would portray as 'joined-up government'. Strategies that take a broader approach to child and family welfare, such as Sure Start, have aimed at improving the future chances of children and their parents by involving health, social and education agencies. These strategies have led to the multi-agency approach currently being developed in the area of child welfare with the creation of child centres and extended schools. Evaluations of the impact of Sure Start have not been positive, with London University researchers reporting that 'possibly the utilisation of services by those with greater human capital left others less access to services than would have been the case had they not lived in SureStart areas' (Ward, 2005).

Criticisms of policy on lifelong learning

Biesta (2005) has commented that 'the dominant policy discourse nowadays sees adult education first and foremost as a lever for economic growth and global competitiveness'. The very instrumental approach to education taken in recent decades involves a narrow view of the purposes of education and can lead to a very restricted curriculum with an unhealthy emphasis on measurable outcomes. Rather than raising educational standards and encouraging involvement of students, this may actually lead to the increasing alienation of certain groups from the education system.

The human capital approach assumes that educating the workforce to a higher level will lead to increased economic performance. However any causal link between educational qualifications and production has never been clearly established. In fact, whether increasing educational provision, particularly in HE, does have a significant economic impact has been increasingly questioned (Wolf, 2002). Gorard (2003) has suggested that the government strategies for the retraining and upskilling of the workforce, with the emphasis on basic low-level skills, have so far had very little impact in spite of the media hype that has surrounded them. Work-based training does not appear to be rising in uptake.

Pause for thought | the value of higher education

In the light of differing views on the value of higher education; discuss the following with your colleagues:

- why you came into higher education;
- why you chose the course you are on at this particular institution.

How might your degree enhance (or not) your quality as a future employee?

It may be that the existence of a risk society and the need to develop an adaptable workforce have been greatly exaggerated and are really little more than social myths encouraged by those with vested interests in capitalist production (Hughes and Tight, 1998). Why might this myth be perpetuated? Crowther (2004) has portrayed lifelong learning as a 'deficit discourse'. By this he meant that responsibility for retraining is placed upon the individual rather than on government. Thus any failure is seen as individual rather than systemic. It is individuals who need to adapt to a lifetime of increasing occupational insecurity, as a consequence of changing employment conditions with more part-time and temporary work. The political rhetoric of lifelong learning involving individuality, adaptability and operating in the 'knowledge economy' may be drawing attention away from real structural inequalities in society by emphasising the importance of individual action.

Also the current emphasis by government, educationalists and employers on acquiring formal qualifications through education, whether part- or full-time, and the requirement of enrolment in vocational or skills training as a prerequisite of entitlement to welfare benefits, means that lifelong learning may actually be a form of compulsion and control over the workforce (Tight, 1998; Minter, 2001; Coffield, 2002). Crowther (2004) saw it as 'a new disciplinary technology to make people more compliant and adaptable for work in the era of flexible capitalism'. Most recently this is seen in the policy arena of FE funding where the Foster Review advocated the cessation of funding for adult learning that was not skills-related (Foster, 2005).

This ideology of lifelong learning does not inevitably have to be the dominant discourse. There are calls for individuals and local communities to have greater involvement in the development of a broader approach to lifelong learning that would encourage informal as well as formal networks (Tight, 1998; Crowther, 2004; Taylor, 2005). This would allow learning to move from being mainly for instrumental purposes alone to becoming an enriching experience for individuals and their communities.

Summary and conclusions

In this chapter we have seen that lifelong learning can have a variety of contestable meanings. It may be used for learning that takes place after the compulsory phase of education. It may be primarily about formal learning and vocational education or it may involve all aspects of learning in an adult's life. In its broadest sense it may be about all the learning that takes place from our birth until we die. Your own personal perspective on lifelong learning is likely to depend upon your ideological stance. You may regard it as being for economic purposes, as a form of social control or as a means to achieving individual fulfilment. You may however reach a compromise position and see a combination of all three purposes in operation in different degrees at different times.

References

Arnove, R (2003) Introduction: reframing comparative education: the dialectic of the global and the local, in Arnove, R and Torres, C (eds) *Comparative education: the dialectic of the global and the local*. Oxford: Rowman and Littlefield.

Bartlett, S (2003) Education for lifelong learning, in Bartlett, S and Burton, D *Education studies: essential issues*. London: Sage.

Bartlett, S, Burton, D and Peim, N (2001) *Introduction to education studies*. London: PCP.

Beck, U (1992) *Risk society: towards a new modernity*. London: Sage.

Biesta, G (2005) The learning democracy? Adult learning and the condition of democratic citizenship. *British Journal of Sociology of Education*, 26(5): 687–703.

Burbules, N and Torres, C (eds) (2000) *Globalisation and education: critical perspectives*. London: Routledge.

Coffield, F (2002) Breaking the consensus, in Edwards, R, Miller, N, Small, N and Tait, A (eds) *Supporting lifelong learning*. London: RoutledgeFalmer.

Crowther, J (2004) 'In and against' lifelong learning: flexibility and the corrosion of character. *International Journal of Lifelong Education*, 23(2): 125–36.

DfEE (1998) *The learning age: a renaissance for a new Britain*. London: Department for Education and Employment/HMSO.

Edwards, R (2000) Lifelong learning, lifelong learning, lifelong learning: a recurrent education?, in Field, J and Leicester, M (eds) *Lifelong learning education across the lifespan*. London: RoutledgeFalmer.

Foster, A (2005) *Review of the future role of FE colleges*. London: DfES/HMSO.

Giddens, A (1998) *The third way: the renewal of social democracy*. Cambridge: Polity Press.

Giddens, A (2000) *The third way and its critcs*. Cambridge: Polity Press.

Gorard, S (2003) Patterns of work-based learning. *Journal of Vocational Education and Training*, 55(1): 47–63.

Hughes, C and Tight, M (1998) The myth of the learning society, in Ransen, S (ed) *Inside the learning society*. London: Cassell.

Kogan, M (2000) Lifelong learning in the UK. *European Journal of Education*, 35(3): 343–59.

Lawton, D (2005) *Education and Labour Party ideologies, 1900–2001 and beyond*. London: RoutledgeFalmer.

Mead, M (1942) *Growing up in New Guinea*. London: Pelican.

Minter, C (2001) Some flaws in the common theory of widening participation. *Research in Post-compulsory Education*, 26(3): 303–19.

NAGCELL (1997) *Learning for the twenty-first century: first report of the National Advisory Group for Continuing Education and Lifelong Learning* (the Fryer Report). London: NAGCELL.

Ritzer, G (2000) *The McDonaldization of society*. Thousand Oaks, CA: Pine Forge Press.

Taylor, R (2005) Lifelong learning and the Labour governments 1997–2004. *Oxford Review of Education*: 31(1):101–18.

Tight, M (1998) Lifelong learning: opportunity or compulsion? *British Journal of Educational Studies*: 46(3):251–63.

Wolf, A (2002) *Does education matter? Myths about education and economic growth*. Harmondsworth: Penguin.

Ward, L (2005) Sure Start sets back the worst placed youngsters, study finds. *Guardian*, 1 December, p5.

Chapter 15

Leadership in education

John Sharp and Graham Meeson

Introduction

Considerable interest in educational leadership over recent times has resulted in a period of unprecedented growth and research in the field. This in turn has led to a rise in the popularity of leadership as a study option on undergraduate and postgraduate university courses and an increase in the provision of professional leadership qualifications. Indeed, it is unlikely that you won't have experienced either leading or being led, whether at school, college, university or the workplace. It would therefore be highly worthwhile for you to reflect and build upon these experiences. The realisation of leadership potential is now widely recognised as a fundamental contributor towards people's personal and professional development and effectiveness and, eventually, their career satisfaction. In this chapter the concept of leadership is introduced and leadership models within a range of educational contexts are presented and explored.

Historical background

Most companies and other organisations remain heavily managed and largely hierarchical in structure, despite some rhetoric to the contrary. Of course, management brings order, control and authority to a hierarchy. The acceptance of this, as a legacy of the European industrial revolution, is perpetuated implicitly and explicitly throughout our own systems of education and training. The German sociologist Max Weber (1864–1920) was perhaps the first to systematically consider the links between social structure and human behaviour in the industrial world (Bush and Bell, 2003). For Weber, the processes involved in industry necessitated the promotion of certain principles, values, beliefs and ideals in the interests of efficiency. This model of industrial efficiency was concerned with the maximisation of output and profit such that the needs of the individual were, at best, of only secondary importance. Problem-solving was applied, which owed more to scientific method and pragmatism than to a deep-rooted understanding of people as individuals. People were, in fact, little more than the human component in an industrial machine. This so-called 'rationalist' approach was characterised by:

- **a strong division of labour in the workforce;**
- **strict adherence to rules, regulations and bureaucracy;**
- **goal-oriented and autocratic management;**
- **minimal opportunities for learning;**
- **meeting production targets;**
- **external accountability.**

The opposite of 'rationalism' might be 'collegiality', a term whose origin can be traced to the colleges of Oxford and Cambridge Universities. Systems that operate 'collegially' do so on principles of collectivity, equality, mutual trust and shared goals; they adopt flat rather than hierarchical management structures (Bush and Bell, 2003). The independence of the organisation and the autonomy of the individual within the workforce are protected at all costs. Decisions are reached and problems solved by way of discussion, compromise and agreement. Opportunities for learning and innovation are maximised. Of course neither approach is perfect, since principles, values, beliefs and ideals can be compromised within each. Indeed, many companies and other organisations are constantly reconsidering the ways in which they operate as they come to terms with the pace of life and expectation in today's world. The principle of hierarchy, entrenched though it is, is slowly giving way to other forms of organisational structure, and the importance of management is slowly giving way to the importance of leadership.

Pause for thought | the nature of educational organisations

The 'politicisation' and external control of education at all levels throughout the UK is seen by many leading authorities on education as a regressive rather than progressive step. Concerns abound over the erosion of academic freedoms, the marginalisation of proper educational debate and the apparent reduction in the status of education to nothing more than a commodity bought by consumers and driven by the forces of a market economy. According to Furedi (2004):

Increasingly, every aspect of education is subjected to rule-making and regulated through inspection and auditing. As a result of a highly centralised system of education managed by an interventionist bureaucracy little is left to chance. It has been noted that even primary school teachers are allowed little initiative to exercise their professional judgement. ... In the university sector, a system of auditing has succeeded in influencing the minutiae of teaching and even of research. The expansion of bureaucratic control is justified on the grounds that it ensures the maintenance of standards of institutions. It is argued that it helps hold teachers, lecturers and their institutions to account. (p9)

Why do you think successive governments have set about intervening and taking more and more control of education? Is the imposition of a 'rationalist' approach, driven as it is by targets, short-term goals, performance indicators and streamlining, the best way forward? Do you feel that criticisms of government intervention and control, particularly where these are seen as attempts at social engineering, are justified? Are the notions of 'rationalism' and 'collegiality' in their purest forms realistic models for any educational organisation to adopt? To what extent have today's educational organisations arrived at compromise or contrived solutions? What role do you think educational leaders might have in resolving some of these issues?

Leadership *vs* Management

Both 'rationalism' and 'collegiality' focus more on the management of organisations than on how they are led. The words leadership and management are often used synonymously or interchangeably but most authors now agree that leadership and management are quite separate constructs. The precise differences between them, however, remain at times blurred and hotly debated. It is often said that the difference between leadership and management is the difference between inspiration and perspiration. But what exactly does this mean? Owen et al (2004) propose a range of behavioural and operational factors that differentiate management from leadership:

- **managers build organisational structures while leaders build organisational cultures;**
- **managers maintain systems while leaders challenge them;**
- **managers focus on structures and doing the right thing while leaders focus on people and doing things right;**
- **managers concern themselves with performance indicators and targets while leaders inspire with shared visions;**
- **managers maintain low levels of emotional attachment while leaders ask for hearts and minds;**
- **managers are programmatic and follow fixed paths while leaders are innovative and find paths;**

- **managers control while leaders empower;**
- **managers are taught by organisations while leaders learn from them;**
- **managers ask how and by when while leaders ask what for and why.**

According to Gronn (1999), however, the importance of leadership and what leadership means in educational settings often suffers from a 'naïve realism' driven by a series of implicit theories or received wisdoms:

- **leaders tend to be formal position holders or figureheads in a hierarchical system and therefore hold more power;**
- **leadership enjoys a status which is different from and more important than management;**
- **there exists qualitative difference between the minority who lead and the majority who follow;**
- **the leader–follower relationship is directional in that leaders act on behalf of and in the best interests of followers;**
- **outcomes can be attributed to the actions of individual leaders;**
- **the variability and uniqueness of contexts in which leadership is exercised are of little significance;**
- **leadership involves the individual rather than the team.**

Pause for thought | the characteristics of leadership

What do you think about the differences between leadership and management presented by Owen et al. (2004)? Are these constructs really separate things or simply either end of a behavioural and operational continuum? In other words, could there be a place for manager-centred leadership or leadership-centred management? Do good leaders necessarily make good managers and vice versa? Reflect upon your own experiences of leadership and management and discuss these with a colleague. Do any other defining features or characteristics of leadership and management occur to you? Is there any substance to the 'implicit theories' view of Gronn (1999) presented above? What might be the implications or consequences of letting 'implicit theories' go unchallenged?

The function of educational leadership in an organisation is, of course, primarily to direct action. As a general rule, individuals become leaders because they are influential among their peers. The ability to influence others, however, is not something that people are born able to do, but is something they learn to do. This means that everyone has leadership potential even if they never actually aspire to being a leader. One of the pressures associated with realising leadership potential in any organisation is knowing when to accept leadership and when to offer it. Barriers to expressing leadership or to realising leadership potential may come in many different forms (Law and Glover, 2000). These might be associated with elements of your own personality, where you work and who you work with. To a large extent leaders can only lead with the consent of those who follow. Trust is an essential component of this often fragile relationship. If the power invested in the leader by virtue of their role is not wielded in an ethically appropriate way that trust will soon be lost. The misuse of power associated with leadership can be problematic. Those who find themselves with power may choose to use it to control people, to get their own way or to advance themselves rather than the interests of those they lead. Leaders who use what power they have in such ways can, in extreme circumstances, become dangerous and damaging individuals.

Pause for thought | assessing your own leadership potential

MacBeath and Myers (1999) offered a self-evaluation protocol which can be used as a starting point for discussion. A modified version appears below. As MacBeath and Myers pointed out, self-evaluation is context-dependent and there may be a difference between how you evaluate yourself and how others might see you. Complete and score the form below yourself and compare outcomes with a colleague. Is this how you really are or how you would like to be? While there may be issues over the nature of certain elements, high overall scores tend towards positive leadership potential.

	Never	1	2	3	4	5	Always
Are you a rule breaker?		1	2	3	4	5	
Are you efficient?		1	2	3	4	5	
Do you have radical views?		1	2	3	4	5	
Do you share power?		1	2	3	4	5	
Are you democratic?		1	2	3	4	5	
Are you charismatic?		1	2	3	4	5	
Do you pursue long-term goals?		1	2	3	4	5	
Are you forgiving?		1	2	3	4	5	
Are you competitive?		1	2	3	4	5	
Do you delegate a lot?		1	2	3	4	5	
Do you embrace change?		1	2	3	4	5	
Do you confront bad practice?		1	2	3	4	5	
Are you reliable?		1	2	3	4	5	
Are you open-minded?		1	2	3	4	5	
Do you attend to detail?		1	2	3	4	5	
Are you gregarious?		1	2	3	4	5	
Are you demanding?		1	2	3	4	5	
Are you a team player?		1	2	3	4	5	
Are you flexible?		1	2	3	4	5	
Are you an optimist?		1	2	3	4	5	
Do you fight for what you believe in?		1	2	3	4	5	
Are you entrepreneurial?		1	2	3	4	5	
Are you unpredictable?		1	2	3	4	5	
Are you a risk-taker?		1	2	3	4	5	
Can you make decisions?		1	2	3	4	5	
Do you take responsibility?		1	2	3	4	5	
Are you straightforward?		1	2	3	4	5	
Are you idealistic?		1	2	3	4	5	
Do you listen?		1	2	3	4	5	
Do you lead by example?		1	2	3	4	5	

Overall score: _____

Take some time to consider the charismatic, situational, transcendental and transactional leadership characteristics presented earlier. Do you recognise any of these qualities in you or those around you? Is it likely that you would see them all exhibited in one person? Would that one person be easy to work with or for?

Contemporary models of educational leadership

As an emergent field, educational leadership has tended to borrow its models from elsewhere (Coleman and Briggs, 2002; Anderson and Bennett, 2003). This approach has not always been helpful as the theoretical frameworks, principles, values, beliefs and ideals involved do not always reside easily in educational circumstances or pay due attention to the constraints within which some educational organisations operate. (Recall 'rationalism' and 'collegiality'.) Models of educational leadership fall into four main categories, each underpinned by its own collection of principles and theories (e.g. Bennis and Nanus, 1985; Mitchell and Tucker, 1992; Bush, 2003; Bush and Middlewood, 2003). While language and terminology may vary, these include:

- **charismatic leadership;**
- **situational leadership;**
- **transcendental leadership;**
- **transformational leadership.**

Of course, no one model of leadership is completely independent of any other, for no two individuals who subscribe to any particular view of leadership ever exhibit exactly the same leadership style, make use of exactly the same leadership strategies or operate within the same context. Effective leaders are, however, generally flexible and adaptable individuals who remain conscious of what is going on around them and respond accordingly and appropriately at all times.

Charismatic leadership

Charismatic leadership concerns itself with individual traits. Individuals, through their charisma and actions are identified as 'great leaders' who then become national role models to inspire others. Such traits often reflect the idealised masculine heroic myth and, traditionally, the most well-known charismatic leaders have been men (Lingard et al., 2004). Charismatic leaders are well known for being successful at finding ways forward in particularly stressful situations or succeeding against all the odds. Models of leadership based upon the charisma or traits of individuals do have disadvantages as they oversimplify the complexity of human relationships and the situations and events that occur in everyday life. Though now regarded with some cynicism, and for reasons that may be obvious, studying charismatic leaders:

- **helps to identify our own notions of what is important in leadership;**
- **provides an understanding of more sophisticated models of leadership.**

Research box

leadership and gender

Much has been written about the differences between men and women as leaders and whether gender has any impact on leadership style and even career progression. On style, women appear to do well. Some 'typical' female characteristics often said to be aligned with effective leadership include the capacity to listen, communicate and share power, a genuine concern for personal and emotional well-being and a person-centred and interactive approach. Rosener (1990) has suggested that women who have broken through the 'glass ceiling' in what is often regarded as a 'man's world' and who have succeeded in certain leadership roles, have done so as a result of, rather than in spite of, their gender. They have not had to 'masculinise' themselves to conform. They have not had to alter how they dress and behave, for example. Gray (1993) has also noted that the similarities in how men and women actually operate in leadership roles are, in reality, far greater than differences, with both genders adopting what might be described as 'feminine' as well as 'masculine' characteristics.

▶

Experience, it would seem, is more important in terms of role fitness than gender stereotyping. The study of leadership in English primary schools, however, is of particular interest (although the ratio of female to male professors in university departments would provide an equally valuable alternative). According to MacBeath and Myers (1999), for example, women make up about 80 per cent of the primary teaching profession at any one time, but only about 50 per cent of head teachers are women (though more women than men occupy middle management positions). Women also lag behind men when age is included as a factor, and women from ethnic minority groups are worst affected. As MacBeath and Myers pointed, out, finding an overall explanation is difficult because some of the same causal factors also appear to apply to some men though not to the same degree. These can include access to relevant role models, perception of teaching as a career, devotion to the job, mobility in the job market, maternity and career breaks.

Situational leadership

Situational leadership is essentially task-driven. It concerns itself with what a leader can attempt to achieve democratically by ensuring the optimal performance of a team in relation to the knowledge and skills base available. Situational leaders are, therefore, good problem-solvers with a talent for matching different individuals to different stages of a project at different times. Leadership is contingent on the environment or situation or task at hand. The characteristics they demonstrate include an understanding of when to delegate, support, coach or direct (Blanchard et al, 1994):

- **when delegating, the leader gives responsibility for day-to-day decision-making away to the able and willing (assumes a high competence and high commitment and enthusiasm on the part of the team member);**
- **when supporting, the leader listens, praises and facilitates (assumes high competence and some commitment and enthusiasm on the part of the team member);**
- **when coaching, the leader trains, directs and supports (assumes some competence but mixed commitment and enthusiasm on the part of the team member);**
- **when directing, the leader structures, controls and supervises (assumes low competence and low commitment and enthusiasm on the part of the team member).**

The disadvantages of situational leadership lie in it being seen as simply a way of getting things done, another form of management. This criticism is particularly evident when situational leaders are viewed as in complete control and overly authoritative when coaching or directing. Situational leadership may easily result in transactional predicaments where work is undertaken in response to 'payback' or to avoid punishment. Opportunities for learning may be stifled.

Pause for thought | approaches to leadership

Consider how you might respond to the following situations. Put yourself in the role of leader and identify strategies that might bring about an appropriate conclusion.

You are part of a group of four on placement (school or other). You have been tasked with organising a drama production. The criteria and expectations are clear. No one else in the group appears prepared to work together to take things forward.

As an active member of your student union you have been asked to plan a series of activities for charity week in order to raise money for a local community project. There are seven other people involved and you have been nominated as leader. All are willing to work for you as their turn will come. Time is short and there is still much left to do.

As part of a departmental summer school project, you have been put in charge of a small group of paid students and other volunteers. For this additional responsibility you receive a small amount of money more than everybody else. The others appear quietly to resent this. Payment is conditional on maintaining and developing the project.

How does your approach to each of these situations relate to the models of charismatic, situational, transcendental and transformational leadership?

Transcendental leadership

Transcendental leadership is essentially relationship- and empathy-driven and may be strongly associated with individuals with high emotional intelligence (Greenleaf, 1996; Cardona, 2000; Goleman et al, 2002). Emotional intelligence concerns itself with our ability to understand our own emotions and how they make us feel and react, as well as the emotions, feelings and reactions of those around us. Recognising what triggers emotional responses helps to maximise the positive aspects of our behaviour and relationships with others (e.g. trust, openness, honesty, motivation, commitment, collaboration) while minimising those that are negative and destructive (e.g. jealousy, resentment). Positive emotions can help to achieve goals, complete tasks and solve problems. Transcendental leadership concerns itself with addressing and supporting the needs and growth of individuals and organisations together and with promoting a strong sense of ownership. By adopting such an approach, individuals are empowered by their leader quite literally to transcend themselves, that is to become more knowledgeable and capable team members while at the same time becoming more autonomous in what they do. Transcendental leaders, who serve their organisations well, can often be identified by the sorts of questions they ask:

- **What can I/we (the organisation) do to … ?**
- **How can I/we (the organisation) enable you to … ?**
- **Where would I/we (the organisation) benefit from … ?**

The disadvantage of transcendental leadership can be found in its rather woolly and diverse approach which may lack sufficient focus and direction. Transcendental leaders may be seen as easily manipulated or as a 'soft touch'.

Transformational leadership

Transformational leadership is essentially change-driven and particularly suited to education (Burns, 1978; Gronn, 1996). Transformational leaders have the vision to identify a need to bring about change or to create something different or new, however large or small that change or creation might be, in order to achieve a particular goal. Transformational leadership is particularly suited to teamwork and to understanding the needs of the individual but in different ways to situational and transcendental leadership. Transformational leaders know how teams are built and maintained and operate and perform. Teams work on the synergy of ideas, practices and responsibilities that allow them to achieve results where individuals or groups might perform less well or fail. Effective team leadership focuses attention, maintains motivation and enthusiasm, and coordinates activities. Within a team, leadership may be transferred from one member to another if particular expertise is required or needs to be brought in from an external source at any point in time. Transformational leaders not only adapt to a situation, and in doing so exemplify the same empathy and emotional awareness as transcendental leaders, they also transform it. Effective transformational leaders can shape the principles, values, beliefs and ideals of a whole organisation. Executed well, transformational leadership can be pivotal in helping to tackle feelings of helplessness within an organisation and improve morale in a disenfranchised workforce by lifting and empowering individuals to higher levels of motivation and commitment. Transformational leaders:

- **recognise and encourage an expression of views;**
- **encourage individual and organisational learning;**
- **acknowledge and reward effort;**
- **strive towards achieving sustainable growth;**
- **relish in and respond positively to uncertainty.**

Transformational leadership suffers from some of the same disadvantages as situational and transcendental leadership. It tends to rely on a single individual as the driving force behind determining change and direction with followers in what might still be described as a compliant role. It is possible to lose sight of goals to be achieved when developing people and maintaining teams. Weak transformational leadership can, for example, lead to the rationality and acceptability of key decisions being called into question and the time taken to reach decisions becoming protracted, all of which can cause progress to falter.

Research box

complexity, chaos and the emergence of distributed leadership

According to Morrison (2002), the tendency towards globalisation, increasing organisational diversity and interdependency, the speed and ease with which we communicate and the rise of an ever-more confident, educated and demanding work force, require a new model of educational leadership which breaks with current practices. Morrison has anticipated that this paradigm shift in thinking about educational leadership will emerge from the application of complexity and chaos theories, which together provide a means of analysing and making sense of how organisations operate as open, dynamic, self-organising and adaptive systems and the ways in which they fail to conform to simple and deterministic cause-and-effect relationships and linear predictability. Handling such everyday variation, in whichever organisation it occurs, requires distributed leadership or leadership at source.

Summary and conclusions

The formal study of leadership within an educational setting is a relatively new and emerging field of enquiry. While there have been several attempts to appropriate models of leadership drawn from outside education, few have been entirely successful. Education is varied, it takes place in a great many different sorts of environment, and educational organisations are usually under a great many internal and external constraints. Educational leaders, therefore, need to be flexible, adaptable, trustworthy and emotionally literate individuals who have the strength and vision to delegate responsibility where appropriate and to be able to motivate and inspire whole teams of people. Seeking out or developing suitable models of educational leadership within which different practices can be analysed and reflected upon is clearly of some importance. Transformational leadership, with its associated principles, values, beliefs, ideals and focus on change, the individual and the team, is perhaps a good place for aspiring educational leaders to look for inspiration. Whether it be in school, college, university or some other place of work, accepting responsibility for the deployment of staff, resources or funding on even the smallest of scales brings with it opportunities to demonstrate leadership potential, opportunities which should be grasped in the interests of personal and professional development and effectiveness. Only trained, educated and visionary educational leaders will ever be in a position to challenge orthodoxy and to liberate citizens of the future.

References

Anderson, L and Bennett, N (eds) (2003) *Developing educational leadership: using evidence for policy and practice*. London: Sage.

Bennis, W and Nanus, B (1985) *Leadership: the strategies for taking charge*. New York: Harper Row.

Blanchard, K, Zigarmi, D and Zigarmi, P (1994) *Leadership and the one-minute manager*. London: Willow.

Burns, JM (1978) *Leadership*. New York: Harper Row.

Bush, T (2003) *Theories of educational leadership and management*. London: Sage.

Bush, T and Bell, L (eds) (2003) *The principles and practice of educational management*. London: Sage.

Bush, T and Middlewood, D (2003) *Leading and managing people in education*. London: Sage.

Cardona, P (2000) Transcendental leadership. *The Leadership and Organisation Development Journal*, 21(4): 201–6.

Coleman, M and Briggs, A (eds) (2002) *Researching educational leadership and management*. London: Paul Chapman.

Furedi, F (2004) The formalisation of relationships in education, in Hayes, D (ed) *The RoutledgeFalmer guide to key debates in education*. London: RoutledgeFalmer.

Goleman, D, Boyatzis, R and McKee, A (2002). *The new leaders: transforming the art of leadership into the science of results*. London: Bloomsbury.

Gray, HL (1993) Gender issues in management training, in Ozga, J (ed) *Women in educational management*. Buckingham: Open University Press.

Greenleaf, RK (1996) *On becoming a servant leader*. San Francisco: Jossey–Bass.

Gronn, P (1996) From transactions to transformations: a new world order in the study of leadership? *Educational Management and Administration*, 24(1): 7–30.

Gronn, P (1999) *The making of educational leaders*. London: Cassell.

Law, S and Glover, D (2000) *Educational leadership and learning*. Buckingham: Open University Press.

Lingard, B, Hayes, D, Mills, M and Christie, P (2004) *Leading learning*. Buckingham: Open University Press.

MacBeath, JEC and Myers, K (1999) *Effective school leaders: how to evaluate and improve your leadership potential*. Harlow: Prentice–Hall.

Mitchell, G and Tucker, S (1992) Leadership as a way of thinking. *Educational Leadership*, 49(5): 30–5.

Morrison, K (2002) *School leadership and complexity theory*. London: RoutledgeFalmer.

Owen, H, Hodgson, V and Gazzard, N (2004) *The leadership manual: your complete practical guide to effective leadership*. London: Pearson–Prentice Hall.

Rosener, JB (1990) Ways women lead. *Harvard Business Review*, 6(6): 119–25.

Chapter 16

Race and education

Nasima Hassan

Introduction

This chapter addresses the issue of race in education through reference to historic and contemporary research and consequent initiatives. Some of the wider issues associated with black and minority ethnic pupils in the classroom are reviewed through an exploration of race and identity. Successive government initiatives to combat racism in schools in response to the socio-political conditions in Britain from the early 1960s onwards are considered. A discussion of the race and achievement nexus draws together conclusions as reflected in the experiences of black pupils in inner London schools which might be considered representative of other geographical locations within the UK.

Educational initiatives to combat racism in education

Successive governments have proved unable to deliver a coherent philosophy and policy to combat racism in education and this has been at an undeniable cost to the nation, its education system and its fragile race relations. Critics argue that the very deracialisation of education policies has failed to address the growing cancer of low expectations of teachers, racist stereotyping and inadequate provisions for children learning English as a second language (Troyna and Williams, 1996). Indeed, the term 'learners of English as an *additional* language', for example, was not formally accepted in place of 'learners of English as a *second* language' by the Teacher Training Agency (now the Teacher Development Agency) until 2002. This can be taken to demonstrate the power of language to perpetuate low teacher expectations and implicitly devalue pupils' diverse skills. A series of reactive recommendations following several major high profile incidents might not have been necessary had diversity been embraced earlier (MacPherson, 1999; Cantle, 2001; Ousley, 2001).

Research box

the roots of racism in the playground

The assumed innocence of children hinders informed debate about children's notion of 'race'. Many studies have identified awareness among even very young children of racial differences and therefore of different values placed upon different skin colour. In addition, the incidence of racial name-calling is an increasingly common feature of the primary school environment, more damaging perhaps than physical acts (Cohen, 1989; Wright, 1992). Swann (DES, 1985) has observed that racial abuse is reference not only to the child but also by extension to their family and indeed more broadly to their ethnic community as a whole. Troyna and Hatcher (1992) have argued that children respond to specific situations more in anger at times than as 'racists'. Interestingly, their research along with that conducted by Gaine (1995) took place in predominantly white primary schools. The discussion therefore explores the socialisation processes on children in their understanding of 'race' and how this impacts on the friendships and relationships they form.

Historically, and in response to the need for successful integration of immigrant children, three policies that received most criticism for their lack of thought and appropriateness were:

- **assimilation;**
- **integration;**
- **racial pluralism.**

These policies were designed to make grassroots impact in textbooks and teaching strategies, as well as addressing the wider notions of race and equal opportunities characterised by legislation in their time. For example, the Race Relations Act 1976 has been heavily criticised for not going far enough to stamp out direct acts of racial discrimination in practice.

Assimilation

To assimilate means to merge and become part of something. It is about the denial and rejection of individuality. The policy of assimilation, which lasted up until the end of the 1960s, was more in reaction to a perceived problem rather than attempting to stabilise and strengthen race relations within the classroom environment. It was understood to calm the concerns of white parents alarmed at the presence of large numbers of immigrant children in their local schools, a state of affairs created by a system of dispersal designed to spread the problem of immigration throughout the country. The implementation of this dispersal policy required statistical data on immigrant pupils, such as their linguistic abilities and the socio-economic status of their parents. This important information was used to secure access to additional funding via Section 11 of the Local Government Act 1966. Local education authorities (LEAs) could now access this fund to aid their dispersal and assimilation work.

This assimilation phase existed against a background of the rise of the political far right and the growing strength of the National Front. It proved a hopelessly problematic policy however, almost impossible to implement, administer or measure in terms of success. It had been created on the very negative assumption that black pupils in the classroom were a problem to be dealt with, through their inability to speak English. Research has shown that bilingual and multilingual immigrant children in America, Canada and Britain opt for a 'silent period' when at first exposed to the new language (Cummins, 2001). This silence can be understood in terms of response to a culture shock. However, in terms of language acquisition it marks a crucial listening period which varies in length, allowing children to learn at their own pace. Assimilation strategies actually pressurised immigrant children to learn English quickly in order to solve the problem of their very presence.

Integration

The dawn of the 1970s, and of a new era of diversity, offered the policy of integration as a suitable replacement to assimilation. Quite simply, integration meant to become part of a bigger picture and to become fully absorbed into it (e.g. the American ideal of throwing everyone together in a melting pot to substitute a new identity of 'coffee coloured people' for the mishmash that had gone before). Integration introduced the first sighting of multiculturalism in education by way of an acknowledgement of cultural diversity (Parekh, 2000). Defining multiculturalism is no exact science. Literally, multiculturalism is about pluralism engaged in social theory. Alleyne (2002) concluded that multiculturalism celebrates difference as an end in itself. Powell and Schwartz (2003) opted for an unambiguous link to racism: 'The notion of multicultural diversity entails exactly the same premise as racism – that one's ideas are determined by one's race and that a source of individual identity is [one's] ethnic heritage.' For some, there exists no incompatibility between multiculturalism and Britishness. For others, however, multiculturalism suggests 'separateness' and is often mistaken to mean that different cultural communities should live their own ways of life in a self-contained manner (Parekh, 2000).

The clear emphasis in developing integration policies was on absorption into the mainstream, while conceding that cultural differences could, when used selectively, be of interest to others. LEAs were now expected to develop and implement multicultural strategies in schools, to facilitate the process of integration. This was done through a 'bolt-on' approach, as something else to push some schools to implement. The anxiety felt by teachers forced into unfamiliar territory was in direct response to ill-considered multiculturalism, resulting in shallow, superficial and barely recognisable global education. This particular brand of multiculturalism had the aim of 'institutional hybridity – a fusion of myriad cultures, Bhangra, Afro, Asian and South Indian with Britishness ... in order to ethnicise schools into integration' (Kundnani, 2001). In an attempt to redress the impact of racial stereotyping and growing prejudices based on ignorance, aspects of the immigrant life experience were to be shared. These included food, music, costumes, rituals, faith practices, festivals and traditional ways of life. Critics summarised this approach as the '3 Ss' – saris, steel pans and samosas – as these were the least threatening element of cultural diversity that might be shared. Exotica was the only way to go to integrate successfully, it seemed (Sarup, 1991). Swann (DES, 1985) was also openly and vehemently critical of integration and multiculturalism in this form. Although some initial barriers were overcome by this first phase of multiculturalism, the strategy was tokenistic and devalued the wealth of heritage that immigrants held so dear. Allowing British society to select elements of cultural diversity that they found particularly palatable, namely the curry, now as British as a bulldog or a pint of beer, could never facilitate social cohesion in the classroom or indeed anywhere.

Cultural pluralism

The principle of cultural pluralism was introduced in the 1980s to find a resolution for the continuing dilemma of racism in education. Two groundbreaking government publications, *West Indian Children in Our Schools*, or the Rampton Report (DES, 1981), and *Education for All*, or the Swann Report (DES, 1985), cited earlier in this chapter, left no doubt that the issues of underachievement as experienced by West Indian pupils in particular were now firmly rooted on the educational agenda. The Swann Report reflected a period of growing social unrest and signified a need to address deeply-rooted ideologies of prejudice and discrimination, thus marking a transition. The title 'Education for All' identified the intent to redress the balance, not only in education policy but in society as a whole. Swann was clear about how we had arrived at this important transition point:

> *All in all, central government appears to have lacked a coherent strategy for fostering the development of multicultural education and thus to have been unable to play a leading role in coordinating or encouraging progress in this field. We regard both the assimilationist and integrationist educational responses to the needs of ethnic minority pupils as, in retrospect, misguided and ill founded.* (1985, p198)

Acknowledgement of recommendations made by Rampton and Swann was of foremost consideration, although traces of assimilation and integration still survived from the troubled 1960s and 1970s. The expectation that shared values and ideals should unite all citizens of the now multiracial, multiethnic Britain of the time was paramount. A sense of belonging was to be cultivated in the sharing of these values. Cultural pluralism rode on the wave of anti-racism policies in all LEAs and schools. Funding from central government sought to employ bilingual support staff where possible. However, a controversial enforced ban on mother tongue in the classroom hindered linguistic progression. When coupled with advice to parents only to 'speak English with your children at home', this compounded the apparent value and status of mother tongue as worthless in the eyes of the education system. As with assimilation, all-white schools were not required to engage with such approaches and often remained oblivious to the need for them. This was no longer acceptable.

The Education Reform Act of 1988, which prepared the ground for the National Curriculum, promoted cultural pluralism through the buzzwords of 'choice and diversity', incorporating non-statutory guidance on multicultural education for all teachers. Despite the rhetoric of antiracism and equality of opportunity, strategies to combat racism in practice continued to prove inadequate. The foundations of successive policies were so deficient in structure and philosophy that they became a self-fulfilling prophecy by virtue of their inevitable failure. Introduced in response to a perceived crisis in education – the presence of immigrant children in schools, the urban race riots in Liverpool and Birmingham, the underachievement of black boys as signalled by league tables – it is difficult to see how could they ever hope to impact positively. The National Curriculum, which made its first appearance in schools in 1989, provided direct strategic guidance to permeate all schools and provide 'a broad and balanced curriculum … an entitlement of all pupils' regardless of their catchments. In the spirit of shared values, the religious education syllabus was to dedicate 50 per cent study time to Christianity and 50 per cent to the main religions represented in Britain, namely Buddhism, Hinduism, Islam, Judaism and Sikhism. This measure was widely perceived as insufficiently progressive to offer a truly multicultural curriculum. The absence of black scientists, artists, poets and role models in general contributed to the mis-education of black pupils throughout the 1960s and 1970s, and it appeared that this institutional racism in education might continue. How could ideals such as the fostering of intelligence and mutual understanding take place within a blanketing white, western worldview? It is important to question the notion of tolerance, a word used happily in school mission statements the length and breadth of Britain. Tolerance means to put up with, perhaps reluctantly. It means to endure or permit grudgingly. It is not about acceptance, understanding and most significantly it is not about equality.

More recent government policy in the 1990s led to various initiatives championing equality of opportunity and high standards for all through parental choice, standards and diversity bringing cultural pluralism into the political mainstream. MacPherson (1999) recommended Ethnic Minority Achievement Grants (EMAG) to replace Section 11 funding of the Local Government Act of the 1960s and all LEAs were directed to appoint EMAG coordinators and teams to make grass roots impact. These teams would be subject to the same accountability through inspection criteria as other sections of education. MacPherson emphasised the continued destructive impact of racism (endemic in the operations of the Metropolitan Police) and condemned 'the collective failure of an organisation to provide a professional service to people because of their colour, culture or ethnic origin. It can be seen in processes which discriminate through unwitting prejudice, ignorance, thoughtlessness and racist stereotyping'.

The incorporation of citizenship as a compulsory secondary curriculum subject in the new millennium, supported by GCSE qualifications in citizenship studies, has helped the 'inclusion' agenda, the replacement for cultural pluralism. A report on 'community cohesion' in the aftermath of race riots in Bradford, Oldham and Burnley, was hailed as a race manifesto advising 'black people to develop a greater acceptance of principal national institutions', including citizenship (Cantle, 2001). Through the embedding of antiracist and multicultural elements into citizenship as a formally assessed and accredited discipline a sea change has taken place which can, at this stage at least, only be considered a start in the battle to combat racism in education (Kundnani, 2001).

Race and achievement

Of the many powerful commonplace generalisations about 'race' and achievement, those around African-Caribbean boys as the lowest-achieving group in comparison to their white and Asian peers, are the most tenacious. Consider these:

West Indian children as a group are underachieving in our education system. (DES, 1981)

There is no doubt that West Indian children as a group, and on average, are underachieving, both by comparison with their fellows in the white majority as well as in terms of their potential. (DES, 1985)

The underachievement of West Indian children is a reinforcement of a stereotype that black people are academically challenged. (Troyna, 1984)

Race, gender and class all impact on achievement. The lowest achieving ethnic groups (Bangladeshi, Pakistani and Caribbean) are disproportionately overrepresented in the lowest socio-economic groups. (Gillborn and Mirza, 2000)

These comments reflect the complexity of the debate on race and underachievement, while at the same time reinforcing the central discourse: that the underachievement of black pupils, in particular black boys, has continued to raise the greatest concerns. As with multiculturalism, underachievement has been defined in fluid terms depending on the subject (ethnic group) and context. The very use of the word 'underachievement' is synonymous with the many stereotypes associated with racial characteristics of black people: that they are lazy, lacking mental capacity, inclined to challenging behaviours, conflict and aggression (particularly boys). However, in terms of educational achievement such powerful stereotypes have been applied both to black pupils and to their rates of learning. Gillborn and Mirza have noted that:

> [i]t is vital to identify differences in attainment but we must be careful to avoid wider beliefs that reinforce wholly stereotypical perceptions that some ethnic groups are naturally talented in some areas or inherently culturally disposed to learning whilst others are not. Thus, simply replacing 'underachievement' with the more recent notions of 'difference' needs to be carefully considered. (2000, p56)

It is vital to point out that the underachievement of black boys is just one facet of the multiplicity of issues when the question of race and achievement is raised. The all-encompassing nature of this debate has preoccupied politicians, journalists and educational professionals alike, with crime, gang culture, binge drinking, the wearing of hoodies, gun restrictions and sink schools all featuring prominently. Since the 1960s when the education system was said to be responding to a crisis in relation to growing numbers of immigrant children in the classroom, institutional racism in its various forms has been blamed for the systematic and consistent failure of Britain's education provision to address the issue of underachievement. Activists within black communities became increasingly vocal in the 1970s, spurring the government to set up its inquiry chaired by Lord Rampton, who noted that: 'Whilst we cannot accept that racism alone accounts for the underachievement of West Indian children, we believe that taken together with negative teacher attitudes and an inappropriate curriculum, racism does play a major part in their underachievement' (DES, 1981).

black pupils' expectations and experiences of schooling

There are many factors that contribute to underachievement as experienced by black pupils. They include the lack of recreational options, high levels of unemployment in the family and poor housing (Modood and Berthoud, 1997), other material deprivation (Modood, 1994; Gillborn and Gipps, 1996), and experiences of racism in wider society (Maughan and Dunn 1988). However, the mismatch between the expectations and experiences of black pupils compounds the entire underachievement debate. Parents from the Indian subcontinent who were educated in English, usually in larger teaching rooms and with the utmost respect for their teacher in a culture that valued discipline, found clear areas of difference in their children's schooling. The 'migrant effect' did not anticipate such lowering of expectations in terms of educational provision. Eade (1995) concluded that parental lack of knowledge about the systems in place might also be a factor in the mismatch experience. Among African-Caribbean pupils the raising of aspirations aimed to combat notions of cultural inadequacy rooted in patterns of disaffection. Coard's (1971) report, *Why the West Indian child is made educationally sub-normal in the British school system*, was endorsed by Swann (DES, 1985): 'Research evidence and our own findings have indicated that the stereotypes teachers tend to have of West Indian children are often particular and generally negative, expectations of academic performance.'

African-Caribbean pupils continue to bear the brunt of concerns about underachievement. A recent review of inner London LEAs concluded that African-Caribbean pupils were the lowest achieving ethnic group, with an average of 22 per cent achieving five GCSEs at grades A*–C, compared with the national average of 46 per cent. In 2002, when the national average achieving five GCSEs grades A*–C was 51 per cent, African-Caribbean pupils were yet again the lowest achieving ethnic group with 30 per cent. Follow-up inspection visits to the LEAs involved in the sample study uncovered a sense of helplessness regarding strategies to raise the achievement of black boys.

Sewell (1997) attempted to demystify the issue, reporting that 'underachievement is strangely decontextualised from wider societal issues such as negative media representations and poverty'. Sewell explored many factors that have exacerbated the dilemma of underachievement, including violent and anti-school masculine culture, the absence of male role models in the classroom, challenging behaviour patterns and the mismatch of masculinity as a process of socialisation linked directly to academic underachievement. For some boys, masculinity means 'hardness', antagonism to school-based learning, sporting prowess and fashion. However, this cannot be interpreted as a standard for all, which is the immediate danger when considering the power of media stereotypes.

Successive studies have also noted *inter alia* low teacher expectations, inappropriate and inconsistent discipline systems leading to increased incidents of disruption and exclusion, misunderstanding about black identity and expressions of culture, lack of role models, the impact of institutional racism in society as a whole and the comprehensive failure of LEAs to embrace inclusion and diversity (Saunders, 1996).

Educationalists in America have reported a similar linked pattern of black boys and underachievement in external examinations, with higher exclusion rates and labelling as the lowest-achieving ethnic group, markedly in comparison with bilingual Latino students. Research has offered a range of possible explanations, including differences in cognitive abilities, aversion to intellectual competition, genetic difference (Hernstein and Murray, 1994), economic disadvantage and manifestations of racism in society. A comparative 'whiteness study' has had limited impact in Britain. 'Whiteness', it was argued, should be considered not as a biological fact but as a social construction, encouraging white teachers to explore how their ethnicity impacts on their work (Pearce, 2003). As with the American research into black underachievement, the ultimate aim of this study was to ensure equality of educational provision for all. Fundamentally, the impact of negative stereotyping and the lack of cultural identification with the system of schooling (and indeed the curriculum) are considered the most powerful of those socio-cultural factors that have contributed to the consistent disaffection and thus underachievement of black boys in American schools (Katz, 1993). American approaches include the successful mass recruitment of black teachers with international teaching qualifications and the delivery of training on black culture in all schools as two initiatives to attempt to understand the 'gangsta' street culture. Ethnic minority teachers made up only 7.4 per cent of London's teaching cohort, whereas ethnic minority pupils made up 43.5 per cent of the total school population. This has prompted some commentators to note that this is unacceptable in the twenty-first century school (Education Commission, 2004).

Pause for thought | cultural racism – a new phenomenon

Multicultural education policies combined with antiracist education policies are now charged with addressing an evolving phenomenon. Identified as 'cultural racism', the emergence of this development is illustrated in the rise of 'Islamophobia' since the Twin Towers disaster in New York in 2001. The classifying of a cultural group prompted Gilroy (1992) to conclude that such 'a form of cultural racism, which has taken a necessary distance from the crude ideas of biological inferiority now seeks to present an imaginary definition of the nation as a unified cultural community'.

Cultural racism may suggest that ethnic groups have a very defined culture that is distinct and easily identifiable. What evidence can you find to support cultural racism in the media? Which other groups are subject to this emerging racialised identification theory? Could it be argued that globalisation challenges such notions of ethnic identification? What should be the response of educationalists to the rise of Islamophobia? Consider the guidance given by the teaching unions, for example the National Union of Teachers (NUT) and the National Association of Schoolmasters and Union of Women Teachers (NASUWT), in response to incidents of 'Islamophobia' in schools. Can multicultural and antiracist education policies have been effective in countering ethnic stereotyping?

Summary and conclusions

This chapter has considered historic government strategies to embrace difference and has reviewed their relative success rates. The ways in which race impacts on language, deciding who belongs and who does not, has added to the notions of identity. In addition, the focus on achievement and attainment in this era of heightened concern around league tables has confirmed the need to celebrate diversity and acknowledge individual needs, in order to promote high aspirations and challenge deeply help stereotypical assumptions.

The contemporary debate around 'race' and education attempts to address the historic 'island race' notion associated with being British. Socio-political debates since the 1990s have explored what it means to be British. Not surprisingly, second- and third-generation immigrants are experiencing their own journeys of discovery, illustrating the complexity and at times controversy of the very nature of the debate. New ethnicities, identities and cultures are a common feature of every town and city, and education policy and governmental initiatives in education need continually to bear this firmly in mind.

References

Alleyne, B (2002) An idea of community and its discontents: towards a more reflexive sense of belonging in multicultural Britain. *Ethnic and Racial Studies*, 25: 607–27.

Cantle, E (2001) *Community Cohesion: a report of the Independent Review Team* (the Cantle Report). London: Home Office.

Coard, B (1971) *How the West Indian child is made educationally sub-normal in the British school system*. London: New Beacon Books.

Cohen, P (1989) *Tackling common sense racism*. University of London: Institute of Education, Centre for Multicultural Education.

Cummins, J (2001) Cultural and linguistic diversity in education: a mainstream issue? *Educational Review*, 49(2): 105–14.

DES (1981) *West Indian Children in Our Schools* (the Rampton Report). London: HMSO/Department of Education and Science.

DES (1985) *Education for All: report of the Committee of Inquiry into the Education of Children from Ethnic Minority Groups* (the Swann Report). Cmnd 9453. London: HMSO/ Department of Education and Science.

Eade, J (1995) *Routes and beyond: voices from educationally successful Bangladeshis*. London: Centre for Bangladeshi Studies.

Education Commission (2004) *Educational experiences and achievements of black boys in London schools, 2000–2003*. The London Development Agency. Available at **www.lda.gov.uk** (accessed 18 April 2006)

Gaine, C (1995) *Still no problem here*. Stoke on Trent: Trentham.

Gillborn, D and Gipps, C (1996) *Recent research on the achievement of ethnic minority pupils*. London: OFSTED/Institute of Education.

Gillborn, D and Mirza, HS (2000) *Inequality*. London: OFSTED.

Gilroy, P (1992) The end of anti-racism, in Donald, J and Rattansi, A (eds) *Race, culture and difference*. London: Sage.

Hernstein, R and Murray, C (1994) *The bell curve: intelligence and class structure in American life*. New York: Free Press.

Katz, M (1993) *The urban underclass*. Princeton, NJ: Princeton University Press.

Kundnani, A (2001) From Oldham to Bradford: the violence of the violated. *Race and Class*, 43(2): 105–31.

MacPherson, W (1999) *The Stephen Lawrence Inquiry*. Cm 4262-I. London: The Stationery Office.

Maughan, B and Dunn, G (1988) Black pupils' progress in secondary school, in Verma, G and Pumfrey, P (eds) *Educational attainments: issues and outcomes in multicultural education*. London: Falmer Press.

Modood, T (1994) *Not easy being British*. London: Runnymede Trust.

Modood, T and Berthoud, R (1997) *Ethnic minorities in Britain*. London: Policy Studies Institute.

Ousley, H (2001) *The Bradford District Race Review*. Bradford: Bradford Vision.

Parekh, B (2000) *The future of multi-ethnic Britain – the Parekh Report*. London: Profile Books.

Pearce, S (2003) Compiling the white inventory: the practice of whiteness in a British primary school, *Cambridge Journal of Education*, 33(2): 62–9.

Powell, T and Schwartz, B (2003) The struggle to define academic multiculturalism. *Cultural Critique*, 55: 152–81.

Sarup, M (1991) *Education and the ideologies of racism*. Stoke on Trent: Trentham.

Saunders, P (1996) A British bell curve? *Sociology Review*, (6)2: 81–8.

Sewell, T (1997) *Black masculinities and schooling*. Stoke on Trent: Trentham.

Troyna, B (1984) Fact or artefact? The 'educational underachievement' of black pupils. *British Journal of Sociology of Education*, 5(2): 153–66.

Troyna, B. and Hatcher, R. (1992) *Racism in children's lives*. London: Routledge.

Troyna, B and Williams, J (1996) *Racism, education and the state*. London: Croom Helm.

Wright, C (1992) *Race relations in the primary school*. London: David Fulton.

Chapter *17*

From special needs to inclusive education

Carol Smith

Introduction

All students of Education Studies bring their own experiences of special needs and learning difficulties to their studies, whether through setbacks they themselves have experienced or through learning alongside peers with a diversity of needs. Few of us have entered higher education without experiencing reverses in learning at some point in our compulsory schooling, perhaps with quadratic equations or with coordination when attempting the triple jump in athletics. So, the accompanying feelings of frustration and low self-esteem are familiar to all, but especially to those who find difficulty in accessing the curriculum daily. When analysing policies and practice for including young people with learning difficulties in the education system, it is essential to draw on this personal experience to evaluate provision critically and consider how issues could be resolved. This chapter reviews developments in provision for pupils and students with special educational needs (SEN) in England and Wales, focusing on the period from the late 1970s onwards, as this has been a time of rapid change. It is important to consider the historical perspective in order to understand the rationale behind the change in emphasis from SEN provision to inclusive education and particularly the models and discourses underpinning these developments. The chapter also examines current provision and discusses critically a range of issues which impact on this provision and which may also influence future developments towards inclusion.

The historical perspective: from 1870 to 1970

From 1870 elementary education became compulsory for all children. However, its provision did not account for children who, for a variety of reasons, were considered ineducable or difficult to educate. The provision of schooling for young people with physical or sensory disabilities developed gradually, and may have been hampered by the system of 'payment by results', by which teachers' wages were determined by the results of tests in the basic subjects. If children with disabilities were likely to lower these results there was no incentive for teachers to include them in their classes or schools. Young people with more severe learning disabilities were labelled as 'idiots' or 'imbeciles', deemed ineducable and therefore considered unfit to be included within the education system, while the 'feeble-minded' were considered to have sufficient ability to benefit from attendance at a special school. The assessment and diagnosis of such people was the responsibility of the medical profession and so a medical discourse evolved, not only to discuss those who were ineducable but also anyone who had a disability or learning difficulty. Therefore a medical model of disability, where the problem was seen to be within the individual, prevailed until the latter half of the twentieth century.

> *Pause for thought* | to what extent does the medical model still influence attitudes towards disability?
>
> The medical (or clinical) model of disability is a product of the nineteenth and early twentieth centuries, but how does it influence our thoughts and language today? In the above paragraph the term 'assessment and diagnosis' was used. Perhaps 'assessment and provision' would have been preferable in an educational context! Support assistants sometimes speak of a child they 'look after', rather than 'support'. Concern is expressed that certain young people will not cope in the school environment because of a physical disability and that they should have the advantage of a special setting, offering them 'the care they need'. Such thoughts and terms locate the difficulty that individuals experience in school within themselves. It is a deficit model. Take a few minutes to reflect about things you have said, or heard, that suggest individuals' inabilities to participate in school or society are because of a deficit within themselves.

Although the 1914 Elementary Education (Defective and Epileptic) Act legislated that local education authorities (LEAs) must provide for these categories of children, and successive legislation made their education compulsory, the move towards provision of compulsory schooling progressed slowly, and continued to be underpinned by a medical and deficit model. Not until 30 years later were *defective* children removed from medical care and into education, frequently but not exclusively in special schools. However, the health authorities retained the responsibility for individuals who were deemed ineducable until legislation in 1970 acknowledged all children's rights to receive an education and the label was abolished.

From 1970 to the new millennium: a shift away from deficit models

If the previous 100 years had seen slow progress in the educational provision for individuals who were considered difficult to teach, these three decades provide a marked contrast as changes in provision became radical and extensive. Human rights movements, at a national and international level, championed the rights of all children and adults to be fully included in society. The disabling barriers created by society, rather than disability, were seen as main causal factors in their marginalisation or exclusion. Legislation has promoted equal opportunities in society and in education. Yet it is important to recognise 'the tensions created between a public rhetoric of equal opportunities and activated government policies which in all areas of public life are deepening inequalities rather than reducing them' (Armstrong et al, 2000).

The Warnock Report (1978) was the first response to dissatisfaction with the education of individuals who were 'handicapped', 'maladjusted' or 'educationally subnormal'. The majority were being educated in day or residential special schools and therefore segregated from their community. A key finding of the Warnock Committee underpinning recommendations in the subsequent report was the anger felt by young people on being isolated from their local community by segregated schooling, a sense of separation which was compounded on leaving school. The main recommendations of the report, identified by Armstrong (1998) were:

- **the abolition of previously used categories in favour of pupils' special educational needs (SEN) being described using educational rather than medical criteria;**
- **recognition that up to 18 per cent of pupils in mainstream schools experience difficulties in learning because of SEN;**
- **that more emphasis should be placed on multi-professional assessment and on parents' involvement in decision-making about their children;**
- **that assessment and provision should be extended to include pre-school children;**
- **that provision should be extended to include the needs of young people in further education.**

A further recommendation was that, wherever possible, pupils with SEN should be educated in mainstream settings. The 1981 Education Act contained many of the recommendations of the report. However, within the teaching profession it was frequently referred to as 'Warnock without resources'. The downturn in the economy and lack of funds to support implementation of the recommendations resulted in 'patchy' integration of pupils into mainstream settings. Nevertheless, the recommendations have influenced subsequent legislation and continue to be strongly reflected in policy-making.

While the aim of the Warnock Report was to remove all but a minority of pupils from segregated settings, discourse revolved around 'integration' rather than 'inclusion'. Unfortunately, these terms are frequently used synonymously in educational discussion. However, integrating individuals into mainstream settings implies their readiness and willingness to change in order to fit into the setting. Three main types of integration were identified by Warnock:

- **locational integration, where pupils are located in a special class or unit, but on the same site as a mainstream school;**
- **social integration, where pupils are again located in a special class or unit on the same site as a mainstream school, but where they are also given the opportunity to socialise with mainstream pupils, perhaps at break or by eating together at lunch-time;**
- **functional integration, where pupils with SEN are taught for part, or all, of the timetable in mainstream classes.**

> *Pause for thought* | are functional integration and inclusion the same?
>
> Functional integration is often confused with inclusion. But are individuals necessarily fully included if they are being taught in a mainstream classroom alongside individuals who do not experience any difficulties in accessing the curriculum? Think of a classroom you have spent time in recently, either in the role of teacher (in its widest interpretation) or learner. Were all pupils equally included and able to share the same experiences? Were pupils with special needs supported in a separate area of the classroom, or were they receiving support alongside and engaging with peers who were not experiencing learning difficulties? Did some pupils choose not to be fully included in the activities or tasks? What do you think was the impact of the level of inclusion or functional integration on the individuals' self-esteem or sense of belonging in the different situations? Is it possible, or in the best interests of all learners, for full inclusion to take place all of the time?

The post-Warnock period has continued to be one of considerable change. The human rights discourse has influenced policy on inclusion. Government legislation has created tensions between a commitment to inclusion and the problems this brings because of the introduction of market forces into the education system. In order to avoid confusion over the use of the term 'inclusion' it must be pointed out that, at the level of government policy-making and legislation, inclusion refers to being included in a mainstream, as opposed to a segregated, setting. To teachers, it can refer to the degree of in-class inclusion. However, the term is frequently used in close proximity in both contexts in discussion.

Two key documents promoting the rights of the child to equal opportunities and inclusion in mainstream education are the UN Convention on the Rights of the Child (United Nations, 1989) and the Salamanca Statement (UNESCO, 1994). The latter was agreed by representatives of 92 governments, of which the UK was one, and 25 international organisations at the World Conference on Special Needs Education at Salamanca in Spain. Lindsay (2003) saw the 'moral imperatives' in the statement as deriving from 'an assertion that children's characteristics, interests, abilities and learning needs are unique to each child and collectively diverse' and that regular schools are the most effective form of provision. And, with regard to governments' responsibilities, Rustemier (2002) stated that:

> *These international human rights texts are not simply guidelines but place obligations on governments to reform education. One of the main strengths of a human rights approach to education is the recognition that the rights of children and young people to enjoy inclusive education are accompanied by the responsibilities of governments to provide it.* (p10)

Successive UK government legislation acknowledged the rights of all children and young people to an inclusive education. The Education Reform Act 1988 introduced a National Curriculum for all children. This development affirmed children's rights to receive a curriculum that was broad and balanced, and also differentiated to accommodate their needs. However, levels of attainment linked to age were introduced, with testing at the end of key stages to measure a school's success. This had an adverse effect on the willingness of mainstream schools to include those who would find it difficult to achieve.

Meanwhile, the Special Needs Code of Practice (DfEE, 1994) provided guidance to schools to support inclusion. This identified eight areas of SEN:

- **learning difficulties;**
- **specific learning difficulties (e.g. dyslexia);**
- **emotional and behavioural difficulties;**
- **physical disabilities;**
- **sensory impairment (visual);**
- **sensory impairment (hearing);**
- **speech and language difficulties;**
- **medical conditions.**

This was accompanied by a five-stage approach to identification and assessment of need, with differentiation of work and monitoring by teaching staff as the first stage and the use of an Individual Education Plan (IEP) from stage two. Later stages included the involvement of outside agencies and finally a Statement of Need outlining provision. It was recommended that IEPs could have a varying number of targets and should be reviewed at least every six months.

Mittler (2000) described the Code of Practice as a 'landmark document' as it promoted inclusion 'by setting out as clearly as possible the principle that all schools and all teachers, without exception, are responsible for the teaching of all children' and that schools are responsible for adapting provision to meet the needs of all individuals. The Code also reflected the social model of disability, locating difficulties encountered by individuals with SEN within society. If barriers created by society and schools were removed, this would improve access to the setting and the curriculum. This was the first time such structured provision had been required and teachers found their workload increased considerably with additional paperwork, while also lacking confidence and expertise in writing IEPs.

To overcome initial difficulties and criticism and to meet the requirements of the Special Needs and Disability Act 2001, a new SEN Code of Practice (DfES, 2001) was introduced into schools in 2002. This attempted to reduce bureaucracy through the reduction of the number of areas of SEN and also the number of stages of intervention. The eight areas of SEN had been reduced to four:

- **communication and interaction;**
- **cognition and learning;**
- **behavioural, emotional and social development;**
- **sensory and/or physical.**

However, a comparison with the areas of need in 1994 shows that categories have been combined, while the same range of need is still included. The three-stage approach of this later Code is clearer, with:

- **School Action (Early Years Action for the Foundation Stage) is provided by the school with support from the Special Needs Coordinator (SENCO);**
- **School (or Early Years) Action Plus involving outside agencies (e.g. the educational psychology service);**
- **Statemented provision.**

Clearer guidance was provided to support the writing of IEPs. No more than three or four short-term and achievable targets now needed to be set, but teaching strategies and resources should be identified and success or exit criteria stated. It now became a requirement that IEPs must be reviewed at least every six months, but preferably every term.

While this clarified teachers' responsibilities, of more significance was the strengthening of the rights of pupils and parents to be involved in any decision-making about their provision. So, parents and children had the right to be involved in target-setting and the reviews to assess the extent to which targets had been met, and in any other decision-making regarding their provision. Research (Armstrong and Galloway, 1992; Brown, 1999) has shown that parents often experience difficulty in making their voices heard. While professionals might listen, parents frequently express concern as to whether their views are taken seriously. In discussing parents' role in the assessment that forms part of the statementing process, Armstrong and Galloway (1992) found that 'many parents felt that their own contribution to the assessment was only taken seriously when it supported what the professionals were saying'. In illustration of the complexities involved, an interesting situation arose with a parent who was also a wheelchair user. She found that with increased school security it was more difficult to make appointments and then obtain entry to the school if a responsible adult was not available to unlock the main door. Her difficulty was further compounded by being in her wheelchair and unable to reach the buzzer.

If parents find it difficult to make their voices heard, it must be more difficult for children, and especially young children with learning difficulties. Yet, pupils can participate in decision-making at two levels. They can contribute to decisions about the effectiveness of their own provision. ('I need more time to change for PE so perhaps I could come in from break a few minutes earlier'; 'Because I'm left-handed it would be better if I sat …'). However, individuals need to be taught how to contribute by developing an understanding of how they learn. Without this understanding they are likely to focus on their own difficulties rather than social barriers. Quicke (2003) expresses some concern about participation in review meetings, where he sees a danger in individuals being asked 'to collude in their own negative labelling'. But pupils can also participate in decision-making at a wider level and thus influence school policy.

Pause for thought | pupils making a difference

In higher education all students have the opportunity to influence practice and initiate change. This could be by articulating their views to staff at an individual level, constructive suggestions in module reviews, Student Union representation on committees (e.g. Equal Opportunities Committee) and representation on programme committees. How can pupils in early years, primary and secondary schools make their voices heard and thus make a positive contribution to developing an inclusive setting?

Booth (1999) has defined inclusion as 'the process of increasing the participation of learners in and reducing their exclusion from the curricula, cultures and communities of neighbourhood mainstream centres of learning'. If learners are not given the opportunity to express what they believe prevents or could facilitate their full inclusion, how can this be achieved?

Research box

listening to young people who have been marginalised

Rose and Shevlin (2004), along with a team of researchers from the UK and the Republic of Ireland, attempted to find out the extent to which young people from marginalised groups, such as minority ethnic groups, young people with disabilities, members of gypsy traveller groups and refugees, had been included in educational settings. They wanted them to relate their experiences in order to 'inform teachers and education policy makers about the steps which may be taken to enable the inclusion agenda to be more thoroughly addressed'. Part of their rationale was a concern that, despite claims of substantial progress in young people's views being recognised, the reality is that their voices frequently go unheard, as it is assumed that immaturity and a lack of competence would prevent them from participating successfully in decision-making. The project's findings were that physical access was still an issue for those with disabilities, and, to a certain degree, access to the curriculum. Negative peer attitudes and low teacher expectations were also mentioned. It also emerged that 'students were expected to assimilate and adapt to mainstream norms'. The research concluded that professionals can still learn from the experiences and opinions of young people, and that as well as listening, must act on their views, removing obstacles to inclusion that still exist within education.

In addition to the Special Needs Code of Practice (DfES, 2001), a Disability Code of Practice (Disability Rights Commission, 2002) was introduced to support the implementation of Part 4 of the Disability Discrimination Act (DDA), which placed new obligations on education providers. Riddell (2003) described these as being:

- **not to treat disabled pupils/prospective pupils less favourably;**
- **to make reasonable adjustments to avoid putting disabled pupils at a substantial disadvantage.**

'Reasonable adjustments' does not include the provision of auxiliary aids and services, because these would be provided by other support services, or the duty to make alterations to the physical features of the school. Nonetheless, the vagueness of the term, and indeed of the term 'less favourably', gives rise to concern that providers could unwittingly act illegally, as only through the build-up of case law will these terms be clarified. However, as with the SEN Code of Practice, the Disability Code reflects the social model of disability in that it seeks to ensure that barriers to inclusion are removed.

Promoting exclusion

Despite the commitment of recent legislation and policy to the ideal of inclusion, its success in breaking down barriers and its potential to continue developments towards inclusion for many years to come, it is interesting that the same legislation has, in many ways, created exclusionary pressures for some. Issues that are raised are:

- **is the social model of disability adequate for our understanding of the needs of and pressures on all people with disabilities?**
- **do the National Curriculum and the ways in which it is provided exclude certain groups who have special needs or who are on the margins of society?**
- **does the effect of market forces exclude those who are less able?**

Crow (1996), a disabled feminist activist, has applauded the success of the social model of disability in enabling people with disabilities to overcome exclusion and discrimination, suggesting that its contribution, 'now and in the future, to achieving equal rights for disabled people is incalculable'. So influential is this model, however, that Crow has also suggested we are at risk of overlooking the impact of impairment on the lives of those with disabilities. While social barriers can be removed, pain or fatigue cannot. Fears for the future are both different and greater for many disabled people. Yet she states that, because of this predominant model of disability, discussion of these is 'taboo'. Swain and French (2000) have concluded that a model, which they call an 'affirmation model', is emerging by building on the social model. This too acknowledges the presence of impairment, but focuses on 'the positive experiences and identity of disabled people from being impaired and disabled'.

The National Curriculum was promoted as an entitlement curriculum for all children. It applies to special schools as well as mainstream settings. Because of this it can be said to be promoting equal opportunities. However, it was also established in order to raise standards in education, both in primary and secondary settings. To this end, it introduced attainment targets and level descriptors, and linked these to age. Furthermore, Standardised Assessment Tasks (SATs now Standard Assessment Tests) were also created to measure achievement in English, mathematics and science at the end of Key Stages 1 and 2 in primary schools and Key Stage 3 in secondary schools, with GCSEs being the mode of assessment at the end of Key Stage 4. While this curricular framework was welcomed, the pressures of 'delivering' the National Curriculum and enabling pupils to achieve the appropriate levels often led to less flexible styles of teaching and a focus on more whole-class teaching. And, although there was government acknowledgement that not all children would achieve the intended levels, there was also an assumption that teachers would teach with a view to all children achieving (Swann, 1992). With schools being encouraged to move towards more flexible approaches again in their teaching styles, the problems experienced by children with special needs, such as coping with the demands placed on concentration by whole-class teaching and the frustration of copious written recording, may be reduced. However 'curricula have always been a means of exclusion' (Clough, 1998) and frustration in finding it difficult to cope with the curriculum, or in understanding its relevance, leads to exclusion through withdrawal and avoidance strategies, truancy or enforced exclusion as a result of disaffection and anti-social behaviour.

This question, of course, is again related to the pressures of the National Curriculum and testing. However the emphasis here is on the publication of results. School performance data based on National Tests (SATs) and GCSE results is available to parents, and many wish to send their children to a school which achieves exemplary results. This has led to pressures on schools to achieve good results in order to compete for pupils with other schools. This 'marketisation' of education is particularly important at a time when numbers on roll are falling, but is seen as detrimental to the inclusion of some children with SEN (Barton, 1995; Ballard, 1999; Armstrong et al, 2000). The process can exclude children with special needs in two distinct ways. The first, as we have seen, is by the approach taken to delivering the curriculum in order that schools can achieve good results, which may be inappropriate for many pupils. The second is in mainstream schools' reluctance to accept children from special schools who may adversely affect their positions in the league tables. Stobbs describes the publication of league tables as 'one of the features of current educational policy that most frustrates and undermines a ready welcome and the development of appropriate provision' (cited in Pyke, 2003). Not until school effectiveness is measured only in terms of value-addedness, where success is calculated on how far individuals have progressed from a base-line assessment, will these exclusionary pressures be overcome.

Future directions

In the past, strategies to support pupils with SEN have been reactive rather than proactive. Initiatives have been directed towards providing for those who have difficulties rather than aiming to prevent them. The influence of the social model has encouraged the removal of barriers to access, and policy has become more proactive in that, often, barriers are no longer there to be taken down. However, there is a need for early intervention, and for support agencies to work together, to ensure that all children achieve their potential. This proactive approach, particularly in areas of high social deprivation, would reduce the need for intervention as a reaction to problems.

In Scotland, services work together through Integrated Community Schools to provide for the needs of pupils through an integrated approach involving teachers, social workers and health professionals (Tett, 2005). This approach is less well developed in England, but can be seen in early intervention programmes such as Sure Start, where not only young children but also their families receive support. Early intervention can support the early identification of and provision for needs, and this may then lessen their impact at a later date. However, the expansion of such schemes depends for its effectiveness on support with adequate resources.

Summary and conclusions

Provision for pupils with SEN has developed from segregated schooling, where a medical model of disability underpinning provision located the problems within the individual. The past 30 years of the twentieth century witnessed a move first of all towards integrating individuals with special needs within mainstream settings and then to encouraging their inclusion in mainstream classes. These changes were driven by local and international human rights movements and also by the recognition that many barriers to inclusion were created by society and, if removed, would increase the degree of access for people with a variety of difficulties. This recognition reflects the social model of disability. However, this model is now criticised as not going far enough.

While much emphasis is placed upon the inclusion of individuals with SEN it is important to stress that inclusion goes further and includes all marginalised groups in society. Concerns have been expressed that policy aimed at promoting inclusion in education can also be exclusionary and that future policy should look towards lessening the disadvantage that excludes individuals from accessing and achieving their potential in education.

However, inclusion is about more than compulsory schooling. If a society is to be promoted where all groups, regardless of ability, ethnicity, faith or culture are to be given equal opportunities, their differences must also be accepted and celebrated. In inclusive schools we see this acceptance and celebration of diversity in the curriculum and the ethos of the setting. In such settings children are able to develop confidence and self-esteem. While there is still a long way to go in the education system as a whole to create such enabling cultures, it is only by doing so that a tolerant and inclusive society will evolve.

References

Armstrong, D (1998) Changing faces, changing places: policy routes to inclusion, in: Clough, P (ed) *Managing inclusive education: from policy to experience*. London: Chapman.

Armstrong, D and Galloway, D (1992) On being a client: conflicting perspectives on assessment, in Booth, T, Swann, W, Masterton, M and Potts, P. (eds) *Policies for diversity in education*. London: Routledge.

Armstrong, F, Armstrong, D and Barton, L (2000) *Inclusive education: policy, contexts and comparative perspectives*. London: Fulton.

Ballard, K (ed) (1999) *Inclusive education: international voices on disability and justice*. London: Falmer.

Barton, L (1995) The politics of Learning for All, in Nind, M, Rix, J, Sheehy, K and Simmons, K (eds) (2003) *Inclusive education: diverse perspectives*. London: Fulton.

Booth, T (1999) Viewing inclusion from a distance: gaining perspectives from comparative study, in Nind, M, Rix, J, Sheehy, K and Simmons, K (eds) (2003) *Inclusive education: diverse perspectives*. London: Fulton.

Brown, C (1999) Parents' voices on advocacy, education, disability and justice, in Ballard, K (ed) *Inclusive education: international voices on disability and justice*. London: Falmer.

Clough, P (1998) *Managing inclusive education: from policy to experience*. London: Chapman.

Crow, L (1996) Including all of our lives: renewing the social model of disability, in Nind, M, Rix, J, Sheehy, K and Simmons, K (eds) (2003) *Inclusive education: diverse perspectives*. London: Fulton.

DfEE (1994) *Code of Practice on the Identification and Assessment of Special Educational Needs*. London: HMSO/Department for Education and Employment.

DfES (2001) *Code of Practice on the Identification and Assessment of Children with Special Educational Needs*. London: HMSO/Department for Education and Skills.

Disability Rights Commission (2002) *Code of Practice for Schools – Disability Discrimination Act 1995; Part 4*. London: DRC.

Education Act 1981. London: HMSO.

Education Reform Act 1988. London: HMSO.

Lindsay, G (2003) Inclusive education: a critical perspective. *British Journal of Special Education*, 30(1): 3–12.

Mittler, P (2000). *Working towards inclusive education: social contexts*. London: Fulton.

Pyke, N (2003) Targets 'unfair' to inclusive schools. *TES Extra for Special Needs*, November.

Quicke, J (2003) Educating the pupil voice. *Support for Learning*, 18(2): 51–7.

Riddell, S. (2003) Devolution and disability equality legislation: the implementation of Part 4 of the Disability Discrimination Act 1995 in England and Scotland. *British Journal of Special Education*, 30(2): 63–9.

Rose, R and Shevlin, M (2004) Encouraging voices: listening to young people who have been marginalised. *Support for Learning*, 19(4): 155–60.

Rustemier, S (2002) *Social and educational justice: the human rights framework for inclusion*. Bristol: CSIE.

Special Educational Needs and Disability Act 2001. London: The Stationery Office.

Swain, J and French, S (2000) Towards an affirmation model of disability, in Nind, M, Rix, J, Sheehy, K and Simmons, K (eds) (2003) *Inclusive education: diverse perspectives*. London: Fulton.

Swann, W (1992) Hardening the hierarchies: the National Curriculum as a system of classification, in Booth, T, Swann, W, Masterton, M, and Potts, P (eds) *Curricula for diversity in education*. London: Routledge.

Tett, L (2005) Inter-agency partnerships and Integrated Community Schools: a Scottish perspective. *Support for Learning*, 20(4): 157–61.

UNESCO (1994) World Conference on Special Educational Needs (Salamanca Statement). Paris: United Nations Educational, Cultural and Scientific Organisation.

United Nations (1989) *Convention on the Rights of the Child*. New York: United Nations.

Warnock, M (1978) *Special Educational Needs: report of the Committee of Enquiry into the Education of Handicapped Children and Young People* (the Warnock Report). London: HMSO.

Chapter 18

Faith in education: what place for faith communities in schools?

Kate Adams and Mark Chater

Introduction

In the British education system there is a long-established but rapidly changing presence of faith communities in schools, manifested not only in multi-faith classrooms, but also in chaplaincy support, church presence on governing bodies, publicly funded church schools, more recently established Islamic schools and very recently-founded City Academies based on Christian principles. This chapter aims to enable readers to pose and explore questions about that presence and how it impacts on pupils, classroom teachers and other educational professionals. This is an important area of knowledge for teachers and students who may work in faith schools or multi-faith schools, or who may collaborate with them in clusters. It is also important for educators in other sectors who engage with members of faith communities.

Religion in education: a historical overview

For a very long time, religious organisations and individuals have paid attention to education and involved themselves in it. They transmit their religious teachings to the young; they advise parents on raising their children; they use places of worship as sites to nurture and develop faith; they run schools; they campaign and advise on education policies; in the UK, churches and other religious groups run schools in the state sector, and business leaders with a personal religious commitment are investing in new Academies. Why all this effort? What is in it for the faith communities, and what is the nature of the evolving relationship between religious faith and education processes? This section will summarise the historical interdependence in the west between pedagogical processes and the Jewish, Christian and Muslim systems of theology. It will show how deeply faith and education are intertwined, and will raise issues about the effects – positive and otherwise – that this mutual involvement can have.

The Jewish, Christian and Muslim traditions, known as the Abrahamic religions, spring from a common ancestral root in the Middle East and have all had major impact on the western European intellectual tradition. Despite their significant differences in theology, the three traditions face some challenges in common: how to express their faith content in intellectual terms; how to communicate their faith to children; how to adjust to a religiously diverse world; and how to respond to a society that is secularising (i.e. losing its explicit commitment to worship, belief and moral norms determined by faith). These four challenges remain paramount for today's followers of Judaism, Christianity and Islam in the UK. While other major faith traditions, such as Hinduism, Buddhism and Sikhism, also have significant communities in the UK, their historical presence in the west is more recent, and therefore has had less long-term impact.

A shared belief in God as creator, law-giver and Lord has common educational implications for Jews, Christians and Muslims:

- **that there are things about God that children and young people need to be taught;**
- **that parents and religious authorities should collaborate to do the teaching;**
- **that growing up in the world involves discovering God's will and obeying it as best one can;**
- **that God can be discovered through the ordinary things of life, such as intellectual study, friendship and nature, as well as through doctrinal and moral precepts.**

Religions have grappled with these issues throughout their history and have generally been at their most educationally creative at times of the most intense theological change. When theology was relatively static, teaching was a matter of routine. When theology was in crisis or changing rapidly, as during the adjustment to scientific modernity of the nineteenth and twentieth centuries, teaching methods would become more intense and innovative (Westerhoff, 1981).

The religions' interest in education grapples with two conflicting and, at times, irreconcilable priorities. The first is their belief that God is revealed in the ordinary; the second is that God is obscured in the ordinary. The implication of the first priority, when considered educationally, is that whenever we educate children about this world we are, implicitly, helping them to discover ultimate meaning. Therefore education is a good thing in itself. But the implication of the second priority is that an ordinary secular education on its own is not sufficient, and that religious and moral issues must be taught explicitly. Therefore education is only a qualified good, and can be harmful.

The first of those two views may be seen as the more positive towards education, and examples are found historically in all three traditions, which have at various times developed models of education designed to affirm the ordinary. Judaism looks to Moses Maimonedes, the twelfth-century Spanish-born philosopher who undertook the gigantic task of integrating classical Greek learning with the teachings of the *Torah* (the Jewish law). Contemporary Jewish leaders recognise the need to embrace secular learning and to be in dialogue with it, even where they disagree (Neuberger, 1997). In Christianity, early theologians, including St Paul and St Augustine, saw themselves as practitioners of education, teaching through culture and experience (1 Corinthians 9: 20–23). Augustine advocated a learner-centred approach (Howie, 1969). Later Christian educators adopted prototypes of differentiation (Jungmann, 1959) and models of child-centred, pluralist learning (Gallagher, 1988). The tradition of Islam, in its earliest stages, invented the concept of universities, developed technological and legal learning independently from the Qur'an and, subsequently, gave the west its first translations of Aristotle (Southern, 1953).

The Christian churches, as the majority religion in Britain, had an additional reason to invest in public education during the nineteenth and early twentieth centuries. Opening schools for the poor and middle classes at a time when state provision was limited, became an expression not only of the churches' sense of mission but also of their wider social duty in response to the industrial revolution. In the same period, Anglican, Methodist and Roman Catholic training colleges were established with the purpose of training qualified teachers for church schools. In the twentieth century, as an expanding state legislated to take over schools and teacher training, the churches' share of this work diminished. Church schools and higher education institutions still exist, working within an equal opportunities framework to provide education for all.

The shared insights of these religiously world-affirming educational communities may be summarised as a belief that there is little or no point in requiring children to memorise sacred texts, digest half-understood theological formulae or conform blindly to moral precepts; that such projects, when attempted, have no educational value and no effect on allegiance to faith. Instead, educational methods were developed that ensured independence of spirit and ownership of ideas, and many of these were later adopted by the state sector.

A belief that education is a good in itself has historically led members of these traditions to found schools and to maintain, when they can, schools in the public sector which advocate a religiously infused vision of learning. Learning is seen as a means to bring the whole person (physical, aesthetic, intellectual, social and spiritual) into being. This is a sacred duty in itself (Groome, 1991) and one that has influenced the curriculum, for instance through the development of a values statement (QCA, 1999).

The more negative view, that education is only a qualified good and that forms of education that do not explicitly address the religious dimension are harmful, is also present in all three western religious traditions. It is a view that places faith communities apart from, and in tension with, modern secular education. In the UK, where Judaism and Islam are minority faiths in a society that could be understood as post-Christian, the impulse is sometimes to resist absorption by conserving traditional values through separate religious and moral teaching, where it is available. To some extent, this impulse informs the growing Muslim interest in Islamic schools. However, it would be a mistake to conclude that all British Muslims wish to separate themselves and their children from state education. The reality is more complex. Muslims have both praise and criticism for British education and the society that evolved it, and they have differing response strategies in education, family life and politics (Seddon et al, 2003). Church schools are being re-evaluated by Christian educators, with a view to making them more distinctive (Arthur, 1995). A new breed of City Academies, some sponsored by Christian organisations or individuals, is emerging.

At the same time, educators of several faiths are concerned that the spiritual and moral dimensions of education should not be lost, or become invisible, in a school system that seems to favour skills over personal development. Partly for this reason, an interest in spirituality, as distinct from religious faith, has been seen as a more productive way forward.

The spiritual development of children

The spiritual development of children is firmly on the educational agenda, being an area that teachers must plan for. It is also an area that the Office for Standards in Education (OFSTED) inspects. Yet spirituality – and spirituality within an educational context – is complex and there are underlying conceptual problems. This section explores some of those problems, with a particular emphasis on those that relate to faith communities.

Considering spirituality in the school is important because that is the first educational environment in which all students encounter the theme. However, the notion of whether or not spirituality can actually be taught in contemporary schools is open to question. Castelli and Trevathan (2005) have outlined three major arguments in the conceptualisation of spirituality. The first contends that spirituality can only be taught in the context of a faith tradition (e.g. Thatcher, 1999), while a second point of view suggests that spirituality is innate and thus not dependent upon a faith stance (e.g. Hay and Nye, 1998).

If teachers adopt either of these two stances it will, of course, have major implications for their practice. For example, a Christian teacher who believes that spirituality can only be taught in the context of the Christian tradition is immediately faced with difficulties in the classroom. Even if they are working in a faith-based school, not all of the children will necessarily be from a Christian background. In situations where there is a small number of children with no religious upbringing, teachers will need to be fully aware of their own beliefs, and also not make assumptions about the secular children's ability or inability to be spiritual. This theme is developed further below.

Conversely, a teacher who believes that spirituality is not dependent upon a faith stance may be better placed to ensure the spiritual development of children of all faiths and none. However, they would need to be aware of different religions' conceptions of spirituality, which may contradict their own ideas. Further, there may be conflicts if children or parents from faith traditions believe that spirituality can only be taught from a faith stance.

Guidance for the teacher

Theoretical issues about the definitions of spirituality – more numerous than this section can accommodate – are important because a third view proposes that it is unrealistic to expect schools to ensure children's spiritual development when there is no consensus over its definition (Castelli and Trevathan, 2005). Until now, whilst reading this section, you may have paused to ask yourself what spirituality is, or you may have been quite comfortable with the terminology. At a national level, the definition of spirituality is an important one for educators.

Academics have long searched for a definition relevant to education, resulting in a range of answers and debates. Brown and Furlong (1996) have described spirituality as a 'weasel word: ... a convenient catch-all, suitably vague and elusive of definition'. As Best (2000) has suggested, the greater the attempts to define spirituality, the more elusive a definition becomes. These authors' comments offer little comfort for teachers, who are required to ensure that pupils' spirituality is developed. Before considering practical guidance for teachers, it is worth exploring your own definitions of spirituality.

> *Pause for thought* | what is spirituality?
>
> Consider answers to the following questions, ideally with colleagues: Would you describe yourself as a spiritual person? If not, who do you know of who could be described in this way? How can this spiritual dimension of the person be described to a Martian who has landed on Earth? Discuss these issues with your colleagues and observe the variety of answers that you have collected. Are there common themes? Are there significant differences? How can those differences be accounted for?
>
> Many people throughout history have claimed to have had a spiritual experience. Have you? If so, how would you describe it? What was it that made the experience a *spiritual* one, rather than one which might be described as purely emotional or psychological?

In attempts to clarify the position for teachers, government bodies have published various guidelines. You will need to examine the current definitions and advice for teachers, but below is a selection of characteristics that OFSTED (2004) seeks to identify in pupils:

- **a set of values, principles and beliefs;**
- **an awareness and understanding of their own and others' beliefs;**
- **a respect for themselves and for others;**
- **a sense of empathy with others, concern and compassion;**
- **an increasing ability to reflect and learn from this reflection;**
- **an appreciation of the intangible;**
- **an expressive and/or creative impulse;**
- **an understanding of feelings and emotions, and their likely impact.**

Do these criteria match with the descriptions of spirituality which you offered earlier? If they are different, it is worth you reconsidering why and how the differences have arisen. The fact that differences are probable does not imply that there are right or wrong answers. What is important is that the differences can reveal insights into your own conceptions, some of which you might not have previously articulated.

The concepts of spirituality and spiritual development need further consideration in view of the presence of faith communities within educational settings. Definitions of spirituality are often largely culturally defined, so in a multi-faith classroom there are additional factors of which teachers need to be aware. Given that different religions perceive spirituality in different ways, students may bring their own perceptions into the classroom with them, partly influenced by their own religious upbringing. For example, a Muslim teenager may experience Ramadan, the month of fasting, as a spiritual experience when they feel closest to Allah.

Further, even within what might be termed a multi-faith classroom in a school setting, there will be children who have not had any religious upbringing. Yet, their spiritual development needs to be attended to as well. This can be a daunting task for teachers, but it is important that adults do not make assumptions about children's capabilities to experience or express the spiritual. In particular, adults must not assume that children with no religious upbringing have no capability to express ideas and/or have experiences which other people might define as being religious. It is children's experience of the spiritual that the next section addresses.

Children's spirituality

Alongside the positioning of spirituality in the curriculum runs research into pupils' spirituality. Contemporary research into children's and adolescents' spiritual experience has provided valuable insights into how young people experience this aspect of being human. At times, children describe their spiritual experiences in terms of their religious background. For example: Muslim children have told researchers how Allah communicates with them through dreams, sending them messages in these dreams (Coles, 1990; Adams, 2004).

However, religion is not necessarily a factor in determining spirituality: people can be spiritual without being religious. For example, secular children may have spiritual experiences, such as seeing or sensing a deceased grandparent. Teachers need to be aware of the distinction between religion and spirituality in the classroom and, as Hay and Nye (1998) have observed, need to be able to distinguish between when religious talk is spiritual and when it is not.

Teachers must learn to listen with care to children, without imposing their views upon the interpretation of the children's talk, and without making assumptions about children's ability to be spiritual. Coles (1990) described a conversation with a 10-year-old girl from the Hopi culture, which illustrates this point perfectly. The girl told how she had not answered her teacher's questions on religion, because the teacher was Anglo-Saxon and, the girl feared, might reject her beliefs, or fail to understand them.

Pause for thought | **what are your assumptions about children's spirituality?**

Imagine you are teaching a class of children comprising Christians, Hindus and those of no faith. You are exploring children's responses to the possibility that there may be life after death, seeking not only their ideas, but any justifications that they have for their views.

- List a series of questions that you would ask the children.
- Now, note down your own views about life after death.
- Reflect carefully on how your views have shaped the questions you intend to ask the children.
- Have your questions been influenced by your own beliefs in any way?
- Have your questions been influenced by your assumptions about children's capabilities to have and to express spiritual ideas?
- Have your questions been influenced by a knowledge of Christian, Hindu or other religious and non-religious views about life after death?

However you answered the above questions, a key element to a successful approach will be to maintain an open mind and to create a forum for open enquiry. Children will need to feel that their views and their expressions of the spiritual, whether religious or not, will be respected by their teacher and by their classmates. The teacher has the capability and responsibility to ensure such an ethos: for some teachers with deeply held convictions, this may not be an easy road to travel.

Deeply held convictions about religion can cause problems not only for spiritual development in education but also for much wider issues. The next section explores religious extremism and its relation to state education, before moving on to explore how the difficulties it creates can be eased.

Faith against education: the new religious extremisms and state education

In the world after the terrorist atrocities of 9/11 in America (2001) and 7/7 in London (2005) it is impossible to deny the existence of religious extremism, usually known as fundamentalism, but it also remains difficult to define it adequately. Several forms of fundamentalism are spreading globally, posing a threat to liberal pluralistic state education systems. Two important modifying statements are necessary. First, although extreme religious behaviour is as old as religion itself, fundamentalism is a more recent phenomenon, both a by-product of modernity and a reaction against it. And although fundamentalist groups are growing rapidly in many religions, and tend to attract publicity and attention, they do not represent all that religious traditions have to say, nor are fundamentalists about to 'take over' in any particular religion (Marty and Appleby, 1994; Muslim Council of Britain, 2002).

Research box

what is fundamentalism?

There is no single definition of fundamentalism but there are recurring characteristics that appear across several fundamentalist groups in many different faiths and cultures. For this reason, it is often more accurate to talk of 'fundamentalisms'. From the research available (e.g. Barr, 1977; Ali, 2002; Bendroth, 1993; Marty and Appleby, 1994; Bush, 2001; Muslim Council of Britain, 2002; Victor, 2005) a basic list of characteristics is presented as follows:

- taking a sacred text literally, even if it disagrees with science, history or common sense, e.g. believing in a literal six-day creation story (sometimes called Creationism, or Intelligent Design, a related modern belief), or adopting a non-literal interpretation only when literal meanings become completely untenable;
- resisting democratic, pluralist values such as the free vote, multi-party systems, freedom of speech and freedom of religion – except when these values will aid the advance of their own group, or when a democratic rhetoric can be used to disguise other motives;
- strong, at times violent, opposition to feminism, gender equality and homosexual rights;
- charismatic male leadership in small sects or cults, where the leader is highly respected and cannot be questioned or held to account;
- dualistic thinking, dividing the world into people who are saved or not, righteous or not: the 'either you are with us, or you are with the terrorists' principle;
- in Christian fundamentalist groups, a belief that the world will end violently in a confrontation between good (the west) and evil (Islam), after which Christ will return to earth; at times, a desire to see this destruction come soon, rather than to avert it;
- a willingness to use violence against the innocent, such as bombing, nerve gas or suicide attack, to advance their cause, in defiance of the mainstream teachings of their faith.

It is important to note how hard many religious leaders and educators are working to point out the dangers of fundamentalism within their own communities (El-Affendi, 2001; Sacks, 2002). It is ironic and instructive that fundamentalist groups, though enemies to each other, have so many key characteristics in common, and seem almost to feed off each other's extremisms (Ali, 2002). Our task is to analyse these characteristics for their impact on educational values such as free open enquiry.

At the very least, fundamentalist allegiance sits uncomfortably with any education system that intends to teach values of critical independent thinking, tolerance, commitment to diversity and equality, and democratic participation. In particular, if schools and universities teach specific scientific and technological propositions, such as that life on the planet has evolved, or that there is a gay gene, or that free access to information and entertainment is desirable, this is likely to encounter profound suspicion and opposition. Literacy, when seen as something more than functional and related to the flexible use of interpretive techniques, is implicitly in opposition to any tendency to privilege and protect one sacred text as being above any criticism.

Educational programmes that engage the young in participative democracy, fostering attitudes of acceptance of religious and moral diversity, may be unfairly suspected by fundamentalists of moral weakness or relativism (Finnis, 1991). Fundamentalists batten upon, or simply invent, narratives of declining morality in order to generate moral panics and sway public opinion in favour of conservative policies. Moral panics are often exploited as an expression of wider social or cultural tensions and so can be manipulated (Goode and Ben-Yehuda, 1994). A healthy political education, taking in aspects of history, psychology, religion and technology, offers young people the skills to engage in complex analysis in which crude dualisms of right and wrong have no place; fundamentalist beliefs thrive on such dualism, and effectively require the young to suspend critical thought.

A late modern condition of uncertainty, in which many teachers shy away from explicit advocacy of moral or religious 'truths', creates fluidity and insecurity for young people. Into this vacuum fundamentalism comes, offering a security and certainty apparently based on reason, goodwill and authority.

Pause for thought | what are the implications of fundamentalism for educational policy and practice?

Reflect on the ways in which the education system should respond to fundamentalism. Consider the following options, alongside your own ideas. Accept, reject or amend any of these options, and explain your reasons:

- changing the law on collective worship in schools, so that it does not have to be Christian;
- making it possible to change the science curriculum, so that Intelligent Design can be taught as an alternative to Darwinism;
- restricting the rights of the public to set up a school, so that it becomes harder for extremist groups of any ideology to engage in educational work.

Faith in education: new paradigms for an old relationship

Fundamentalism is not the whole of any religion, but it exists and, like spirituality, is an area that educational professionals need to be informed about, particularly with reference to faith communities. So, while faith and education have a close relationship, there are tensions and the final part of the chapter poses the question: what might be the best way forward to secure an appropriate future for the presence of faith in education?

Whether or not faith schools are justifiable is not the issue under discussion here. This is a major debate which is dealt with elsewhere (see Gardner et al, 2004 for arguments both for and against faith schools). Rather, this chapter's conclusions work on the basis that faith schools exist, and that there are also increasing numbers of multi-faith communities within non-denominational schools and other educational settings.

In all schools, the coverage of religions must go beyond Christianity. In addition, the five other main religions which are represented in Great Britain must also be covered across the Key Stages. These are:

- **Islam;**
- **Judaism;**
- **Buddhism;**
- **Sikhism;**
- **Hinduism.**

For some pupils, teachers and parents, particularly those with a strong commitment to a faith, this may pose difficulties. Naturally, for some (though not all) devout religious people, the process of engaging with different religious beliefs may pose difficulties. Learning about different points of view can be uncomfortable, even painful, perhaps leading to reflection on one's own beliefs which may have been held for a lifetime.

However, the process of becoming a reflective practitioner is fundamental to an educator's job. As Pollard (2002) has written, it is essential that teachers are fully aware of their own identity. Pollard's view encourages teachers to reflect upon different aspects of themselves, including how they appear to others, their values, aims and commitments, and their perceptions of pupils. Given that religious beliefs – in addition to atheistic or agnostic views – form part of a person's identity, it is inevitable that teachers will have to confront other people's views on religion. This can occur in the course of either teaching about religion in a variety of educational settings or in conversations with members of faith communities in other contexts.

Educators seeking to offer a balanced, unbiased view of religion and spirituality in the classroom, must ensure that the fundamentalist tendencies of religion are reduced yet not ignored. Fundamentalist tendencies are best reduced by exposure to open enquiry of the sort that takes place within religious education and spiritual development in schools. For example, effective religious education moves beyond pupils simply learning facts about different religions, to learning from religion also. This latter concept includes pupils reflecting upon their own and others' experiences in light of what they have learnt about religion, and interpreting and evaluating what they have learnt.

Children should be encouraged to:

- **listen to others' views;**
- **reflect on their own views;**
- **engage in debate with others;**
- **respect others' views.**

Exposure to other opinions and beliefs in such an environment of respect could aid a reduction in religions' potentially damaging fundamentalist tendencies. Young people can then take these attitudes and skills into adult life.

Summary and conclusions

This chapter has shown: how the west and Britain have had a close historical relationship between faith and education; how schools need to ensure children's spiritual development; how fundamentalist tendencies in several religions pose a threat to secular education; and how educators can model open critical enquiry in matters of faith and spirituality.

Education has the power to change the potentially damaging fundamentalist tendencies of religions. If teachers in faith schools and non-denominational schools alike are aware of these tendencies and actively encourage open enquiry into them, this should help pupils develop into critical thinkers. By taking a critically reflective approach to views about religion and spirituality, educators can help students make informed judgements. While this process can at times present some with awkward challenges, it can also be a healthy way for the faith presence to raise issues that might not otherwise be given exposure. It is only through open discussion and genuine dialogue in which students and educators hear each other that pertinent issues can be raised and moved forward.

References

Adams, K (2004) Scriptural symbolic dreams: relevant or redundant in the 21st century? *Sleep and Hypnosis: an international journal of sleep, dream and hypnosis*, 6(3): 11–118.

Ali, T (2002) *The clash of the fundamentalisms: crusades, jihads and modernity*. London: Verso.

Arthur, J (1995) *The ebbing tide: policy and principles of Catholic education*. Leominster: Gracewing.

Barr, J (1977) *Fundamentalism*. London: SCM.

Bendroth, M (1993) *Fundamentalism and gender*. New Haven, CT: Yale University Press.

Best, R (2000) (ed) *Education for spiritual, moral, social and cultural development*. London: Continuum.

Brown, A and Furlong, J (1996) *Spiritual development in schools*. London: The National Society.

Bush, G (2001) Address to joint session of congress and the American people. Available at **www.whitehouse.gov/news/releases/2001** (accessed 9 April 2006).

Castelli, M and Trevathan, A (2005) The English public space: developing spirituality in English Muslim schools *The International Journal of Children's Spirituality*, 10(2): 123–31.

Coles, R (1990) *The spiritual life of children*. Boston, MA: Peter Davison.

El-Affendi, A. (2001) (ed) *Rethinking Islam and modernity*. Leicester: Islamic Foundation.

Finnis, J (1991) *Moral absolutes: tradition, revision and truth*. Washington, DC: Catholic University of America Press.

Gallagher, J (1988) *Our schools and our faith*. London: Collins.

Gardner, R, Cairns, J and Lawton, D (2004) *Faith schools: consensus or conflict?* London: Routledge.

Goode, E and Ben-Yehuda, N (1994) *Moral panics: social construction of deviance*. Oxford: Blackwell.

Groome, T (1991) *Sharing faith: the way of shared praxis*. San Francisco: Harper Collins.

Hay, D and Nye, R (1998) *The spirit of the child*. London: Fount.

Howie, G (1969) *Educational theory and practice in St Augustine*. London: Routledge and Kegan Paul.

Jungmann, J (1959) *Handing on the faith*. New York: Herder and Herder.

Marty, M and Appleby, R (1994) *Fundamentalisms observed*. Chicago University Press.

Muslim Council of Britain (2002) *The quest for sanity: reflections on 9/11 and the aftermath*. London: MCB.

Neuberger, J (1997) *On being Jewish*. London: Arrow.

OFSTED (2004) *Promoting and evaluating pupils' spiritual, moral, social and cultural development*. London: OFSTED.

Pollard, A (2002) *Reflective teaching*. London: Continuum.

QCA (1999) *National Curriculum Handbook for primary teachers*. London: Qualifications and Curriculum Authority.

Sacks, J (2002) *The dignity of difference: how to avoid the clash of civilisations*. London: Continuum.

Seddon, M, Hussain, D and Malik, N (2003) *British Muslims: loyalty and belonging*. Leicester: The Islamic Foundation.

Southern, R (1953) *The making of the middle ages*. London: Hutchinson.

Thatcher, A (ed) (1999) *Spirituality and the curriculum*. London: Cassell.

Victor, B (2005) *The last crusade: religion and the politics of misdirection*. London: Constable.

Westerhoff, J (1981) *A faithful church: issues in the history of catechesis*. Wilton, CT: Morehouse Barlow.

Chapter 19

Education for citizenship and democracy

Howard Gibson

Introduction

In 1998, and under the guidance of Professor Bernard Crick, an Advisory Group on Citizenship issued its report on *Education for Citizenship and the Teaching of Democracy in Schools* (QCA, 1998). The outcome of this report was the introduction of citizenship education to primary-aged pupils from September 2000, and to secondary pupils from September 2002. Crick had concluded that there were three principal strands of the citizenship curriculum: social and moral responsibility, community involvement and political literacy. The third of these, political literacy, or education for democracy, has had less attention than citizenship education and Crick acknowledged that his committee's recommendations for teaching politics were limited. This chapter looks at different versions of 'democracy' and examines the causes of political apathy in young people. There is a critique of the citizenship education suggested by the Crick Report, which fails to recognise the power and influence of the media and the diminished role of the state in the global economy. An alternative curriculum is suggested which, through such areas as media studies, would make pupils aware of the 'constructed' nature of political discourse and would encourage them to engage in political action.

What does 'democracy' mean?

The origin of the word democracy lies in the Greek *demos*, meaning 'people in a community'. The ending '...ocracy', from the Greek *kratos*, meaning 'power or strength', implies rule. So democracy is the rule of the people. However, the concept of 'democracy' is problematic and there are various versions and views of democracy in different societies and cultures. Some might say that democracy should involve having a 'parliament'. But while the United States of America, for example, claims to be democratic, it does not have a parliament (although it does have two elected legislative assemblies). Perhaps democracy has nothing to do with an institutional name but with having the right to vote for who represents you in that institution, in which case a more 'direct' form of democracy might be appropriate, such as voting via the web. It might be argued that, instead of representative parliamentary democracy, where a party is elected for a period of time to make the decisions, there should be a referendum where everyone votes on all the big issues as they come along. There are also worries about democracy when it can allow minority racist parties, such as that of Le Pen in France, to gain representation and influence. There are also problems with how democracy is implemented; General Pervez Musharraf, who carried out a military coup in Pakistan in October 1999, declared he was instituting:

> ... not martial law, only another path to democracy. The armed forces have no intention to stay in charge any longer than is absolutely necessary to pave the way for true democracy to flourish in Pakistan ... what Pakistan has experienced in recent years has merely been a label of democracy, not the essence of it ... I shall not allow the people to be taken back to the era of sham democracy but to a true one. (Goldenberg, 1999)

It might be argued that states with military rulers are more effective than democratically elected governments. There is also a question as to whether we have a true democracy when members of the public have the right to participate in an election but do not bother to vote. In 1997, for example, Labour was elected by only 31 per cent of those qualified to vote. In 1932, Hitler's Nazi Party came to power in Germany with 37 per cent support among the democratic electorate. For these reasons, some question whether democracy is always 'a good thing'. It is not easy to talk about democracy with clarity, let alone define it. Saward (2003) has suggested that it is 'an enormously rich, suggestive, evocative political term, and it is partly this fact that makes it such a potential political weapon'.

Democracy and the curriculum

While a clear definition of democracy is not easy to give, from the Crick Report (QCA ,1998) and the curriculum documentation we get glimpses of how it is represented.

- *Participation*. There is a concern for the problem of apathy and dwindling commitment of young people in political life and the need to reverse this lack of interest and engagement. These worrying levels of apathy, ignorance and cynicism about public life need to be tackled at every level.
- *Communication*. There is a need to communicate views and opinions and engage in open discussion with others. Talk or discourse is obviously fundamental to active citizenship. Thus, to the need for pupils to participate in their community and become active in politics, we can now add the important skill of learning how to debate and engage with others.
- *Rule of law*. There is the requirement for members of the democratic community to obey the law. The assumption is that once debate has progressed sufficiently and decisions reached, however unpopular they may be with some individuals, the rule of law should apply. Respect for the rule of law is a necessary condition of social order and a necessary component of education.

But this apparently self-evident account of what democracy is, and how schools should prepare pupils for it, is both questionable and contentious.

Pause for thought | political apathy

Political apathy is said to be a key problem for democracies and one of the reasons for citizenship becoming mandatory for primary and secondary schools in England. However, while the government's response has been to emphasise the need to increase participation by encouraging the democratic involvement of pupils in school councils and the like, an alternative could have been to investigate *why* British democracy might be producing apathetic citizens and what consequences this might have for the teaching of citizenship in schools. Discuss political apathy with friends and colleagues. Do you think it really exists? Do you vote yourself, or take an active part in politics at any level? Why are governments interested in the political views of a nation's youth?

Participation

The claim about the need for more commitment and participation is unconvincing because, although it rails against the problem of apathy, it fails to examine the historical decline of political commitment and ignores the huge changes to the nation state in recent years, which have come primarily from the effects of globalisation:

- the idea of national autonomy which used to define the democratic state can no longer be assumed;
- cultural pluralism and multiple identities in societies present complex challenges for national governments;
- the inability of states to deal with global problems, such as the environment, inequality and poverty makes them appear ineffective and powerless.

These are some of the issues that affect modern democracies and which may account for apathy. James Anderson (2002) has described the stark effects of globalisation on national democracies:

Globalisation is putting democracy in question and is itself being questioned as undemocratic. Its border crossings are undermining the traditional territorial basis of democracy and creating new political spaces which need democratising. 'Global forces' are disrupting the supposedly independent, sovereign states and national communities which have provided democracy's main framework. And these 'global forces' are apparently beyond control or, more specifically, beyond democratic control. The political implications are wide reaching and far from clear … . National democracy's problems are experienced most immediately in perception that the national state is losing its sovereignty to 'outside' bodies and is being infiltrated by them. Actions taken in or by other states are having increasing impact on supposedly 'sovereign' neighbours. State electorates are more directly affected by decisions made in other jurisdictions, including supra-state bodies like the EU. Private multinational corporations have become more powerful, and foreign-owned ones may determine the success or otherwise of national economies. States are losing some of their autonomy, as power 'goes upwards' to other, supra-state, political institutions, 'sideways' to privatised operations, or in some respects 'goes nowhere' or just 'evaporates', as economics outruns politics and political control is simply lost to the global market. (pp6–9)

By putting much of the decision-making processes beyond the borders of individual countries, there has been a decline in the economic, political and social effectiveness of the national state. As private multinational corporations have become more powerful they have affected the success or otherwise of national economies. Hertz (2001) went so far as to suggest that modern democracies are now resigned to the fact that multinationals are taking the place of elected governments and that shopping may be now more effective than voting: 'This is the world of the Silent Takeover … Governments' hands are tied and we are increasingly dependent on corporations'. Since the Thatcher era of government in the 1980s, 'rolling back the state' has been policy in the UK, relaxing regulation on business and encouraging private health care and education. Bottery (2003) argued that a consequence is the undermining of loyalty to the state. Put another way, as the nation state's influence on its citizens withers, so does their allegiance to it.

Democratic theory, from Locke to Rousseau and Bentham to Mill, has always been vigilant in separating the public from the private realm, and liberal democracies have tended to preserve free market economies. Within the walls of a factory or beyond a nation's borders can be found the economic freedoms for individuals to innovate, produce, market and sell. The point for democracies is this, while those economic freedoms that accompany capitalism whet consumers' appetites for more products, dealing with the less pleasant by-products such as global warming becomes problematic. To reduce global warming, for example, it might be considered sensible to reduce dramatically the use of private motor vehicles (though the link remains subject to intense scientific debate), but a government which does this will probably not be elected the next time round. A democratically elected government finds it difficult to limit the freedom of its voters.

Research box

market sovereignty or democracy?

The historian Eric Hobsbawn (2001) has argued that 'democracy can be bad for you' and that the market and democracy are mutually exclusive. Is he right?

Market sovereignty is not a complement to liberal democracy; it is an alternative to it. Indeed, it is an alternative to any kind of politics, as it denies the need for political decisions, which are precisely decisions about common or group interests as distinct from the sum of choices, rational or otherwise, of individuals pursuing private preferences. Participation in the market replaces participation in politics. The consumer takes the place of the citizen … . [We] face an age when the impact of human action on nature and the globe has become a force of geological proportions. Their solution, or mitigation, will require measures for which, almost certainly, no support will be found by counting votes or measuring consumer preferences. This is not encouraging for the long-term prospects of either democracy or the globe. (p26)

Because of colonisation, globalisation and increasing mobility, many citizens within national states now have multiple identities. One can, for example, be a UK citizen, British, a Muslim, a member of the EU, have a commitment to another country by birth or marriage, and so on. The state today is plural and diverse and no longer consists of a single people. In consequence, according to Parekh (2002), the state 'cannot claim to embody and legitimate itself in terms of [its inhabitants'] sense of collective identity either, both because many of them no longer place much emphasis on their national identity or privilege it over their other identities, and because some of them increasingly cherish trans-national ties and identities'. The publication of Salman Rushdie's *Satanic Verses* in 1988, for example, produced a strong reaction from some members of the Muslim community and led to a conflict which lies at the heart of modern democracies: freedom of speech versus blasphemy.

Such issues as these place great pressure on democratic governments. It was suggested above that the citizenship education curriculum (QCA, 1998) recognises the need to engender participation and commitment to counter the alienation and cynicism of the young, but it skirts around the causes. To say that 'trust in society's core institutions has been falling steadily' does not explain the phenomenon. Given the complexity of issues attending globalisation, including the expansion of corporate capitalism, the withering power of the nation state, the proximity within single nations of people with diverse and sometimes conflicting identities, it seems reasonable to explain dwindling participation not simply in terms of individual apathy but in recognition of the challenges that face modern, complex democracies.

Pause for thought | spin, sleaze and political apathy

It is sometimes argued that voter apathy is the consequence of spin and the so-called 'dumbing-down' of modern political life. In Britain, examples of political sleaze are easy to come by and you can use the internet to remind yourself of examples. You might research the questions that arose about the legality of the 2003 war with Iraq. Allegations about lies in political life and the spoon-feeding of the public with sound bites all perhaps contribute to political apathy. Pupils' trust in politics and politicians remains constantly at 'low levels' according to attitude surveys (Cleaver et al., 2005). Furedi (2004) has suggested that the government's response to such claims has only reduced its credibility:

> Apathy and disengagement breed both anti-political and apolitical reactions. The political class is aware of this: but instead of attempting to address the underlying malaise and disillusionment through developing challenging political ideals that could inspire the electorate to vote, its response has been to acquiesce in dumbing down. (p80)

It might be argued that rather than instead of merely reminding young citizens of their duty to participate in their local community or to become more charitable (QCA, 1998), there should be a curriculum that attempts to explain the complex causes of apathy and the actions of government.

Communication skills

Earlier it was suggested that the education for democracy component of the citizenship education curriculum emphasises debate and discussion: 'Talk or discourse is obviously fundamental to active citizenship ... [because] open and informed debate is vital for a healthy democracy'. For some, echoing John Stuart Mill (1806–73), free communication is one of the central pillars of liberal democracy. For Mill (1969) there was no test for the adequacy of a claim to a good idea or 'truth' other than the force of better public argument: put your idea on the table, await critical scrutiny, argue your case when challenged, but be prepared to accede to new and better ideas.

However, while Mill's rationale for open and free communication seems convincing in theory, in practice it is a different matter because powers of communication are not equally distributed. In the real world, media-moguls have the power to persuade and to influence the views of others. As Karl Marx argued, the free exchange of ideas may be good in principle but, when tied to the market and the free exchange of commodities, the reality of freedom becomes illusory for the majority of ordinary people. Habermas (1972) similarly warned against 'the fiction that Socratic dialogue is possible everywhere and at any time'. To put it simply, liberal democratic philosophy presupposes the existence of the very sense of community that dialogue is intended to develop and, in so doing, overlooks the reality that debate rarely takes place on a level playing field.

In the citizenship education curriculum, discussion is not problematised and the term 'communication' is preferred, portraying debate as if it were a content-free skill (see Cameron, 2000). It presents classroom discourse as if it should mimic the procedures of debates that go on outside – in Parliament, in town councils, between parties and the electorate, and so on. This failure to acknowledge the power structures that determine or distort free communication has two main consequences for citizenship and democracy:

- **Political activity is 'mediated'. Political issues are most often communicated to us via television, radio or newspaper and so we need to understand how media discourses are constructed. Understanding the media is fundamental to an understanding of politics.**
- **Because teachers largely mediate what pupils can or cannot say in school, there needs to be more clarity regarding the power structures that determine, restrict or enable 'open' discussion. In other words, we need to be clear about where the boundaries lie if our aim is to democratise schools through school councils and pupil involvement.**

These two points are addressed in turn. First, there is inadequate theory or critique of the link between the media and modern democracy. This link is crucial in understanding democracy:

> *So-called 'spin' originates in a bottom-line desire to look good. So it's essential to assert you are right, providing explanations and then reasons for why it has to be as you've presented it. If all else fails … everything becomes a question of opinion … Most people find this process unedifying. It is certainly deeply damaging to democracy.* (Brighouse, 2004, pp18–19)

A curriculum designed to prepare pupils for the realities of debate in a modern democracy might therefore include a variety of media themes:

- **it could explain the links between media ownership and political discourses (e.g. between the newspaper and publishing magnate Rupert Murdoch and the Prime Minister's office);**
- **it might examine work that has helped our understanding of the way the rhetorical styles of politicians are constructed (e.g. Margaret Thatcher was taught to lower her voice to sound more authoritative);**
- **it might grapple with democratically complex issues concerning the control of information during periods of international conflict (e.g. the Falklands, Afghanistan or Gulf wars);**
- **it could attempt to account for the rise and effect of 'synthetic conversation' in the tabloid press in the presentation of public policy;**
- **it could provide an understanding of the symbiosis between politicians and the media and how each exploits the other.**

In short, while the citizenship curriculum makes a passing reference to media education, there is little hint about how pupils might develop an awareness of the constructedness of political discourses. Debate is not problematised and the political structures within modern democracy that obfuscate or enable genuine encounter are not explained.

The second point is that, within the school environment, the issue of free communication remains unproblematised. Education for democracy says it wishes to establish 'a classroom climate in which all pupils are free from any fear of expressing *reasonable points of view* which contradict those held either by their class teacher or by their peers' (QCA, 1998). But the notion that teachers are responsible for what is reasonable classroom discourse glosses over complex and questionable areas. To illustrate the effect of the embedded nature of communication within the socio-cultural practices of the school as an institution, consider the effect that market-funding mechanisms might have on open debate in schools like City Academies which are owned by private corporations. If the governing body has welcomed sponsorship of the school's computer suite by, say, Nescafé, Burger King or Nike, it could be difficult to hold a critical discussion of the use of child labour, or the merchandising policies of the companies that help augment the excesses of western consumption.

Research box

school councils

The Crick Report (QCA, 1998) recommended the formation of school councils, although it did not suggest making them compulsory. There seems to be a consensus regarding the value of their consultative nature insofar as they give pupils responsibility and enable them to experience democracy first hand in a way that mimics the parliamentary process (Print et al., 2002; Hannam, 2003). Others have their doubts. Control of the agenda or topic, for example, is a major way of limiting such debate. Rudduck and Flutter (2000) have suggested that school council discussions often revolve around 'the charmed circle of lockers, dinners and uniform'. For Fielding (2001) debate and discussion is often tokenistic:

> *How many school councils can we all think of that have flourished for a while but have subsequently declined from their former vibrancy and engagement with real issues into a mechanistic and largely tokenistic set of procedures for recycling the minimum and predictable minutiae of the status quo? (p105)*

In this section it has been suggested that the liberal philosophy of discussion and debate always needs to be grounded in social, political and educational contexts where it then becomes a much more complex notion than the education for democracy curriculum seems to acknowledge. There is inadequate coverage about how pupils might become aware of the constructedness of media discourses, and debate. Discussion is presented in an unproblematic way that prevents understanding of how social and political power limits the ability of some groups to engage, both within and outside the school.

The rule of law

The third element of education for democracy is that it should foster 'respect for law, justice, democracy' (QCA, 1998). Because of the difficulty with words like 'justice' we need to approach this issue with care, just as we should the rather provocative suggestion that young citizens should be helped to 'distinguish between law and justice'. This appears to suggest that democratic citizens could, under certain circumstances, move their political ambitions *outside* the law and is perhaps what Her Majesty's Chief Inspector of Schools had in mind when he insisted that citizenship education should lead to 'genuine action' (Bell, 2005).

Democratic theorists have often accepted the possibility of unlawful dissent. They distinguish between principled unlawful dissent and other unlawful practices, like theft, which do not aim to change the law. The examples the curriculum documents give of illegal acts, like theft and glue-sniffing, are thus not *politically* disobedient for they imply no desire to engage in issues of social justice. The second point theorists frequently make is that there has been a long history of unlawful dissent within liberal democracies which has not toppled them. Healthy democracies, some say, can and should absorb these challenges.

Pause for thought | law or justice?

What is 'law' and what is 'just' are not synonymous in democracies. Think of the illegal acts performed by the women's suffragette movement; of Gandhi's peaceful march to take salt from the Indian Ocean in defiance of the colonial law that raised tax by selling it; or the occupation of woods around airports and supermarkets in protest at environmental degradation. Consider also how a senior Vatican official insisted that good Catholics should oppose Spain's law permitting marriage between gay couples since 'a law as profoundly iniquitous as this one is not an obligation, it cannot be an obligation. One cannot say that a law is right simply because it is a law' (cited in Gledhill, 2005). Where do you stand on the issue of law and justice?

It is possible to imagine a classroom scenario in which the disparity between law and justice could open and flourish. Reaction in schools to the 2003 Iraq war is an example, with UK pupils taking illegal action to join street protests against the threatened war – illegal in that it was school truancy. The issue is not whether their action was appropriate and just, or simply naïve and ineffective. The point is whether this type of action is an appropriate activity in an education for democracy curriculum. We need to be clear that the stated aim of education for democracy is not just to *know* about politics but to take action: pupils should be encouraged 'to recognise, reflect upon and act upon these values and dispositions … this is vital in developing pupils into *active* citizens' (QCA, 1998; see also Bell, 2005).

Over a period of study about the war in Iraq these pupils could be shown to have demonstrated many of the skills and qualities valued by the citizenship curriculum. They have shown:

- **a sense of *commitment* to the issue;**
- **they are able to *communicate* well and counter alternative views in a reasonable and responsible manner;**
- **they have developed a caring attitude to both their *local* and *global community*;**
- **they *understand* how liberal democracies work, as well as some of their limitations, such as governments refusing to change direction despite huge opposition by the public; or that in the past some, particularly colonial, wars have been fought to secure natural resources and not for reasons of justice;**
- **they have learnt about *the media* and about 'camera consciousness' and how politicians and members of the public use it to gain mainstream attention and maximum publicity for their cause.**

In short, these hypothetical pupils are far from apathetic, have a good understanding of the issues and, as responsible citizens and as the recipients of a lively curriculum, have come to the point of conviction about their moral duty to take *political* action.

There are different ways of managing pupil action. The first is *containment*, where the citizenship education and education for democracy curriculum is akin to dramatic role-play, possibly enjoyable and active, but consequence-free and devoid of 'genuine action' (Bell, 2005). This would quite possibly reinforce pupils' cynicism and increase their apathy.

A second scenario is that political action would be permitted but only if closely *controlled and monitored* by what the Crick Report (QCA, 1998) calls 'those in authority'. Action would be legitimated, but only when the topics under discussion involved recycling or fundraising for charities, or where it addressed problems such as street litter. In this scenario, the school would permit action to raise money for new playground equipment for the local primary school, but forbid a demonstration against insufficient public funding in state schools.

A third scenario would be the fragmentation of views into what the curriculum calls '*personal opinions*' (DfEE/QCA, 2000). Here a pupil would be permitted to write to a councillor or to the Prime Minister with an argument about the war, but only in a personal capacity and not as the representative of the class or school. This is to 'personalise' the opinion – to diminish it as simply the view of an individual – and to remove its public legitimacy. The tag (merely) 'personal' can be applied to those who are recalcitrant, intractable or intolerable, and serves to de-activate them. If teachers are 'in authority' to decide who is or is not a responsible student, or what or is not a responsible personal opinion, the rules for deciding whether pupils' views and actions should remain personal or become public rests squarely with them.

Summary and conclusions

It has been suggested that defining a citizen involves understanding democracy and it has been shown that the problematic nature of what a modern democracy might be is not evident in the curriculum for citizenship. There needs to be a debate about what it is and what it could become in the light of the threats to the nation state today. Pupils should be part of this. The power structures underlying debate and discussion need to be far more clear and media studies should become a much more important and integral aspect of citizenship education and education for democracy. Teachers are a relatively powerless group required to teach citizenship. They need to see beyond a curriculum that bores pupils with the facts of government and to raise the stakes by looking very carefully at where their energised and enlightened pupils may roam. Responsibility for the success or failure of democracy is likely to rest with teachers, rather than government. A final question is: whose responsibility would it be if pupils actually made the decision to take un-civil action?

References

Anderson, J (2002) Questions of democracy, territoriality and globalisation, in Anderson, J (ed) *Transnational democracy: political spaces and border crossings*. London: Routledge.

Bell, D (2005) *Education for democratic citizenship*. Roscoe Lecture by Her Majesty's Chief Inspector of Schools, Liverpool, 2 November. Available at **www.ofsted.gov.uk/publications/** (accessed 12 April 2006).

Bottery, M (2003) The end of citizenship? The nation state, threats to its legitimacy, and citizenship education in the twenty-first century. *Cambridge Journal of Education*, 33(1): 101–22.

Brighouse, T (2004) Tough on the causes of Tony. *The Times Educational Supplement*, 29 October.

Cameron, D (2000) *Good to talk? Living and working in a communication culture*. London: Sage.

Cleaver, E, Ireland, E, Kerr, D and Lopes, E (2005) *Citizenship education longitudinal study: second cross-sectional survey 2004. Listening to young people: citizenship education in England*. Slough: National Foundation for Education Research.

DfEE/QCA (2000) *National Curriculum – Citizenship*. London: Department for Education and Employment/Qualifications and Curriculum Authority.

Fielding, M (2001) Beyond the rhetoric of student voice: new departures and new constraints in the transformation of twenty-first century schooling? *Forum*, 43(2): 100–10.

Furedi, F (2004) *Where have all the intellectuals gone? Confronting 21st century philistinism*. London: Continuum.

Gledhill, R (2005) Vatican attack on Spain's gay marriage law. Available at **www.timesonline.co.uk/article/0,, 20709-1580888,00.html** (accessed 12 April 2006).

Goldenberg, S (1999) Coup to 'save Pakistan from ruin'. *Guardian*, 18 October.

Habermas, J (1972) *Knowledge and human interests*. London: Heinemann.

Hannam, D (2003) Participation and responsible action for all students: the critical ingredient for success. *Teaching Citizenship*, 5: 24–33.

Hertz, N (2001) *The Silent Takeover: global capitalism and the death of democracy*. London: Heinemann.

Hobsbawm, E (2001) Democracy can be bad for you. *New Statesman*, 5 March, pp25–7.

Mill, JS (1969) On the liberty of thought and discussion, in Warnock, M (ed) *Utilitarianism*. London: Fontana.

Parekh, B (2002) Reconstituting the modern state, in Anderson, J (ed), *Transnational democracy: political spaces and border crossings*. London: Routledge.

Print, M, Ornstrom, S and Skovgaard, N (2002) Education for democratic processes in schools and classrooms. *European Journal of Education*, 37(2): 193–210.

QCA (1998) *Education for Citizenship and the Teaching of Democracy in Schools: final report of the Advisory Group on Citizenship* (the Crick Report). London: Qualifications and Curriculum Authority.

Rudduck, J and Flutter, J (2000) Pupil participation and pupil perspective: carving a new order of experience. *Cambridge Journal of Education*, 30(1): 75–89.

Rushdie, S (1988) *The Satanic Verses*. London: Penguin.

Saward, M (2003) *Democracy*. Cambridge: Polity Press.

Chapter 20

Comparative education

Les Hankin

Introduction

The term 'comparative education' identifies a tradition of academic studies that compares educational systems, and seeks to understand how education relates to wider social forces. This tradition has many strands, all curious to explore the processes, structures and dynamics of different countries, regions or educational systems for meaningful similarities and contrasts between them. Comparative educationists (often known as comparativists) unite in a belief that analysis of the practices and outcomes of any educational system or grouping is instructive, on the broad principle of learning from others. However not all agree about whether comparisons actually enlighten educational practice. This chapter considers similarities and variations between education systems and how comparative studies might illuminate educational development in a rapidly changing world.

The dimensions and purposes of comparative education

Drawing together the views of comparativists, Phillips (2000) has listed a number of purposes whose consequences tend towards copying successful practice, 'generally known as borrowing'. Comparative studies:

- **show what is possible by examining alternatives to provision 'at home';**
- **offer yardsticks by which to judge the performance of education systems;**
- **anticipate the consequences of certain educational policy choices by looking at experience in other countries;**
- **play a supportive and instructional role in the development of plans for educational reform, by reference to experience elsewhere;**
- **help foster cooperation and understanding among nations by discussing and explaining cultural differences and similarities.**

Phillips noted a further role for comparative education in providing objective data with which to test the assertions of politicians and administrators who, in order to exert political influence, might present their country's education provision as 'under- or overperforming in comparison to other nations'.

Arnove and Torres (2003) have suggested that the frame within which comparative education works is shifting with the rising significance of the global dimension, to add to its scientific (building theories about school systems) and pragmatic dimensions (improving policy and practice by drawing practical lessons from other systems). They show how comparativists, by responding to the effects of globalisation, can contribute to international understanding and peace by promoting examples of equity in education.

Influences on education across nations

The warp speed of global change has indeed altered the integrity and identity of nation states . Those bonds of culture, tradition and territoriality that once clearly defined countries and held them together have been loosened by the effects of trade, conflict and population movement. Once, societies might have looked within themselves to find answers to the complex questions about freedom, responsibility, truth, control and achievement now taxing their educational systems. Now they must look further afield to emulate success.

Paradoxically, the absence of external threat after half a century of relative world peace has undermined the solidarity that once united countries around their national distinctiveness. The sense of common purpose that was the one true dividend of two world wars has not survived the long peace. Kinship and allegiance have given way in most nations to confusion, anomie and uncertainty in the way people experience their lives (Hedges, 2003). Social bonds, networks and identity have become threatened by the dissolution of communities and the fragmentation of the family. The pressures of a global economy, where 'there are no hiding places for the under-equipped', have led governments to undervalue their own distinctive and precious cultural heritage (McLean, 1995).

Many states have adopted uniform and narrowed school curricula they have seen introduced elsewhere to drive the vast educational improvements needed to keep their place in the world. What has been most eroded in this process has been motivation. Education has lost some of its power to attract populations to learning for its own sake rather than as a pressing economic necessity (Beauchamp, 2002; Crossley and Watson, 2003).

Cross-national trends in education

Common imperatives can be seen emerging as countries strive to shape their educational policy initiatives and strategies to ensure equity and economic survival in the punishing climate of globalisation. A set of trends can be drawn from sources including the OECD. While not exhaustive, these give some sense of how educational systems have to deal with similar convergent and insistent phenomena.

- **A greater proportion of populations is engaged in education than ever before.**
- **Life chances and educational success still depend upon socio-economic background and inheritance, evident in the take-up of post-compulsory education.**
- **A correlation persists between the educational success of parents and that of their children.**
- **Principles of lifelong learning and widening access have led to the 'massification' of higher education.**
- **Female educational attainment outstrips male, swelling concerns about male underachievement and disaffection (subject choice and consequent career direction remain gender-influenced).**
- **Careers are ever harder to sustain without educational qualifications, as knowledge-based economies take root and low-skill occupations disappear.**
- **The educational success of ethnic communities falls into predictable patterns.**
- **Cost influences policies of fairness and widening participation purporting to integrate students with special needs within mainstream education.**
- **The relentless growth of digital education is creating a 'digital divide' of excluded groups who will never catch up.**
- **The balance of power between governments and practitioners may be shifting, as education is increasingly expected to serve as an agent of social change.**

Many of these trends follow the movement of societies to become economies where the production, transfer and refinement of knowledge must be fed by new armies of flexible 'knowledge workers'. Such economic necessity may need to give ground to educational values involving 'the emotional, perhaps even the spiritual, lives of those who learn' (Newby, 2002).

Pause for thought | education as a universal human right

The proclamation of education as the inalienable right of all in the human family, adopted in the Universal Declaration of Human Rights of 1948, might suggest that a standard exists for education to progress towards common goals among nations. The requirement of the Declaration, that education should not only be free in its fundamental stages but also 'directed to the full development of the human personality' (Article 26) illustrates how the values, norms and needs of systems at varying stages of economic and political development would inevitably diverge in their response to this edict. Societies whose economic and philosophical circumstances require them to work towards more generalised well-being rather than individual opportunity, would have to approach this right entirely differently from developed industrial nations. Spring (2000) has shown that the proclamation was couched in such general terms that principles and philosophies of learning and development did not need to be confronted or harmonised before full acceptance was given by member states. Do you feel that such a right can realistically be justified for all peoples in all nations, regardless of differences in culture, religion and political and social circumstance? What would interfere with the working of such a universal aspiration if no stable universal concept of education exists that is linked to the defence of human rights?

Difficulties of comparison

The presence of common educational threads and concerns suggests that meaningful contrasts can be drawn between systems. Comparative analysis becomes highly problematic, however, in the face of global disorganisation, social fragmentation and the decline of clear-cut national systems. We are advised always to be alive not only to the circumstances in which particular decisions are made about education, but also to 'the forces impelling countries to make often uncomfortable and unwelcome decisions to change old and familiar ways of doing things, as well as the limits imposed on free choice by each country's context' (Noah and Eckstein, 1975).

The essence of any educational system will always lie in its particular cultural map, so that concepts, variables and indicators of educational effectiveness can never be confidently treated as directly comparable when setting evidence about one system against that of another. Every detail is open to question on these terms. Simply establishing age and stage equivalence between systems is problematic (Steedman, 1999). The very word 'education' is itself loaded with associations and nuances within and between languages, so that in every country it has a different scope and range of meanings (Corner and Grant, 2004).

If there are great variations between countries educationally, then the power and relevance of comparative education might lie in the reasons behind such difference. No two countries possess quite the same educational contours, because these are the legacy of history and are shaped by unique traditions and cultures. So questions arise about the social forces and factors in knowledge production that are considered so vital to each country's success. What economic, political, cultural and community influences have been at work? Do judgements about such factors combine to give a valid or appropriate picture and do they account for the influence each education system has in turn exerted on all the other structures in its own society?

Pause for thought | an example of international comparison

Despite reservations about the comparability of data, the propensity for government-sponsored cross-national research is increasing with advances in communications. The International Adult Literacy Survey, for example, considered factors influencing the development of adult skills across the 20 OECD countries, whose combined populations account for over half of the world's entire gross domestic product. It measured levels of advanced literacy, defined as the ability to cope with written material in the information age. A vast underclass was revealed, with nearly a quarter of 16- to 65-year-olds in the richest countries shown to be functionally illiterate. Significant differences in the level and distribution of literacy skills within and between countries were revealed, against such parameters as the changing demand for skills in a knowledge economy. The survey concluded that policies to develop skills should be directed at the workplace and family settings, as well as towards high-quality learning in schools (OECD and Statistics Canada, 2000). The young people of Britain appeared less well qualified for the world of work than those in other industrialised countries and a connection was drawn between the British television-addiction and their comparative weakness in advanced reading skills, with 22 per cent proving functionally illiterate. However, 35 per cent of young people gained a university degree in the UK, compared with fewer than 20 per cent a decade previously and against an average of 23 per cent for the countries surveyed. The Survey demonstrated more than a link between the possession of good literacy skills, better pay and a longer life. It showed that every country involved had a literacy problem, but that responses were very different: most funded proactive bodies equivalent to Britain's Basic Skills Agency because poor reading is considered the easiest of the poverty indicators to tackle. In contrast some states, such as Germany, took few steps to acknowledge the seriousness of functional illiteracy. What do you think are the most important skills for the effective functioning of labour markets and for the economic success and social advancement of individuals and society wherever they live?

Shared principles

What is the common ground among educational systems as they have developed over time? Certain shared fundamental principles have emerged. Take the ancient belief coming down to us from Plato that education should be provided for the masses through the action of the state. This may now seem self-evident and only right and just, but was strikingly revolutionary once. It may have taken two millennia to become universally adopted, but it has not been seriously destabilised in any country by movements such as the 'deschoolers', whose sustained critique of the corrupting effect of educational institutions reflects a wider scepticism about the competence of governments anywhere to make them work (Tooley, 2005).

One of the earliest principles to emerge was the perception that children were not simply adults waiting to happen, but that childhood had a value in its own right as a distinctive stage in every person's life. This can be traced to Rousseau, whose eighteenth-century insight that children were naturally good but vulnerable, that they learned differently and needed the support of mentors to learn how to live, marked a paradigm shift in the understanding of the child (Darling, 1993). This vision took root unevenly in different countries but made space for the child-centred thinking of subsequent influential educationists, including Pestalozzi, Steiner, Piaget and Froebel in Europe and Dewey in the United States (McLean, 1995).

All such principles are, of course, modified by circumstance. Descriptions of the nature of childhood in a range of present-day societies show how market forces distort educational opportunities for children as their families seek simply to survive (Penn, 2005). At the other end of the spectrum from concern for the child's interests is the dual belief that education has the power to deliver the will of a country's political elites and that it is the key to that country's future economic prosperity (Halsey et al., 1997).

Some principles are of their time and owe less to tradition than to modern expediency and developing notions of equity, expressed forcefully in the OECD's watchword that 'society's most important investment is in the education of its people'. The Organisation notes how educational policy is formulated under intense pressures, ranging from the demographic to the social and economic, as education systems seek to be more sensitive to the needs of individual learners than to those of the systems themselves. Lifelong learning, widening participation, extended schools, are all markers of a universalised recognition of the shifting purpose of education in the twenty-first century.

Research box

extending the boundaries of education

Schuller (2003) has problematised the 'remorseless extension of initial education', where more students are encouraged by widening participation policies to stay at school beyond the compulsory years. This has become a benchmark for countries' relative achievement and economic success. Evidence increasingly suggests, however, that stretching education reduces motivation for learning and impinges on equity.

However wide the net is spread for access into higher education, it will not equalise life chances if it is too closely tied to the initial phase. [Another issue] is gender. Can we assume that men and women will tend to follow the same life-course patterns, and, if not, how does this affect their motivation to learn? Arguably, we are heading for a major crisis in the socialisation of young males. Should the response be to retain them in formal education, or to help them to learn elsewhere? (p27)

Lessons from systems and social structures

Comparativists are also concerned with the role and function of education systems *within* societies and how they interact with other components of the social structure. By this understanding, comparative education is forever looking backwards, because it is always assessing inherited systems of education that will have been formulated around societal needs that will inevitably have shifted. At its extreme, the historical slant to such tensions can be read into Santayana's famous axiom that 'Those who do not remember the past are condemned to repeat it'. This statement confronts visitors to the memorial to the victims of the Holocaust, at the Auschwitz concentration camp. Writ large in that dreadful place is the terrible lesson that an education system somehow germinated a generation capable of the 'banality of evil' that made genocide so easy in the middle of the twentieth century, and that such conditions must not be allowed to arise again anywhere (Rees, 2005).

King (2000) shows how the focus, concerns and intentions of comparativists have shifted over the past century as governments have coveted, and often sought to blueprint, educational institutions and practices that appear to have succeeded in other countries. Often this process has been driven by military and economic rivalry and competition for international esteem and influence. This impulse to imitate contributes to the global convergence of educational systems, where 'the curious look abroad to discover the future' (McLean, 1995). An example is the way that the British government looked to Taiwan for superior teaching methods in mathematics. Reynolds and Farrell (1996) noted the methods used in Taiwan and David Reynolds went on to chair the Numeracy Task Force which formulated the National Numeracy Strategy in England.

Studies of education systems, and their relative effectiveness, are often driven by statistics, particularly through the work of dedicated monolithic inter-governmental agencies such as those of the United Nations or the European Union. These agencies provide open access to data on countries, using indicators drawn from education and related disciplines (including sociology, political science, economics and anthropology) to enable international and cross-cultural comparisons to be made. However, a society's philosophical, ideological and structural hinterland must also be considered, along with the social, cultural, economic, political and pedagogical developments that have shaped its national and regional variants. The north European countries of Norway, Denmark and Sweden are notable for having a late start to formal schooling, usually around the age of six or seven years, whereas formal schooling begins at four-plus in the UK. To assume that either country should change to imitate the other would perhaps ignore the culturally different views of childhood which are held.

That there are tensions around what constitutes unequivocal evidence in analysing education systems is illustrated by the presence of independent indices of educational success, although the level of claimed independence needs to be examined. An example of this is the Human Development Report, a composite of measures that claims neutrality but is commissioned by the United Nations Development Programme. This gauges the development of nations in terms of educational progress, life expectancy and gross domestic product (UNDP, 2005). The Programme is concerned to explore progress towards the Millennium Development Goals, eight targets for the eradication of poverty on earth by 2015, as agreed by all 191 UN member states and the world's leading development institutions. The second of these goals, after the eradication of extreme poverty and hunger, is the achievement of universal primary education (United Nations, 2005). Despite addressing persistent problems of deprivation and inequality, the goals have been challenged over their North–South divide, since they address the endemic conditions of the developing world, the South, yet ignore the poverty and discrimination that exists in the developed countries of the North.

The Qualifications and Curriculum Authority for England projects its mission in comparative and competitive terms, claiming 'a pivotal role in helping the UK become the most dynamic knowledge-based economy in the world' (QCA, 2005). Its INCA (International Review of Curriculum and Assessment) programme of comparative education provides system summaries of governments' policies on teaching 3–19 and teacher training in a range of countries. It also offers *thematic probes* and summaries, comparing strands across countries such as learner motivation and skills and curriculum progression.

The impulse to compare and judge educational arrangements in other societies, from information that can never be complete, carries its own dangers, such as those of prejudice. Wainaina (2005) has condemned the stereotyping of western writing about Africa and the exploitative undertow of its supposedly comparative approach: 'Broad brushstrokes throughout are good. Avoid having the African characters laugh, or struggle to educate their kids … Have them illuminate Europe or America in Africa'.

Against such dangers, the variety of contrasts between parts of the world may grow in importance as globalisation acts to draw systems towards compliance with supposed ideals and norms of what is 'best' in education for every human being, regardless of the conditions in which they live. Could it be that there is a set of irreducible principles of education to which all systems should subscribe, by looking for the best in each other in pursuit of the best of all possible educational worlds?

Pause for thought | **are there universal principles of education?**

Consider the idea that there might be universal assumptions, principles and goals of education that every country must account for, to serve both the interests of their learners and the economic imperatives of the state. Attempts to isolate such truths are illustrated in a three-nation comparison of the literacy and numeracy expectations of six-year-olds (OFSTED, 2003). This survey compared some very fundamental underlying principles, including the age at which children should properly start formal schooling and the extent to which teachers should be able to determine what they teach and how they teach it. It also pointed to evidence of the importance a broad and balanced curriculum has in encouraging literacy. Consider this list of general principles that may be held by most education systems. Do you agree with them? Can you add to them?

- A country's education provision is best regulated nationally but organised and delivered locally.
- Education is most successful when parents, teachers and local and national government work together.
- Teachers need freedom to teach.
- Children must attain functional levels of literacy and numeracy close to the expectations of their age group.
- Personal and social education is important.
- There should be coherence and continuity between the different stages of a child's education.

Explanations and perspectives on the development of nations

Comparative education draws much of its relevance from the view that the professional, political and moral decisions of any nation are intimately tied to those of all other nations through their interplay within a global society. As knowledge and information become among the most valued commodities in world trade, yet are less and less restrained by any precise physical location, this fusion becomes more pronounced (Coulby and Jones, 1995). There are also shifts in the balance of economic power: a rich 'North', of member countries of the OECD, is being challenged by the much higher growth rates of the 'newly industrialised countries' (NICs) of Asia. Where that continent so recently contained half of humanity, it now holds five-sixths (Boyd, 1998). The movement from the South to the North, with large-scale migration from the Third to the First Worlds, as they were once labelled, means that such contrasts are no longer 'out there' but are replicated within each of the world's major cities (Held et al, 1999).

Conflicting accounts explain the development of nations, ranging from *modernisation* or *modernity* theory to *convergence* and *dependency* paradigms. The modernisation perspective finds its model in the evolution of so-called traditional western societies, where all nations have followed a similar evolutionary arc through pre-ordained stages. Such an interpretation locates developmental factors *within* societies, in that a society's values are what govern its economic performance. In contrast, dependency theorists look *outwards*. They conclude that subjugated societies such as the colonies were deliberately underdeveloped by their conquerors, in a form of exploitation that has continued into the post-colonial phase through unequal trade arrangements (McMichael, 2000; Hoogvelt, 2001).

The learning paths of developing nations are not following those of developed states. Consider how technology, not previously so prominent in the moulding of educational systems, is being harnessed to leapfrog severe shortages of resources. India, needing 10,000 new schools a year to meet targets to cut her 35 per cent illiteracy rate, has bypassed the old constraints of landlines crossing vast distances by launching the world's first dedicated education satellite linked to cheap mass computers and offering virtual classrooms. In Africa, a pan-continental e-school programme is on course to provide all 600,000 of its schools with computers, internet access and links (NEPAD, 2005).

Research box

networks of comparative education

The meteoric expansion of the internet has given power to informal groupings that are motivated to share and develop ideas across national boundaries. They are prepared to engage with and challenge the findings of official organisations about the purposes and direction of education. One example of this development is the Global Social Change Research Project, which seeks to explain change and its influences on education as well as on social and political systems. This website sets out its global credentials, including its affiliations to international learned societies.

The future: post-comparative education

It has been argued that comparative education is still at a very early stage as a distinct field of study, but faces unique challenges. Broadfoot concludes that while comparativists might be uniquely placed to 'make the familiar strange' and offer educational policy-makers a vision of what is possible, their work has often served only to reinforce the status quo. Comparative approaches could valuably be remodelled around a *comparative learnology* to do justice to the new century's aspirations (Broadfoot, 1999; 2000). Learning should reassert itself over education in a new climate of 'potentially limitless access and lifelong commitment to educational activity' (Broadfoot, 2003). A re-examination of what learning is for is also needed, by returning to a discourse about learning that 'predates contemporary mass education systems and their universalistic notions of courses of study, examinations and grades; a vision in which it is once again the individual that is the focus of attention and their diverse talents, needs and inclinations' (Broadfoot, 2000). This new phase of searching for more general insights about how the key building blocks of education work together in an era of constant change has been labelled neo- or post-comparative education.

Despite such rich developments, uncertainty hangs over the literature about whether a canon of work identifiable as comparative education exists, and whether it has exerted influence or enjoyed any impact (Cook et al, 2004). Those cross-national forces of change that characterise globalisation are themselves exerting pressures to make countries converge and grow alike, in their education systems as much as in their other institutions (Bray, 2003). This befits an arena where 'any worthwhile education today is education for uncertainty' (King, 2000).

Summary and conclusions

Education is the engine of change in most societies. States have learnt from comparison and cooperation to shape enlightened policies around urgent ideas that they must mesh with their cherished ideals. They have sought to bring fairness as well as efficiency to their systems to meet the demanding conditions of the changing world order. Where these systems might once have preserved privilege, they now include changing structures of opportunity to address disparities of access: lifelong learning, widening participation and principles of inclusion. Social cohesion and the renewal of young people's social commitment have been pressing themes; inherited forms of privilege in education (such as selection) have been scrutinised to relieve problems around social disadvantage, the underclass and exclusion. It is through these grand concerns that nations, regions and locales can continue to learn from each other. The tradition of comparative education continues to inform this debate and is itself responding to the onrush of globalisation.

In the light of all this, comparative education is said to be enjoying a renaissance as an academic specialisation. It has been described as a discipline of easy virtue, lacking in distinctiveness, with 'almost anything vaguely educational' serving as grist to its mill. It is essentially boundless, riven by different viewpoints about its value and purpose, and beset by fundamental difficulties around the validity and reliability of data for cross-cultural comparison. What does unite comparativists is a willingness to look outwards, as well as to engage with other cultures and be optimistic and receptive to international understanding.

References

Arnove, R and Torres, C (2003) *Comparative education: the dialectic of the global and the local*. Oxford: Rowman and Littlefield.

Beauchamp, E (2002) *The comparative education reader*. London: Routledge.

Boyd, A (1998) *An atlas of world affairs*. London: Routledge.

Bray, M (2003) Comparative education in the era of globalisation: evolution, missions and roles. *Policy Futures in Education*, 1(2): 209–24.

Broadfoot, P (1999) Stones from other hills may serve to polish the jade of this one. *Compare*, 29(3): 217–31.

Broadfoot, P (2000) Comparative education for the 21st century: retrospect and prospect. *Comparative Education*, 36(3): 357–71.

Broadfoot, P (2003) Editorial: post-comparative education? *Comparative Education*, 39(3): 275–8.

Cook, B, Hite, S and Epstein, E (2004) Discerning trends, contours and boundaries in comparative education: a survey of comparativists and their literature. *Comparative Education Review*, 48(2): 123–49.

Corner, T and Grant, N (2004) Comparing educational systems, in Matheson, D (ed) *An introduction to the study of education*. London: David Fulton.

Coulby, D and Jones, C (1995) *Postmodernity and European education systems*. Stoke on Trent: Trentham.

Crossley, M and Watson, K (2003) *Comparative and international research in education: globalisation, context and difference*. London: RoutledgeFalmer.

Darling, J (1993) *Child-centred education and its critics*. London: Paul Chapman.

Global Social Change Research Project: social, economic and political change. Available at **gsociology. icaap.org/** (accessed 12 April 2006).

Halsey, A, Lauder, H, Brown, P and Wells, A (eds) (1997) *Education: culture, economy, society*. Oxford: Oxford University Press.

Hedges, C (2003) *War is a force that gives us meaning*. London: Anchor.

Held, D, McGrew, A, Goldblatt, D and Perraton, J (1999) *Global transformations: politics, economics and culture*. Cambridge: Polity Press.

Hoogvelt, A (2001) *Globalisation and the postcolonial world: the new political economy of development*. London: Palgrave Macmillan.

INCA (2006) International Review of Curriculum and Assessment Frameworks Internet Archive. Available at **www.inca.org.uk/** (accessed 12 April 2006).

King, E (2000) A century of evolution in comparative studies. *Comparative Education*, 36(3): 267–77

McLean, M (1995) *Educational traditions compared: content, teaching and learning in industrialised countries*. London: David Fulton.

McMichael, P (2000) *Development and social change: a global perspective*. London: Pine Forge Press.

Newby, N (2002) Foreword to Gearon, L (2002) *Education in the United Kingdom: structures and organisation*. London: David Fulton.

Noah, H and Eckstein, M (1975) Review of King, E (1973) Other schools and ours. *Comparative Education Review* 19: 290–5.

NEPAD (New African Partnership for Africa's Development) Available at **www.nepad.org/2005/ files/home.php** (accessed 12 April 2006).

OFSTED (2003) *The education of six year olds in England, Denmark and Finland: an international comparative study*. HMI 1660. London: OFSTED.

OECD (2004) *Handbook for internationally comparative education statistics: concepts, standards, definitions and classifications*. Paris: Organisation for Economic Co-operation and Development.

OECD and Statistics Canada (2000) *Literacy in the information age: final report of the International Adult Literacy Survey*. Paris: OECD.

QCA (2005) *About us: what we do*. Qualifications and Curriculum Authority for England. Available at **www.qca.org.uk/7.html** (accessed 12 April 2006).

Penn, H (2005) *Unequal childhoods: young children's lives in poor countries*. London: Routledge.

Phillips, D (2000) Learning from elsewhere in education: some perennial problems revisited with reference to British interest in Germany. *Comparative Education*, 36(3): 297–307.

Rees, L (2005) *Auschwitz: the Nazis and the Final Solution*. London: BBC Books.

Reynolds, D and Farrell, S (1996) *Worlds apart? A review of international surveys of educational achievement involving England*. London: HMSO.

Schuller, T (2003) Deschooling revisited: lessons for lifelong learning? *Adults Learning*, 14(5): 27.

Spring, J (2000) *The universal right to education: justification, definition, and guidelines*. Hillsdale, NJ: Lawrence Erlbaum Associates.

Steedman, H (1999) Measuring the quality of educational outputs: some unresolved problems, in Alexander, R, Broadfoot, P and Phillips, D (eds) *Learning from comparing: new directions in comparative education research*, vol. 1. Oxford: Symposium.

Tooley, J (2005) *Reclaiming education*. London: Continuum.

UNDP (2005) *Human development report*. New York: United Nations Development Programme.

United Nations (2005) *UN Millennium Development Goals: keep the promise*. Available at **www.un.org/ millenniumgoals/** (accessed 12 April 2006).

Wainaina, B (2005) How to write about Africa. *Granta* 92.

Chapter *21*

Globalisation and global education

Les Hankin and Wendy Bignold

Introduction

Ours is an ever-more interconnected, interdependent, information-driven world. Ours is also an unsustainable world. It is said that we will need three planet Earths to supply all the natural resources to keep us going on our present course. All these aspects are covered in the term 'globalisation'. Globalisation has come to be regarded as the central organising principle of the world, yet it has been described as the most pervasive while least understood concept of our time. Is it a force of nature that cannot be checked or a creation of humanity that can be tamed? As globalisation has taken increasing hold and its effects on every one of the world's peoples recognised, an allied concept has arisen, that of *global education*, the need to prepare the world's citizens for their roles and responsibilities. This chapter considers what globalisation entails and what part education might play in influencing its course for the benefit of all individuals, wherever they live.

The globalisation debate

So rapid and so visible has been the transformation of the world, particularly over the past few decades, that its effects can be seen as a quake at whose epicentre lies the creation of a global economy. The survival of all nations depends crucially on the quality of education each can command. This is one argument in a debate as intensive as the forces it seeks to explain. Views over globalisation fall into one of three main camps (Held and McGrew, 2003; Cambridge and Thompson, 2004):

- **the hyperglobalists;**
- **the sceptics;**
- **the transformationalists.**

The hyperglobalists see in today's world the onset of an era in which the fusion of history, ecology and economics is creating a new world order, where states must converge economically and politically or be rendered irrelevant by the unfettered activities of transnational business. This has echoes in the environmentalist view that the world is about to change more profoundly than at any time in the history of human civilisation. The sense that we are living through a period of irreversible transformation is contested by the sceptics, who argue that national governments, nationalism and geopolitics continue to dominate and determine the course of history. The transformationalists are concerned more with the shifting locus of power across the world's major regions and continents. There is visible evidence of a huge, inexorable power shift from the rich world towards China and India, who together account for 40 per cent of humanity, with as many people as the next twenty countries combined (Starke, 2006).

That the world is merging in some way, by force of some irresistible dynamic, is generally accepted as a reality which is good for the short term because technological change is breaking down the barriers that exist between peoples of different nations. It trails paradoxes, however, for just as connectivity and mobility of culture and labour are dissolving traditional national boundaries and widening horizons, so our world seems to be turning into a place of greater individualism rather than community. Whatever people gain by way of longer lifespan and greater material wealth, they pay a human price in losing the narrative thread about who they themselves might be and their place in society. As corporations alter working conditions in favour of short-term employment rather than long-term careers, their workforce loses those anchoring relationships with other workers and with their employers around which communities once coalesced. Women become marginalised when they cannot match their family and childcare commitments to less socially responsive work patterns and longer shift hours. Communities are eroded as workers are driven out of districts increasingly gentrified and made too expensive by market forces. Indeed, the reassurances given by governments that growth is good, against the harsh reality that freeing global market competition from tax and the regulatory burdens of government brings the very opposite of rising standards of living, is rarely acknowledged. On most indicators of social, and ecological life, some evidence suggests that the restructuring of societies for corporate globalisation has been increasingly life-destructive.

As the world's horizons shrink so fast that extreme wealth draws cheek by jowl with unremitting poverty both locally and internationally, how is it that, despite increases in rates of global economic growth, the gap between rich and poor countries, regions and peoples, persists and even shows signs of widening (UN, 2005)? And how is it that the experience of childhood can remain so unequal across the world (Penn, 2005)? This highly partial revolution of our world challenges us to develop education to nurture global responsibility. By this it is meant that the observance of human rights is now an issue for each one of us, wherever we live and however prosperous or secure we may feel ourselves to be. Instability in any state or region anywhere in the world now affects us all (Mepham and Cooper, 2004).

The narrative of globalisation

Globalisation is most usually depicted as a relentless economic imperative that is concentrating wealth in multinational corporate hands, aided by advances in education, in the knowledge economy, and in technology (Coulby and Zambeta, 2005). The term describes the trend by which all corners of the world have been edging closer together since the Middle Ages, when territoriality and the divinity of monarchs took root as the organising logic of nations. Historians have noted that from the time of the voyages of discovery of the sixteenth century, societies have been converging towards an interdependent, interconnected world economy in their search for the most efficient use of capital and labour. This process has accelerated through exponential increases in trade, cultural exchange and breakthroughs in travel and communications since 1870, when an economic system of free markets and the free movement of money around the world, anchored only to the gold standard, was allowed to flourish.

Interrupted by two world wars and a third, cold, war of the 1950s and 1960s, globalisation has gained unstoppable momentum since the early 1970s. While the economic system has grown less flexible and more protective of national economies, with rules preventing people from following work freely around the world, the force of immigration has itself broken all bounds, with 200 million of the world's 6 billion people now living as migrants (Sassen, 1999). At the same time the advent of world electronic communications has brought about what Cairncross (2001) has called the 'death of distance'. The satellite news revolution has also brought about the death of ignorance, for no longer can we pretend not to know what is happening elsewhere. Economies and societies are becoming increasingly enmeshed as events in one country impact directly on others, as the constraints of space and time dissolve and socio-economic activity is less and less constrained as borders and geographical barriers erode (Held and McGrew, 2003).

An alternative view suggests, however, that there never has been a true global economy. Today, for example, a group of the world's eight most economically powerful nations (the G8) directs world activity now just exactly as eight great self-interested powers held sway before the First World War (Hirst and Thompson, 2000). The world's richer countries are able to exert so much control that the poorer nations seem mired in a fatalistic belief that they can do little to change the world order and so take control of their own destinies (Held, 2000).

The global citizen

Convergence around global markets has led to international conventions by which states have set common standards on fundamental human rights, including the status of women and of refugees. Emerging from this new world order is a yearning for the global citizen, a responsible and responsive person who has been educated to owe allegiance to the world as much as to the nation state into which they were born. These citizens demonstrate their cosmopolitan loyalty by being actively concerned for the fate of all humanity, upholding the ideals of peace, justice, respect and sustainability as ways to achieve a better future for everyone. Global citizens are 'bound to other human beings by ties of recognition and concern' (Nussbaum, 1998). With this level of concern comes a sense of complicity, culpability and responsibility for the state of the world. It has been argued that it is wrong to burden school children with such depressing truths, particularly as education for global citizenship is made to carry a range of ideas that may be innovative but are not necessarily connected (Young, 2004). Yet there is a growing international consensus that education must be directed to encourage a global ethic among young people. Such an ethic would require all of us to recognise a duty to respect the fundamental and inalienable rights of all other human beings through an early understanding of the new realities of unprecedented global change (Claire, 2001; Dower, 2003).

A study across nine nations of what policy-makers judged such change to require of people by the year 2020 showed consensus around certain essential *citizen characteristics*. These include:

- **cooperation;**
- **tolerance;**
- **a willingness to resolve conflict non-violently;**
- **a willingness to modify lifestyle habits to safeguard the environment;**
- **a readiness to defend human rights.**

Engaging in politics at local, national and international levels was deemed essential (Cogan and Derricott, 2000). Oxfam (1997) has gone further by requiring the global citizen to be 'outraged by social injustice', infused with 'a belief that we can make a difference' and hence be 'willing to act in order to make the world a more equitable and sustainable place'.

The momentum within world events may be advancing nations and individuals fitfully towards a wider sense of community and social cohesion. As nations shoulder their responsibility to uphold democracy, to combat terrorism and to find greater economic harmony, their peoples can be seen taking on this mantle of global citizenship and working for world peace, sustenance and sustainability in a multi-ethnic, multicultural world where national boundaries no longer define their total reality. Many of these advances have been denied to *majority world countries,* the term favoured by Oxfam to characterise more fairly 'those countries described as developing' (Young and Commins, 2002). Dogged as they are by poverty, injustice and disease, these nations have little real influence over superpowers ready to act against the wishes of the United Nations, an organisation which stands as the only approximation of a world government upon which the concept of a world citizenry must in some way depend.

Pause for thought | the characteristics of the global citizen

As never before, we live and work alongside people from all over the world. A survey of almost any decent-sized group or gathering of students, for example, will show that many locate their origins in different countries. We treat our origins as a source of pride in ourselves. Indeed the added value that students with diverse origins bring to learning communities is recognised in the recruitment policies of most universities (Khamis, 2005). Our culture is shaped by global influences. We can plot the significance of every decision each of us makes as consumers. Our culture is shaped by global influences. We travel where we wish as of right and we become global citizens the moment we step onto other soil, or surf the web to find similarities or differences with our counterparts abroad.

The dimensions of global citizenship

Global citizenship finds its essential expression through four interlocking themes which gain force when they are set against their alternatives:

- **equality *vs* inequality;**
- **justice *vs* injustice;**
- **peace *vs* conflict;**
- **environmental sustainability *vs* damage.**

The resolution of these tensions is taken by many commentators to be the fundamental purpose of all schooling. At school, if children are to gain the knowledge, skills and attitudes to respond to these tensions, a whole-school approach becomes essential. This is a radical view because the production of global citizens depends more on cooperation and a dynamic regard for social justice than on the competition that is said more usually to characterise young people's taught experience (Young and Commins, 2002; Davies et al, 2005). In terms of environmental sustainability *vs* damage, for example, the closing decades of the twentieth century have thrown up movements that have worked around and beyond the concerns of governments to unite populations in concerns about where the planet is heading (e.g. visible climate change and global warming). Vast popular movements galvanised by rock stars, together with the dawning recognition of global warming and energy shortages, laid fertile ground for global citizenship to force its way onto the curriculum. The countries of the UK have adopted a global dimension in the syllabus (e.g. DfEE, 2000). Parallel but distinctive developments can be seen in every Council of Europe member state (Council of Europe, 2005).

Globalisation and a global dimension in the school curriculum

In the English school system all National Curriculum subjects at all phases are called upon to contribute to the global dimension of learning. Eight key concepts are taken to encompass the enduring values and essential learning about global issues:

- **citizenship;**
- **sustainable development;**
- **social justice;**
- **values and perceptions;**
- **diversity;**
- **interdependence;**
- **conflict resolution;**
- **human rights.**

National strategies encourage excellence in teaching and enjoyment of learning by allowing schools to take more control of the curriculum and be more innovative and creative in how children are educated. Such a concession has been seized by educators, keen to secure those concepts for children (DEA, 2004; Hicks, 2004). Official guidance on the teaching of controversial issues specifically places globalisation at the heart of a range of concerns that have personal impact or deal with questions of value and belief (QCA, 2003; DFID, 2006).

Research has shown that even children in the early years are able to show that they are forming rudimentary conceptions, and indeed misconceptions, about issues of peace and conflict, human rights, racism, sexism, global development and the environment (Fountain, 1990). Globalisation can be made accessible to young children by linking them to their own immediate world. For example, young children will complain and protest about classroom rules that they regard as unfair. This could be seen as the beginning of an awareness of human rights. In contrast to this, students in higher education have significant life histories upon which to draw in becoming global citizens. In line with such practical issues, there is a growing view that the whole concept of global commitment is shifting as it takes the weight of world change (Nelson and Carr, 2005; Osler and Starkey, 2005).

With improved communications between national governments and peoples, and as a result of a greater understanding of the differences in societies and a recognition of haves and have-nots, more and more people are calling for modern day responses to historical events. This can be seen as an impulse among global citizens to ensure that countries and groups of people take responsibility for the past actions of their forebears, from which they continue to benefit.

Pause for thought | global issues, curriculum projects and your locality

One of the more sinister, if mostly historical, impacts of globalisation as it has unfolded over the years, and which can be demonstrated easily to young people, involves the trade in humans. A significant economic activity of the past, in terms of wealth created and people involved, was the triangular trade in slaves between Europe, Africa and America. At its height in the 1700s, nearly 80,000 Africans a year were being sold as commodities. Despite the abolition of the slave trade in Britain in 1807, the fruits of slave labour have had a fundamental effect on society here and the repercussions of the human traffic are still resonating around the world. Walvin's *Atlas of slavery* (2005) has shown graphically how the diaspora of the enslaved, far from being a remote phenomenon, has proved instrumental in shaping the modern world. Research in maritime cities once heavily involved in the slave trade, such as Liverpool, is identifying educational projects that have the potential to confront the legacies of slavery in Africa, the Americas and Europe, and to heal the wounds of society. Educationalists in Liverpool have recognised the role that education can play in helping individual citizens and groups develop a better understanding of others and of the ways in which actions by one group can have far-reaching consequences on others, both planned and unplanned. Consider how the four main legacies of the Atlantic Slave Trade relate to where you live:

- migration;
- the economy;
- cultural values;
- racism.

How might education address issues related to each? Consider the hierarchy of languages in the UK today. Which languages are at the top and what do they have in common? Which languages are at the bottom? How is the hierarchy reinforced by society? What role do you think education plays in this? In what ways do we see racism manifesting itself in Britain today? What common stereotypes might racist incidents be fuelled by? How could these be overcome in our global society? What role can education play in combating racism? Does slavery exist today?

Where is globalisation going?

Many of the world's problems may not be directly caused by the impacts of world integration. For example, 'weaker' nations and their citizens need help to beat poverty exacerbated by global market inequalities and to share in globalisation's benefits. The World Trade Organization (WTO), founded as recently as 1995, presides over the new economic order. Its remit is to make life more efficient and, through economic prosperity, to bring peace and good government everywhere (WTO, 2005). However, there are signs that globalisation has ground to a halt and may be in retreat. Saul (2005) has found evidence for this in the emergence of ad hoc alliances of China, India, Brazil, South Africa and others to counter the WTO's unfavourable economic policies (viewed as imperialistic and neo-colonial) and the huge demonstrations against the effects of globalisation that attend every economic summit meeting of the world's most powerful nations. In one example, outrage has been expressed over the pricing policies of western drug companies in the fight against disease.

Most world events, from the phenomenon of asylum-seeking through to the unfavourable state of certain African nations and all points between, including natural disasters, which are popularly seen to be caused by the wholesale economic abuse of the planet, can be read in terms of the progress of the WTO's philosophy of prosperity. The United States in particular has been held to be the driving force behind globalisation. As its foreign policy has taken more nationalistic turns, its economic policies could possibly turn inwards against the threat of the vast economic rise of China and India. The closing of American and European borders, as protectionism against the influx of cheap goods from the East, can be seen as one natural historical symptom of resistance to such economic dangers.

There are difficulties in labelling the disparate movement that has massed to oppose the impacts of globalisation, rather than the underlying process, which itself may be inexorable. It is difficult, if not hypocritical, to castigate globalisation without renouncing so much of modern life, such as air travel, the internet or any international contact. This tension has led to the rise of alliances such as the *Global Justice Movement*, an array of groups concerned with popular education to mitigate the unequal effects of globalisation. Naomi Klein, a standard-bearer for those groups lobbying decision-makers to stop policies that hurt the world's poor, called for global justice in her seminal book *No logo* (2001), a devastating critique of the damage inflicted by world marketing brands. Klein proceeds from 'the simple hypothesis that, as more people discover the brand-name secrets of the global logo web, their outrage will fuel the next big political movement, a vast wave of opposition squarely targeting transnational corporations, particularly those with very high name-brand recognition'.

Klein's critique of the competitive branding of the world unfolds from the way that the 'manufactured sameness' of mass production required that 'difference had to be manufactured along with the product'. The age of the logo arrived when the 'essence' of a brand became more significant than the individual product. Once morphed into a logo, a brand has the propensity to expand virally, encouraging in consumers the fetishisation of their lifestyle choices around over-priced designer labels. There is highly visible evidence of this dynamic in the universal spread of advertising across every medium, and the way that companies lend their logos to products wildly unrelated to their core business. Klein concluded that the politics of identity and symbolic representation have turned out to be immeasurably problematic because accelerating economic trends 'have all been about massive redistribution and stratification of world resources: of jobs, goods, and money'. The rise of the logo has concealed grossly exploitative relations of production. Other horrors, such as religious fundamentalism, have shaded Klein's fears of corporate world dominance in the reshaping of the political landscape since the disastrous events of 9/11. The democratic theme represented in her work, that all people should be given the understanding and power to shape global society, remains however as persuasive and critical as ever.

Research box

The global dimension in the higher education curriculum

Several UK government initiatives have been set in train to stimulate a global dimension in the curriculum of universities. Pivotal among these is the international strategy for education, Putting the World into World Class Education (DfES, 2004), which seeks specifically to integrate international considerations into existing programmes of study. It sets three interrelated goals that will help the UK keep its 'unique position' as a confident, outward-looking society and leading edge economy playing its full part in the world:

▶

Research box continued

- *Goal 1*: equipping our children, young people and adults for life in a global society and work in a global economy. This involves instilling a strong global dimension into the learning experience of all young people, transforming the national capability to speak and use other languages and moving towards the international mutual recognition and improved transparency of qualifications.
- *Goal 2*: engaging with our international partners to achieve their goals and ours. This will require the benchmarking of UK performance against world-class standards, drawing on best practice everywhere, developing the capacity to engage strategically with a wide range of partners across the world, working with European partners to realise the goal that the EU should become 'the most competitive and dynamic knowledge-based economy in the world'. It also demands that expertise and resources are shared in support of the improvement of education and children's services worldwide, particularly in Africa.
- *Goal 3*: maximising the contribution of the UK education and training sector and university research to overseas trade and inward investment. This calls for further expansion in the number of international HE students in the UK, making the UK an international leader in the creative and supportive use of ICT for education, promoting UK universities as international hubs for learning and research and encouraging education and training providers to work internationally in partnership with business.

Compare these major goals with the grassroots work of the Development Education Association (DEA), an umbrella body for a raft of organisations working to raise awareness of global issues and the role people play within them. The Higher Education section of its website sets out projects (many of them student-led) illustrative of the role of higher education in global responsibility.

Summary and conclusions

This chapter has considered what globalisation means to different groups, what globalisation entails and what the impacts of globalisation might be. The enduring image of globalisation is of a vast watering hole where the herds of nations converge to draw their sustenance and ensure their survival by competing in the one huge world market. It is responsive to none but the most competitive and has gained acceptance as the most efficient system for creating the wealth and prosperity that all nations must seek and share. The challenge must be to find ways to ensure that all members of all societies have their share, including the least enfranchised who cannot fight so well for their place at the trough. The need for global citizenship and people with a global ethic in the twenty-first century are paramount. In relation to this, the role of education in creating global citizens is crucial.

There is nothing new in thinking that we are all ultimately more answerable to the global arena than to the narrow concerns of the country we call our own. Whilst many resist the equation of global citizenship with the international doing of good and condescending philanthropy, education for global citizenship must go beyond mere awareness to become an animated concern for social justice. The changed global security environment and the uncertain climate in which we must all now live merely add urgency to the understanding that respect for human rights, hand-in-hand with a commitment to a prosperous, clean and socially just world economy, is now more than ever the best defence against the world instability that might engulf the planet.

References

Cairncross, F (2001) *The death of distance: how the communications revolution will change our lives*. Boston, MA: Harvard Business School Press.

Cambridge, J and Thompson, J (2004) Internationalism and globalization as contexts for international education. *Compare*, 34(2): 161–75.

Claire, H (2001) *Not aliens: primary school children and the Citizenship/PSHE curriculum*. Stoke on Trent: Trentham Books.

Cogan, J and Derricott, R (2000). *Citizenship for the 21st century: an international perspective on education*. London: Kogan Page.

Coulby, D and Zambeta, E (eds) (2005) *Globalisation and nationalism in education: world year book of education 2005*. London: RoutledgeFalmer.

Council of Europe (2005) The Europe of cultural co-operation: education: country profiles. Available at **www.coe.int/T/E/Cultural_Co-operation/education/E.D.C/Country_profiles/** (accessed 22 February 2006).

Davies, L, Harber, C and Yamashita, H (2005) *Global citizenship education: the needs of teachers and learners*. Birmingham: Centre for International Education and Research.

DEA (2004) *Global perspectives and teachers in training*. Gloucester: Development Education Association.

DfEE (2000) *Developing a global dimension in the school curriculum*. London: Department for Education and Employment

DfES (2004) Putting the World into World Class Education. London: Department for Education and Skills.

DFID (Department for International Development) (2006) Global dimension. Available at **www.globaldimension.org.uk/** (accessed 22 February 2006).

Dower, N (2003) *An introduction to global citizenship*. Edinburgh: Edinburgh University Press

Fountain, S (1990) *Learning together, global education 4–7*. Cheltenham: Stanley Thornes.

Held, D (2000) *A globalising world: culture, economics, politics.* Buckingham: Open University Press.

Held, D and McGrew, A (eds) (2003) *The global transformations reader: an introduction to the globalisation debate*. Cambridge: Polity Press.

Hicks, D (2004) Global education: what does it mean? in Kent, A and Morgan, A (eds) *The challenge of the global dimension in education*. London: Institute of Education.

Hirst, P and Thompson, G (2000) *Globalization in question: the international economy and the possibilities of governance*. Cambridge: Polity Press.

Khamis, A (2005) Global partnerships workshop report, in *Conference report on graduates as global citizens: quality education for life in the 21st century*. Gloucester: Development Education Association.

Klein, N (2001) *No logo*. London: HarperCollins.

Mepham, D and Cooper, J (2004) *Human rights and global responsibility: an international agenda for the UK*. London: Institute for Public Policy Research.

Nelson, J and Carr, D (2005) *Active citizenship: definitions, goals and practice*. London: QCA/INCA.

Nussbaum, M (1998) Cultivating humanity. *Liberal Education*, 84(2): 38–46.

Osler, A and Starkey, H (2005) *Changing citizenship: democracy and inclusion in education*. Maidenhead: Open University Press.

Oxfam (1997) *A curriculum for global citizenship*. Oxford: Oxfam.

Penn, H (2005) *Unequal childhoods: young children's lives in poor countries*. London: Routledge.

QCA (2003) *Citizenship: a scheme of work for KS3. Teachers Guide, Appendix 9: guidance on the teaching of sensitive and controversial issues*. London: QCA/DfES.

Sassen, S (1999) *Globalisation and its discontents: essays on the new mobility of people and money*. New York: The New Press.

Saul, J (2005) *The collapse of globalism*. London: Atlantic.

Starke, L (ed) (2006) *State of the world 2006*. London: Worldwatch Institute.

UN (2005) *Report on the World Social Situation*. National Assembly.

Walvin, J (2005) *Atlas of slavery*. London: Pearson.

WTO (World Trade Organization) (2005) Understanding the WTO. Available at **www.wto.org** (accessed 22 February 2006).

Young, B (2004) *Global Citizens Unite*. TES, 3 September.

Young, M and Commins, E (2002) *Global citizenship: the handbook for primary teaching*. Cambridge: Oxfam/Chris Kington Publishing.

Index

academic freedom 108
achievement 137–9
action research 16
activity theory 101
Adey, P 93
Alleyne, B 135
Anderson, J 84, 161
Armstrong, D 143, 146
Arnove, R 121, 167
auditory modalities 43, 44

Bacon, R 91
banking concept 22
Barnett, R 113
Bartlett, S 12, 54
Beck, U 119–20
Becker, GS 5
Bee, H 67
Bell, A 59
Benlloch, M 9
Best, R 153
Biesta, G 123
biological determinism 72
Black, P 94
Blair, T 33
Bloom, BS 42
Boal, A 23
Board Schools 60
Booth, T 146
Bottery, M 161
Boyd, D 67
brain, the 37–9
Brighouse, H 31–2
Broadfoot, P 173–4
Brown, A 153
Bullock Report 77–8
Burbules, N 119
Burton, D 12, 54
Butler, RA 61
Bynner, J 88

Cairncross, F 177
Campbell, A 48
Carr, W 13, 15, 16, 18
Cassidy, S 43, 45
Castelli, M 152
Certificate of Secondary Education (CSE) 61
chaos and cognition 42
childcare, and government 70
children
    see also young children

rights 144–5
spirituality 152–54
Children Act 2004 53
Children's Services, integration 47, 55
    see also Every Child Matters
    allied professionals 48–50
    challenges 53–4
    common assessment framework (CAF) 54
    external providers 50–51
    implications for professionals 54
    multi-agency involvement 51, 53–4
    multi-disciplinary professional development 54
    support workers 50–51
    teachers' role 47–8
Children's workforce strategy 54
Chomsky, N 79
citizenship see also democracy
Clark, D 44
Climbié, V 47, 51
Coard, B 138
Cockcroft Report 85, 87
Coffield, F 43
cognitive development, and science education 92–3
cognitive psychology 40–41, 42, 43
Cohen, B 6
Coles, R 154
Colwell, M 47, 51
Comenius, J 91
commodification of knowledge 112
Common Assessment Framework (CAF) 54
communities of practice, theory 101
community education 20, 27
    concept of community 23–4
    expectations 22–4
    groups 26–7
    history 21–2
    intervention 24–6
    projects 26–7
    range 20–21
community projects 26–7
community schools 64
comparative education 167, 174
    see also education
    cross-national trends 168–9
    and development of nations 173
    difficulties 169–71
    future approaches 173–4
    and globalisation 168, 174
    influences on education 168
    networks 173
    purposes 167

shared principles 170–71
and social structures 171–2
computers
see also technology
and learning theories 100–101
rationales for use 98–100
Cox Report 76–7
Crick Report 159, 164 165
critical social science 15–16
Crook, D 14, 101
Crosland, A 109
Crow, L 147
Crowther, J 123
cultural pluralism 136–7
curriculum development 62, 63
Cuthell, J 104

Davey, I 60
Dearing Report 110
Delanty, G 113
Democracy
and communication skills 162–4
and the curriculum 160
definition 159–60
education in 159, 165–6
global citizenship 178–9
and globalisation 160–62
and market sovereignty 161
and participation 160–62
political action 164–5
political apathy 160, 162
Disability Discrimination Act 1995 147
Dixon, J 76
Doyle, ME 22
Drefus, HL 17
Driscoll, MP 37, 41
Driver, R 42, 92
Dryden, G 48
Dunn, R 43

Eade, J 138
Early Years education 67, 70, 71, 73
see also young children
education 5, 10–11
see also community education; comparative
education
definitions 5, 7–8
extending boundaries 171
flexi-time 10
formal 8, 20
informal 8–9, 22–3
opportunities 8–10
peri-formal 9
philosophical approach 6–7
and schooling, learning, training 6
state-controlled 62–3
universal principles 172

Education Act 1902 60–1
Education Act 1944 61
Education Action Zones (EAZ) 63
Education Reform Act 1988 32
Education Studies 12, 18–19
and action research 16
and critical social science 15–16
phenomenological epistemology 17–18
reflective practice 14–15
and teacher education 12–13
theory and practice 14
educational organisations *see also* leadership
Edwards, R 117
Elementary Education Act 1870 60
Elementary Education (Defective and Epileptic) Act
1914 143
Elliott, J 16
Ellis, W 111
Engeström, Y 93
English teaching 75, 80–81
cross-phase discontinuity 80
future 80
in higher education 79
and literacy teaching 78
literature v literacy 75–6, 78–9
multitextuality/multimodality 76
naming the subject 78–9
rationales 76–8
subject concept 75–6
epistemology, phenomenological 17–18
equal opportunities approach 143–7
Every Child Matters
agenda for change 52–3
audit data 52
Children's workforce strategy 54
outcomes framework 52–3
sectors covered 51–2
external providers 50–51
Eysenck, MW 40

Fairbairn, G 48
faith communities *see also* religious education
family 68–9
Farrell, S 171
feminism 22, 72
see also gender
Fernández, G 9
Findlay, F 77
flexi-time education 10
Flutter, J 164
formal education 8, 20
see also schools
and technology 103–4
Forster, WE 60
Foster, A 123
foundation schools 64

free market 29, 35
    Adam Smith 30
    critiques 33–4
    Education Reform Act 1988 32
    educational critiques 34
    Lowe's Revised Code 30–31
    moral critiques 34
    parental choice 31–2
    political critiques 33
    principle 29–30
Freire, P 22, 23
French, S 147
Frowe, I 63
Fryer Report 120–21
Furedi, F 112, 126, 162
Furlong, J 153
further education 60–61

Gadamer, H-G 16, 17
Gagné, RM 41
Galloway, D 146
Galton, M 94
Gardner, L 26
Gender
    see also feminism
    issues 60
    and leadership 129
    socialisation 68–9, 72–3
General Certificate of Secondary Education (GCSE)
    61
Giddens, A 120
Gilborn, D 138
Gipps, CV 33
global citizenship 178–9
globalisation 119–20, 176, 182
    and comparative education 168, 174
    and curriculum issues 179–80, 181–82
    debate 176–7
    and democracy 160–62
    future 180–81
    history 177
Goodwyn, A 77
Gorard, S 123
Gordon, C 59
Gorwood, B 94
Government
    see also state-controlled education
    and childcare 70
    and lifelong learning 120–21
    and university education 108–9
Gray, HL 129
Greenfield, S 38
Gregory, I 5, 10
Gronn, P 127
Grosseteste, R 91

Habermas, J 15, 162–3
Hadow Report 61
Hall, H 17
Hall, S 13
Halpin, D 63
Hanney, S 108, 109
Hatcher, R 134
Hay, D 154
Heidegger, M 17–18
Heppell, S 103–4
Hertz, N 161
higher education 106, 114
    see also university education
    academic v vocational 109
    commodification of knowledge 112
    and economy 110
    and employment 111–112
    globalisation and the curriculum 181–2
    infantilisation 112
    marketisation 110–1, 112
    and performative skills 113
    postmodern 112–113
Higher Level Teaching Assistants (HLTAs) 49
Hirst, P 13
Hirst, PH 5
Hitler, A 160
Hobsbawm, E 161
Hodson, D 42
human brain 37–9
human rights 144–5
    universal 169
Humboldt, W 108, 112

ICT
    attainment standards 103
    development 119
    and learner agency 104
inclusion *see also* Special Educational Needs (SEN)
Individual Education Plans (IEPs) 145
informal education 8–9, 22–3
information and computer technology *see also* ICT
information literacy 102
interventionist theatre 24–6

Jeffs, T 95
John, P 100
Joseph, K 31

Kant I 29, 33, 108
Kay-Shuttleworth, J 60
Keane, MT 40
Kemmis, S 15, 16, 18
Kershaw, B 26
kinaesthetic modalities 43, 45
King, E 171
Klein, N 181

Kogan, M 108, 109
Kuerbis, P 42, 93

laissez-faire economics 29–30
Lancaster, J 59
Lang, P 7
Lave, J 93
Lawton, D 23, 32, 33
leadership 125, 132
    approaches 130
    characteristics 127
    charismatic 129–30
    contemporary models 129–32
    distributed 132
    and educational organisations 126
    and gender 129
    hierarchy principle 126
    history of approaches 125–6
    and management 126–7
    rationalism v collegiality 125–6
    self-evaluation protocol 128
    situational 130
    transcendental 131
    transformational 131
learner agency 104
learning 37, 45
    see also VAK instrumentation
    and the brain 37–9
    chaos and cognition 42
    condition of 41
    definition 37
    and education, schooling, training 6
    educational context 41–2
    and memory 40–41
    mentors 49
    process 118
Learning Style Inventory (LSI) 43
learning theories, and computers 100–101
Lennie, L 94
lifelong learning 117, 124
    definition 117
    government responses 120–21
    human resource approach 123
    instrumental approach 118
    policies 121–2
    as self-fulfillment 117–18
    and societal changes 118–20
Linder, CJ 42
Literacies
    information 102
    technology 101–102
literacy teaching 78, 80
    and numeracy 88–9
Loveless, A 99, 104
Lowe, R 30–31
Luffiego, M 42
Lukasiewicz, J-F 113

McBeath, JEC 128, 130
McCulloch, G 14
McFarlane, A 103
MacPherson, W 137
management *see also* leadership
Mansfield, S 22
Maslow, A 49, 50
mathematics teaching 83, 89
    concerns 83–4
    international comparisons 84
    investigations 85–6
    and numeracy 87–9
    public perceptions 86–7
    and underachievement 89
    understanding requirements 85–6
Matheson, D 5
Media
    literacy 101–2
    and young children 69
Meighan, R 10
memory 40–41
meta-cognition 43
Mill, JS 13, 108–9, 162
Millar, R 92
Miller, P 60
Millwood, R 100
Mirza, HS 138
Mittler, P 145
monitorial system 59
Morle, P 23, 25
Morrison, K 132
multi-agency involvement 51, 53–4
multitextuality/multimodality 76
Musharraf, P 159
Myers, K 128, 130

National Curriculum 62, 64–5
    and democracy 160
    and English teaching 76, 80
    and exclusion 147–8
    and globalisation 179–82
    and mathematics teaching 84–5
    and science education 94–5
nature v nurture 72
Neave, G 108
Neelands, J 24
Newbolt Report 75
Newman, S 8
Nicholson, H 24
Nixon, H 76
numeracy 87–8
    and literacy 88–9
Nye, R 154

objective principles 29
Office for Standards in Education (OFSTED) 63

Osborne, J 95
O'Shea, M 38
Owen, H 126, 127

Papadopoulous, G 6
Papert, S 100–101
para-professionals 48–50
Parekh, B 162
parental choice 31–2
Parsons, S 88
payment by results 60
Peacock, A 9
peer influence 70–71
Peim, N 12
people's theatre 24
performative skills 113
phenomenological epistemology 17–18
Piaget, J 100
Plato 37, 107
Pollard, A 157
polytechnics 109
Powell, T 135
primary socialisation 68
principles 29
professionals 48–50
    multidisciplinary 54
pupils *see also* children

Quicke, J 146

race 134, 139–40
    and achievement 137–9
    assimilation 135
    children's notions 134
    cultural pluralism 136–7
    initiatives on racism 134–5
    integration 135–6
ragged schools 59
Raikes, R 59
Rampton Report 136, 138
Raynor, S 43
reflective practice 14–15
religious education 150, 157
    coverage of religions 156–7
    and fundamentalism 155–6
    history 150–52
    and spirituality 152–4
Reynolds, D 171
Riding, RJ 43
Rose, J 21
Rose, R 146
Rosener, JB 129
Rousseau, J-J 170
Rudduck, J 164
Rushdie, S 162
Rustemier, S 144

Santayana, G 171
Saward, M 160
Schechner, R 24
Schön, D 14–15
Schools
    board 60, 65
    and education, learning, training 6
    gender issues 60
    history 59–61
    mainstream types 64–5
    monitorial system 59
    National Curriculum 62
    payment by results 60
    political intervention 62–3
    publicly funded 59–60
    and vocational learning 61
schools councils 164
Schuller, T 171
Schwartz, B 135
science education 41–2, 91, 96
    and cognitive development 92–3
    definitions 91–2
    elements 91
    induction/deduction 91
    justification 92
    primary/secondary transition 93–5
    and supply of scientists 95
    Zone of Proximal Development (ZPD) 93
secondary education 60–61
secondary socialisation 69–71
Sefton-Green, J 76
self awareness 67–8
Selwyn, N 103
Sewell, T 138
Sharp, JG 42, 93
Shayer, M 93
Shevlin, M 146
Siraj-Blatchford, I 10, 72
Skemp, R 86–7
slave trade, project 180
Smith, A 39
Smith, Adam 30, 32
Smith, MK 95
Smith Report 85
social science 15–16
socialisation 68–71, 72–3
Special Educational Needs (SEN) 48–9, 142, 148–9
    areas of need 145
    equal opportunities approach 143–7
    exclusionary pressures 147–8
    functional integration 144
    medical model 142–3
    proactive initiatives 148
    pupils' involvement 146
Specialist Teaching Assistants (STAs) 49
Speering, W 94

spirituality *see* religious education
state-controlled education 62–3
    see also government
Stevens, R 111
Stone, J 69
subjective principles 29
Suffrage Movement 22
sunday schools 22, 59
support workers 50–51
Swain, J 147
Swann Report 134, 136, 138

Tall, D 85
Taylor, R 122
Teacher
    education 12–13
    role 47–8
    and spirituality 152–3
technology 98, 104
    see also computers
    and formal education 103–4
    ICT, attainment standards 103
    literacies 101–102
    and micro/macro politics 102–3
    rationales for use 98–100
Thatcher, M 161
Theatre-in-education (TIE) 22, 23, 24–6
third way, the 23, 120
Torres, C 119, 167
Tout, D 87
training, and education, learning, schooling 6
Trevathan, A 152
Troyna, B 134
Twining, P 98, 97

underachievement 89, 137–9
university education 106
    see also higher education
    academic freedom 108
    ancient/medieval 107
    binary system 109
    fees 111
    hierarchy of status 110
    modern 107–8
    and the state 108–9

VAK instrumentation 43–5
    application 44–5
    dimensionality 43–4
    origin 43
    reliability 43–4
    terminology 43
    universality 44–5
    validity 43–4
Van Erven, E 25
visual modalities 43, 44
vocational learning 65
voluntary aided schools 64
voluntary controlled schools 64
Vos, J 48
Vygotsky, LS 93, 101

Walton, RJ 92
Walvin, J 180
Ward, S 13
Warnock Report 143–4
Webb, J 8
Weber, M 125
Wellington, JJ 92
Wells, P 5
Wenger, E 93
Wilkins, M 14
Williams, R 34, 35
Wittgenstein, L 6, 7
Wolf, A 110, 111
women's movements 22, 72
working people's clubs/institutes 21
Wrigley, T 63

young children 67, 73–4
    see also children
    early years practitioners 71
    and family 68–9
    gender socialisation 68–9
    and government 70
    and media 69
    nature v nurture 72
    peer influence 70–71
    practitioners 71, 73
    primary socialisation 68
    secondary socialisation 69–71
    self awareness 67–8

Zaslavsky, C 89
Zone of Proximal Development (ZPD) 93